SHAPING THE JOURNEY OF EMERGING ADULTS

*Life-Giving Rhythms
for Spiritual Transformation*

JANA L. SUNDENE
AND RICHARD R. DUNN

IVP Books
An imprint of InterVarsity Press
Downers Grove, Illinois

InterVarsity Press
P.O. Box 1400, Downers Grove, IL 60515-1426
World Wide Web: www.ivpress.com
E-mail: email@ivpress.com

InterVarsity Press® is the book-publishing division of InterVarsity Christian Fellowship/USA®, a movement of students and faculty active on campus at hundreds of universities, colleges and schools of nursing in the United States of America, and a member movement of the International Fellowship of Evangelical Students. For information about local and regional activities, write Public Relations Dept., InterVarsity Christian Fellowship/USA, 6400 Schroeder Rd., P.O. Box 7895, Madison, WI 53707-7895, or visit the IVCF website at <www.intervarsity.org>.

Scripture quotations, unless otherwise noted, are from The Holy Bible, English Standard Version, copyright © 2001 by Crossway Bibles, a division of Good News Publishers. Used by permission. All rights reserved.

While all stories in this book are true, some names and identifying information in this book have been changed to protect the privacy of the individuals involved.

Cover design: Cindy Kiple
Interior design: Beth Hagenberg
Images: © Lesley Aggar/Trevillion Images

ISBN 978-0-8308-3469-3

Printed in the United States of America ∞

Library of Congress Cataloging-in-Publication Data

Sundene, Jana L., 1958-
  Shaping the journey of emerging adults: life-giving rhythms for spiritual transformation / Jana L. Sundene and Richard R. Dunn.
      p. cm.
  Includes bibliographical references (p.   )
  ISBN 978-0-8308-3469-3 (pbk.: alk. paper)
  1. Church work with young adults. 2. Young adults—Religious life.
3. Discipling (Christianity) I. Dunn, Richard R. II. Title.
  BV4446.S86 2012
  259'.25—dc23

                                                                    2011047336

P	19	18	17	16	15	14	13	12	11	10	9	8	7	6	5	4	3	2	1
Y	28	27	26	25	24	23	22	21	20	19	18	17	16	15	14	13	12			

From Jana

To the BSGE

Thank you for letting me journey with you over the years and for teaching me so much about the amazing potential as well as the challenges of your generation. You truly are the Best Small Group Ever!

From Rick

To Jessica

Always my baby girl, but increasingly an amazingly gifted young woman who changes the world every day simply by loving well with Christ's love.

To Zach

Absolutely the most uniquely creative person I have ever known, who every day takes another step toward manhood and the full expression for Christ's glory of your seemingly limitless gifts.

To Ben

A warrior from birth, whose strength and passion astound me and whose impact increases every day as you grow into the leader Christ called and created you to be.

To Stephen

Thank you for the authenticity of your journey, the strength of your character, and the integrity of your love for Christ and my daughter.

CONTENTS

FOREWORDS

by Some Emerging Adults

AFTER EXPERIENCING spiritual transformation through Rick's shepherding for the past twenty years, I have committed myself to reproduce this same shepherding in my ministry to the next generation. As a result, I have seen the significant impact that flows out of simply following God's heart and design for making disciples who disciple.

As a local church pastor, I know there is nothing more important than shepherding well! *Shaping the Journey of Emerging Adults* thoroughly communicates the process that God has used to shape my heart as well as my calling to invest in others. The wealth of biblical truth and the principles of discipleship Rick and Jana write about, if applied, will change lives. I know this to be true firsthand.

However, as I reflect on the desperate need to invest strategically in this generation of emerging adults, I know not everyone has had the opportunity to see this modeled in their lives. As one who has experienced this privilege, I can only hope that the vision and practices modeled in *Shaping the Journey of Emerging Adults* will ultimately provide its readers with the depth of motivation and preparation that has been formed in my heart through my emerging adult years.

Doug Miller, lead pastor, Plum Creek Community Church,
Castle Rock, Colorado

■ ■ ■

For eight years, a small group of us have been meeting together regularly. We lovingly refer to ourselves as "the best small group ever." This community has been God's gift to each of our lives; we often wonder who we would be today if not for one another. We are a group of women comprised of four emerging adults and one established adult, Jana. Although the age difference creates a dynamic that we wrestle through from time to time, Jana's presence in our group as our equal (rather than "the leader") has been a unique strength. Her wisdom and life experience have distinctively shaped us.

For the four of us, the presence of mentors like Jana has anchored us in the fast-moving and sometimes threatening course of our lives. When we have faced vast uncertainty and the dreaded need to "rise to the occasion" of adulthood, the voice of reassurance from an established adult has countered our disorientation with a stability that is founded in Christ. When the waters around us have changed too rapidly or at times too slowly, the men and women who have journeyed beside us have taught us not only to wait upon the Lord with expectancy but also to recognize his presence in the heart of the chaos. When a myriad of voices have drawn us into confusion, we have benefitted from the perspective of mentors who have challenged us to attend to the one Voice who speaks through his Spirit, his Word and his community.

We were in our early twenties when the group began, and Jana has been an anchor for each of us as we have individually and collectively journeyed through many stages: transitioning into adulthood, encountering spiritual breakthroughs as well as faith crises, sorting through the pain of abusive childhoods, and experiencing romantic relationships as well as break-ups. Although her advice has frequently been vital, our lives have ultimately been shaped by the immense privilege of doing life with her. It is primarily as we have observed her in the ebb and flow of her own challenges and as we have been invited to trace the choreography of God in her daily life that we have been gripped by the wild and yet unchanging goodness of God.

In this book she shares insights about what it means to minister to emerging adults who need other adults as they search out both their own identity and God's and seek to live openly inside of both of those realities. We believe many in the church will benefit from Rick and Jana's vision for purposefully walking alongside emerging adults in their journeys.

THE BSGE

Susanne Osborne, 31, is pursuing a doctoral degree in historical theology at Wheaton College and is a mentor for many young adults.

Sarah Beyer, 30, is an admissions counselor at Trinity International University and works with the youth group at Trinity Community Church in Libertyville, Illinois.

Annie Palubicki, 31, is the senior campaign manager for Light the Night at the Leukemia and Lymphoma Society and is an active leader in her church.

Emily Hennings, 33, is an occupational therapist in the Grayslake, Illinois, area and a prayer minister for her church.

INTRODUCTION

An Emerging Adult's Plea for Disciplemakers

ON MONDAY MORNING, August 29, 2005, Hurricane Katrina made landfall in the southeastern United States, slamming into the Louisiana coast as a category three hurricane and then hammering coastal areas from Alabama to Texas with torrential winds and rain. It was the aftermath of Katrina that wrought the greatest devastation in New Orleans, however. Massive levees designed to protect the city failed in the wake of the storm's surge, to the extent that words like *catastrophic* and *apocalyptic* best describe the impact of the floods that followed Katrina. The city of New Orleans became a community characterized by chaos and desperation.

Using images of post-Katrina New Orleans, I (Rick) challenged my congregation to be a "levee" of Christ's grace and truth in the midst of the rising tide of post-Christian Western culture, comparing post-Katrina New Orleans with the impact that follows when mature adults fail to care well for the spiritual and moral health of the next generation in our communities. In response to that sermon, twenty-seven-year-old Megan wrote the following poignant email:

> I was struck by the imagery of Hurricane Katrina in describing the post-Christian era. Being a 27-year-old, I am so much a product of the times. However, most importantly—being a Christ-follower—I am more so a product of God's grace. In keeping with the imagery, I feel like my parents and elders in the church I grew up in represent the levee, which had broken probably even before I was born and became of a highly influen-

tial age. I somewhat see my generation drowning, and just holding so tightly to lampposts and road signs on the streets of New Orleans—grasping for anything that seems rooted in something. The problem is, the levee has already broken and the roads are flooded with several feet of water and they're under it all. I see so many of my peers—even fellow "Christians"—with empty hopes, drowning.

Again, I praise God that it seems like the generation after mine is being well-kept [in our church] and the levee is stronger! But I can't help but break for the young adults my age, in their 20s and 30s. Where does that leave us? In my own experience, Christ redeemed my life—literally, I did nothing but continue finding ways to drown. I pray that his grace will fall upon them and bring them to repentance so they will know him. As one who is set free of the floodwaters and no longer trapped on the streets of New Orleans, I want to do more and more for my peers. When I reflect backwards, I know it's all in God's perfect plan, but I am hurt by that indifference, especially when I see the brokenness that has been a result.

I am involved in the Gathering [a community of young adults] and have been able to get to know several people through the group. In these relationships, I have heard a few people mention that they wish for a connection to older generations to disciple, guide, lead, encourage, challenge and protect. . . . My fear is that history will repeat and that indifference will spill over again—something I have seen and experience with my Christian brothers and sisters even now. My intention in writing isn't just to lament about the brokenness I see in those around me, but to figure out where we fit into ministry. It's obviously up to the Father how he uses older generations to minister and disciple the already-grown adults in my age group, but I pray deeply for movement in this area.[1]

If your heart, like ours, deeply desires to be a part of the Father's answer to Megan's prayers, then you are reading the right book! *Shaping the Journey of Emerging Adults* was written with a vision for motivating and equipping the movement Megan so wholeheartedly desires. For the sake of her generation we pray that you will not simply be informed by your reading but rather that you will be transformed in the midst of it. And we pray with Megan that ultimately this transformation will lead you on a search-and-rescue mission into the spiritual and moral apocalyptic devastation that characterizes the first adult generation of the twenty-first century.

DISCIPLEMAKING RELATIONSHIPS: A MISSION-CRITICAL URGENCY

"Growing up is hard, Daddy."

My (Rick) nineteen-year-old daughter, Jessica, spoke from experience. Having endured an exceptionally painful breakup with a college boyfriend, she now found herself severely questioning every belief she had ever held—including her faith in God and her confidence in herself. Jessica's initial adventure into young adulthood left her with a bruised soul.

Reaching for fatherly words that would validate her pain as well as point her toward renewed hope, I offered, "Yes, honey, growing up is hard. That's why a lot of people choose not to do it."

In every generation and in every culture, the road to adult maturity is paved with hard choices. (The road to adult immaturity, on the other hand, offers an enticing alternative: the path of least resistance.) To suggest otherwise tragically ignores the teachings of Scripture as well as the findings of social science. For Jessica and her peers all over the world, growing into the mature adult God created you to be is, universally and unequivocally, a series of challenges to be met and conquered. Spiritual growth into the likeness of Christ in young adulthood therefore requires perseverance, courage, and a willingness to wrestle with sin and failure. Consider these Scriptures on the journey of faith:

> Not that I have already obtained this or am already perfect, but I press on to make it my own, because Christ Jesus has made me his own. Brothers, I do not consider that I have made it my own. But one thing I do: forgetting what lies behind and straining forward to what lies ahead, I press on toward the goal for the prize of the upward call of God in Christ Jesus. (Phil 3:12-14)

> Let us also lay aside every weight, and sin which clings so closely, and let us run with endurance the race that is set before us, looking to Jesus, the founder and perfecter of our faith, who for the joy that was set before him endured the cross, despising the shame, and is seated at the right hand of the throne of God. (Heb 12:1-2)

> For this very reason, make every effort to supplement your faith with virtue, and virtue with knowledge, and knowledge with self-control, and self-control with steadfastness, and steadfastness with godliness, and godliness with brotherly affection, and brotherly affection with love. For

> if these qualities are yours and are increasing, they keep you from being
> ineffective or unfruitful in the knowledge of our Lord Jesus Christ. (2 Pet
> 1:5-8)

These verses apply to all who live by faith in Christ, regardless of age.
However, they are especially applicable to the rugged passage from
being a teenager to becoming a fully independent, mature, responsibil-
ity-taking adult.

Growing up in faith as teens grow into mental, emotional and relational adulthood can be done, but Scripture and the personal experiences of generations of young adults clearly demonstrate the necessity of
purposeful relationships in young adults' lives. Fully mature spiritual
adulthood cannot be reached without intentional relationships that invest Christ's grace, truth and love into the young adult's life. Consider
the roles of relationships in these biblical passages:

> Let us consider how to stir up one another to love and good works, not ne-
> glecting to meet together, as is the habit of some, but encouraging one an-
> other, and all the more as you see the Day drawing near. (Heb 10:24-25)

> Speaking the truth in love, we are to grow up in every way into him who
> is the head, into Christ, from whom the whole body, joined and held to-
> gether by every joint with which it is equipped, when each part is work-
> ing properly, makes the body grow so that it builds itself up in love. (Eph
> 4:15-16)

My daughter's successful passage through the initial disillusionment
and disappointments of young adulthood was encouraged, facilitated
and enabled by a network of significant relationships that stretched from
the mountains of Vermont to the hills of Birmingham, Alabama. Lauren,
Diane, Carol, Juanita, Lindsey and Jana were among those who directly
spoke into Jessica's soul with the wisdom, character and love of Christ.

Jessica's early-adult experiences illustrate two crucial rationales for investing our life significantly in the spiritual journey of a young adult. These
two rationales, and their correlation with the urgent pleas contained in
Megan's email, form our primary motivation for creating this book.

The first rationale is that Jessica's young-adult spiritual adventures
are *typical* of young-adult development all over the world. Whether in
the city dumps of Tijuana, Mexico, or the wealthy northern suburbs of

Chicago, whether in the agnostic religious climate of Szczecin, Poland, or the Bible belt of Birmingham, Alabama, we continually encounter young adults wrestling with foundational questions related to identity, faith, morality and romantic attraction.

In his seminal work *Emerging Adulthood: The Winding Road from the Late Teens Through the Twenties,* Jeffrey Jensen Arnett identifies five distinguishing features that universally characterize the post-adolescent journey:

1. It is the age of *identity exploration.*

2. It is the age of *instability.*

3. It is the most *self-focused* age of life.

4. It is the age of feeling *in-between,* in transition.

5. It is the age of *possibilities,* when hope flourishes, when people have an unparalleled opportunity to transform their lives.[2]

As a mentor in an educational setting and a pastor in a local church, the two of us respond to this list with passion that stirs us to action. We're continually asking ourselves, *What can we do in this generation to empower and equip emerging young adults to reach their God-designed potential for spiritual transformation?*

We agree with Arnett that the term "emerging adult" seems appropriate to describe the challenge for this generation in becoming fully functional adults. In his recent book *Lost in Transition: The Dark Side of Emerging Adulthood,* Christian Smith also embraces this term because, "rather than viewing these years as simply the last hurrah of adolescence or an early stage of real adulthood, it recognizes the very unique characteristics of this new and peculiar phase of life."[3] Some have chosen to define emerging adulthood as encompassing the ages of eighteen to twenty-nine,[4] while others have expanded the season to stretch from twenty-one to forty-five years of age.[5] For our purposes, however, we will use the terms "young adult" and "emerging adult" interchangeably to refer to adults ranging from ages nineteen to thirty-five. We believe that adults in this span consistently share the five distinguishing developmental characteristics outlined by Arnett.

With that said, we will call those who have achieved higher life stability, increased self-confidence in their personal identity and less self-focus *established* adults (approximately thirty-five to sixty years old) and *seasoned* adults (approximately sixty and up). We do acknowledge, however, that a young adult *may* achieve some or all of these characteristics at *any* point within the ages of nineteen to thirty-five. Furthermore, we believe that *each* stage of adulthood holds hope and possibilities for the follower of Christ (Arnett's fifth indicator). For established and seasoned adults, one of the areas of greatest potential for hope and possibilities is choosing to invest in disciplemaking relationships with emerging adults.

Our years of experience, spanning two generations of young adults, have convinced us that effective disciplemaking with emerging adults is not based on external factors such as age, marital status or career achievements. Rather, effectiveness is rooted primarily in a willingness to submit to Christ and an openness to invest intentionally and reflectively in an emerging adult's life. Facilitating the formation of such relationships is our answer to the question above of what we can do in this generation to empower and equip emerging adults to reach their God-designed potential for spiritual transformation.

The significance of disciplemaking relationships in young-adult lives provides the backdrop for the second compelling rationale illustrated by Jessica's early-adult experiences: While emerging adults all over the globe share the same developmental journey as Jessica, her connection to a vibrant relational spiritual community is *atypical* for young adults we've observed in cultures all over the world. Rarely does a week go by without both of us encountering a young adult longing for and lacking a relationship that will encourage and facilitate spiritual maturity in Christ. While the location may vary, from America to Asia to Africa, the intensity of the need for spiritual disciplemakers in the lives of emerging adults does not.

In one sense, the absence of spiritual shepherds is a universal reality, spanning not only the globe but even the history of the Christian faith. Jesus himself encountered this same reality:

> And Jesus went throughout all the cities and villages, teaching in their synagogues and proclaiming the gospel of the kingdom and healing every disease and every affliction. When he saw the crowds, he had compassion for them, because they were harassed and helpless, like sheep with-

out a shepherd. Then he said to his disciples, "The harvest is plentiful, but the laborers are few; therefore pray earnestly to the Lord of the harvest to send out laborers into his harvest." (Mt 9:35-38)

Jesus knew the opportunity and the urgency of the need that lay in front of his disciples. He also knew what the devastating impact of failing to respond to those needs through relationships would be. The need among young adults in this generation, however, has reached an acute level of spiritual crisis. Continued failure to prayerfully and proactively gather local communities of Christ's disciples to invest relationally in the spiritual journeys of young adults will ultimately have catastrophic spiritual consequences. Consider the following representative snapshots taken from around the globe:

1. Over the past few years, I (Rick) have travelled throughout western and eastern Europe, observing the daily lives of men and women who are deeply invested in shaping the journeys of emerging adults. These passionate, courageous, compassionate disciplemakers make their homes as educators and business leaders and pastors in extraordinarily spiritually challenging cities like Szczecin, Budapest and Prague. Most do so, however, with a sense of being profoundly alone and "other." The educational, social and religious ethos of these cities demonstrates the accumulated effects of the gospel not being entrusted from generation to generation.

   Christ is virtually unknown to the young adults in these communities; he's recognizable only as a historical religious figure memorialized in religious relics and works of art primarily observed by tourists in cathedrals or museums. One young leader in Germany shared with me, "If you want to talk about Christ with the students in our university, you must assume nothing—no knowledge of Christ or the Bible or any of the stories of the Bible." In the land of Luther, my friend has discovered that educated young adults have zero knowledge of the most basic elements of the Christian faith.

2. Having concluded my sermon titled "The Love of God, the Father" in a village church just outside Kampala, Uganda, I (Rick) was approached by a young youth pastor following the service. Our conversation quickly revealed to me his strength and humility. He was cur-

rently organizing creative outreach events on the campuses of universities in Kampala. Having heard my teaching, he responded with words of deep gratitude, followed by this statement: "We need your message in Uganda because we do not have many fathers [disciplemakers] who teach us such love."

3. In American culture, the trend of "losing the next generation" has become a crisis of equally epic proportions. According to Robert Wuthnow's research, there is both a decline in the number of young adults who attend religious services regularly and an increase in the number who seldom or never attend.[6] This growing exodus of young people from churches, especially after they leave home and live on their own, is echoed in a 2007 study by Lifeway Research which reported that 70 percent of young Protestant adults between eighteen and twenty-two stop attending church regularly.[7] The Barna Group's research reveals an equally startling statistic: "Perhaps the most striking reality of twentysomethings' faith is their relative absence from Christian churches. Only 3 out of 10 twentysomethings (31%) attend church in a typical week, compared to 4 out of 10 of those in their 30s (42%) and nearly half of all adults age 40 and older (49%)."[8]

An overall lack of heart connection between young adults and the church has reached the level of a spiritual global pandemic in the first generation of twenty-first-century adults. In response, *Shaping the Journey of Emerging Adults* presents a call to vision and action. We see so many in this generation living harassed and helpless, like sheep without a shepherd. Yet, in every country where we've traveled and in every culture we've engaged, we have also repeatedly encountered emerging-adult men and women living in Christ-filled hope. Whether in the desperate slums of Kampala or the affluent neighborhoods of Chicago's suburbs or the overcrowded streets of Saigon, we stand amazed at the passion with which emerging adults are pursuing radical Christ-centered, kingdom-based visions for change. And, in every country and culture, the key factor that determines whether young adults are thriving or simply surviving is always the same: the availability and accessibility of teachers, coaches, pastors, friends and mentors who are committed to investing in their spiritual vitality.

An inspiring and compelling example is London's multisite church Holy Trinity Brompton (or HTB, as it's called by the locals). The church has become an urban center for spiritual revival among the next generation in London. How did this happen? The leadership of the church has been consumed by a sense of urgency and purpose, mission and prayer, specifically focused on reaching and investing spiritually in the journeys of emerging adults in the city of London. Even the most casual experience of worship and community at HTB stands in stark contrast to the pervasively spiritual barrenness left by the loss of gospel vision and passion in previous generations.

On a personal level, this heart cry of the Father has been echoing in our lives for almost thirty years. We are both now in our sixth decade of life. A quarter of a century ago we were young, energetic, "edgy," next-generation leaders with a vision for changing the world. Since then, our bodies have changed dramatically (slower). The world in which we live and serve has changed even more dramatically (faster). Our hearts, however, are fundamentally the same. And we see the same promise for relational impact today as we did in the late 1980s. If our years of working with successive generations of students and young adults have taught us anything, it's this: shaping the next generation through disciplemaking remains by far the most powerful strategy Christ has given to us for shaping the church and changing the world.

We are convinced, therefore, that this relational strategy is mission-critical to the future of the church in the world. No country or culture is exempt. In fact, the need is increasingly acute in countries such as Europe and the United States whose cultural ethos has radically departed from its formerly supportive attitude toward Christianity. In this moment in history, creating a legacy of spiritual vitality for the twenty-first-century church that is just now emerging is crucial for the body of Christ. We must rebuild the spiritual levees of our communities with an uncompromising faith, an unwavering hope and a relentless love.

THE COMPLEX WORLD OF EARLY ADULTHOOD

Why Young Adults Need Guidance

GROWING UP, AS WE HAVE already noted, is never easy. Growing up during the emerging-adult season, however, can be an amazing adventure, one that presents surprising plotlines and intriguing new characters. Still, upon closer examination, even the most positive stories about the emerging-adult years contain evidence of a powerful longing for spiritual companionship, community and guidance on the journey.

Jon and Sarah met and fell in love at the Christian college they attended.[1] Soon after graduation they were married. One of them grew up in a stable Christian home while the other did not. Driven by a shared desire to make a difference in the film world, they relocated to Hollywood, hoping to be the aroma of Christ in this unique mission field. Though finding work didn't take long, being so far away from family wasn't easy, and finding a church that fit them in this unique stage of their lives took three years of on-and-off searching. Weekends found them exploring the distinctive landscape and attractions of California. Friends were envious of their life—as much for its adventure as for its impact on nonbelievers. They might have stayed longer, but family concerns motivated them to move back to the Midwest toward the end of their twenties.

Once back, Jon and Sarah had new decisions to make, such as what the next season of their life would look like. They had pursued their dream of working in Hollywood; they'd also made enough money to live an adventurous life and felt free to focus on themselves. Should they now start a family or enjoy having the freedom to reinvent their lives without factoring in children? They watched as some of their friends "settled down" while others lived to please themselves. The question they felt compelled to face was, What does it mean to be an adult, and how do I know if I am one?

Jon got a stable, non-film-related job and Sarah got pregnant when they were both about twenty-nine. Any sooner would have felt too early to them. Two children later, they are successfully "launched" into adulthood by conventional markers. They live on a budget, plan for the future, are involved in a local church and make decisions now that are not only about them. Sarah says they had to accept "a new reality" as they transitioned from the flexible years of their twenties to a more settled stage of life. They look back on their experience as emerging adults with a mixture of relief and sadness; it was a time of exploration *and* confusion in which they were carefree but often floundering and idealistic. Many times they were discouraged, but it was also a time during which they felt empowered and yet eventually paralyzed. Now in their mid-thirties, Jon and Sarah realize that the risks they took in their twenties were great, the rewards greater—and the longing during that season for relationships with people who would invest *in them*, greater still.

Emerging adults desire the guidance of seasoned Christians—not because they can't "make it" in this world or because the challenges they face are completely insurmountable but because they are charting new territory. Emerging adulthood has been characterized as a "new phase of individual exploration and uncertainty" brought on by both economic and cultural changes that have globally affected young adults.[2] Christian Smith, in his book *Souls in Transition,* suggests that the years between eighteen and thirty have "morphed into a different experience from that of previous generations."[3] Defining characteristics of this "different experience" are a tendency to delay marriage and parenthood, a more meandering path to a stable career, and difficulty in attaining financial and emotional independence.

The pressing question, however, remains the same: What *does* it mean to be an "adult"? Previous generations tended to recognize someone as an adult when they entered into marriage and family life or embarked on a "serious" career path. In an effort to go beyond these more external markers (marriage, children, stable career) and after consulting a number of studies, Jeffrey Arnett identified three criteria as universal markers of adulthood: accepting responsibility for yourself, making independent decisions and becoming financially independent.[4]

The transition from adolescence to traditional adulthood still includes many of the same challenges. It's just that the landscape is different and, as a result, the journey may take a bit longer. Sarah and Jon are an emerging-adult success story: even in the midst of the challenges of navigating their twenties, they followed Christ as best as they could, developing confidence in his wisdom and discovering satisfying ways to engage in his purposes for them in each stage of their lives. However, their *journey*—like most journeys—was a mixture of success and failure. On the long road through her twenties, Sarah longed for a mentor who would help her navigate what was often a lonely journey. If only someone could have modeled how to pursue a career while maintaining a stable Christian marriage in the entertainment world (an environment that cannot comprehend why anyone would want to be married at such a young age). Jon craved the guidance of an older man or even a peer to help him gain a vision for how to be a godly father and husband, especially as they moved back to the Midwest. Even though they survived intact, the journey was hard and the church helped very little. (We are exceedingly thankful that the lack of mentors in this very vibrant couple's lives has not caused them, like so many of their peers, to walk away from the church.)

Emerging adults long for mentors who will provide navigational guidance as they face a changing societal landscape where values and markers are no longer clear. This could be a peer who comes alongside them as a powerful fellow traveler or a grandparent who proactively engages in the holistic growth of their adult grandchild. The key is the disciplemaker's willingness to listen, learn and walk the path to Christian maturity themselves as they journey with the young adult.

Those who wish to be disciplemakers for this generation need not feel lost in this new territory. The remainder of this chapter will examine several important developmental factors as well as make sense of essential aspects of the multifaceted landscape emerging adults encounter.

Chapters seven through eleven will specifically explore how to engage some of the challenges mentioned here, providing a clearer picture of the kind of shepherding that will allow these adults to experience the freeing rhythms of living the Christlife.

THE DEVELOPMENT OF EMERGING ADULTS

Developmental theorists point to two common phases that characterize this journey into adulthood. The first phase comes as young adults (ranging in age from twenty-one to thirty) move from a still relatively dependent *pre-adult* stage (eighteen to twenty-four) into the functional adult world. Those who go straight from high school to full-time employment or marriage may experience this transition earlier. However, the majority of young adults (nearly 70%) spend at least some time in college,[5] and many prolong the pre-adult stage by pursuing even more education (nearly 40%[6]).

In this phase, pre-adults engage in a battle aimed at proving to themselves and their family that they are no longer dependent children. They seek resolutions to questions about how to define themselves as adults as well as what it means to form lasting relational bonds. They wonder how adult friendships should look and consider whether they want to be married. Developmental theorists describe the twenties as a somewhat chaotic season of high-stakes decision making about jobs, lifestyle, housing and relationships. Young adults at this stage have been characterized as *transitional, idling, flexible, trying* or *tinkering*[7] as they seek to actualize their answers to the question they were asked as children, "What do you want to be when you grow up?" How prepared young adults feel to live out their answer to that question affects the complexity of the transition from home or college to independence.

Journalist Gail Sheehy calls the twenties "provisional" and comments, "The age of Provisional Adulthood today is lived at a breathlessly accelerated pace, even though many of the responsibilities of full adulthood are delayed."[8] Her statement captures something typical of this age group. They are often untethered and hurried—untethered because they resist making commitments amidst the pressure of having to decide about their career, relationships and living situations, and hurried as they struggle with life-pacing. Lifestyles that emerge in the college years (a time of greater physical energy and social capacity) feel like they must be sustained—doing less feels like "getting old." This clashes with the daily job of being self-sufficient (doing dishes, doing laundry, cooking, paying bills, cleaning, etc.); many will therefore choose to live spontaneously, avoiding commitments that force them to limit options. Doing so allows them to maintain an active lifestyle and postpone action regarding impending decisions hanging over their heads.

Developmentally, the second phase of young adulthood (mid-twenties to mid-thirties; also called *functional* adulthood) is about moving from the uncertainty of entering into the adult world to a more stable place within it. As emerging adults become more established in both identity and relationships, they begin to focus on personal impact. Different questions arise, questions like What is my purpose? Why am I here? What does it mean to be a contributing member of society? How can I make a purposeful contribution in the midst of the demands in my life? As twenty-nine-year-old Annie, for example, adjusted to a job that was "finally a good fit" and became more settled in her identity, she simultaneously felt a little lost. *What am I supposed to do with all the energy I was putting toward figuring out who I am and what career I should be pursuing?* she wondered.

Typically around age thirty, young adults experience this shift in life's questions as a transitional crisis. According to Erik Erikson, a developmental crisis is "a crucial period in which a decisive turn *one way or another* is unavoidable."[9] In this second stage of adulthood the "unavoidable turn" is away from the flexibility of the twenties to a more established season of life, representing a shift from a transitional identity into a more concrete or settled adult identity.

Few emerging adults experience the turning point from pre-adult to functional adult or from a flexible to a more settled lifestyle in the same way or with the same level of intensity. Erikson points out, "Such crises occur in man's total development sometimes more noisily, as it were, when new instinctual needs meet abrupt prohibitions, sometimes more quietly when new capacities yearn to match new opportunities, and when new aspirations make it more obvious how limited one (as yet) is."[10] Emerging adults that experience this shift more quietly might identify with the following sentiments:

We may at one time have expected our lives to be in sort of grown-up order by thirty, but many of us have taken so long considering our many options and questioning this order or that, that expectation now seems unreasonable. We've stayed in school longer, we're getting married and having children later. We've grown up learning that our job futures will probably never be as secure as those of generations past, and this has meant that the once defining commitment of career choices is also now more malleable. . . . Many of us talk about a kind of unease with the decisions of adulthood, and of feelings of being overwhelmed at the many alternatives we see before us. . . . Often this generational unease is interpreted by those older than us as a kind of proclivity for sluggishness.[11]

This "generational unease" has been explored in recent literature. For example, Arnett's *Emerging Adulthood* notes a shift that has occurred in the eagerness that once existed for entering the adult roles of spouse and parent, or settling down into a career. Adulthood and its obligations "are seen by most of them not as achievements to be pursued but as perils to be avoided."[12] The majority of young adults still desire adult things—to own a home, get married, have children—but they don't feel ready for them as soon as other generations did. Apparently the security and stability of established adulthood don't sufficiently offset the perceived loss of independence, spontaneity and a sense of wide-open possibilities that emerging adults have come to value.

Present cultural norms also affect the way this turning point is experienced. This perceptual shift was recognized in a *Newsweek* article about the twentysomething's tendency to postpone adulthood. The article used the term "adultolescents" to capture a season of adolescence that bleeds into adulthood. The author explains:

Relying on your folks to light the shadowy path to the future has become so accepted that even the ultimate loser move—returning home to live with your parents—has lost its stigma. . . .

Most adultolescents no longer hope, or even desire, to hit the traditional benchmarks of independence—marriage, kids, owning a home, financial autonomy—in the years following college. The average age for a first marriage is now 26, four years later than it was in 1970, and child-bearing is often postponed for a decade or more after that. Jobs are scarce, and increasingly, high-paying careers require a graduate degree. The decades-long run-up in the housing market has made a starter home a pipe dream for most people under 30.[13]

Though the economic decline's effect on housing prices and mortgage rates have made owning a home more achievable for the emerging adult in 2010, the percentage of adults between the ages of twenty-five and thirty-four living with their parents is still rising. According to a 2010 current population survey data on young adults living at home, approximately 27 percent of twenty-five- to thirty-four-year-olds lived with their parents in 2010 compared to 21 percent in 2000.[14]

Recent sociological efforts from authors like Christian Smith *(Souls in Transition* and *Lost in Transition)*, Jeffrey Arnett *(Emerging Adulthood)* and Robert Wuthnow *(After the Baby Boomers)* resist identifying this new way of experiencing early adulthood as an *extension* of adolescence. Wuthnow says it is a mistake to think we can understand the decisions and interests of young adults by studying teenagers,[15] and Arnett argues that emerging adulthood is not the same as "late adolescence." He points out, for example, that dramatic changes in puberty are no longer a factor and legal rights have changed.[16] Likewise, true parental and financial independence is typically not possible in adolescence whereas it can be obtained by those in their twenties.

What *is* similar to the adolescent stage is the task of navigating new responsibilities on one's own. However, in adolescence, students still have parental and institutional support (school, youth groups, sports teams, etc.). No one expects a teenager to have it all together. For eighteen- to thirty-year-olds, however, supportive life-stage programming is lacking in churches, beyond age-targeted social events.[17] The emerging adult's challenge, especially beyond the college years, is to travel into this new territory with all its confusing options and instability *without* institutional support. This makes the need for adult disciplemakers even more critical. Perhaps the church can best be responsive to this lack by mobilizing adults to respond personally to the call to "make disciples" among this generation.

THE LANDSCAPE OF EMERGING ADULTS

Added to these developmental factors that affect a young adult's historically unique emergence into adulthood are important facets of the emerging adult's cultural landscape.

Chanda is twenty-four. She recently moved into her own apartment and feels good about being out on her own again (she was mostly on her own in college but then moved back home to save money). Sometimes she worries about whether she will be able to keep her job for the length of her lease; she's pretty sure, though, that she'd be able to rely on her parents for financial help every now and then if she needed to. If that doesn't work out, she knows she can consider going back to school for a master's degree or looking for a job in an exotic place like Alaska or Hawaii. She goes to church, but her connections there aren't strong enough to keep her from exploring other possibilities.

Lisette and Roger got married when they were both twenty-six and now have two little girls who are one and three. In order to stay gainfully employed, they have already moved three times. Lisette works from home in a part-time position that allows her to connect with clients remotely. Roger takes the train to work and is occasionally required to fly to other countries on business. Their connection to a local congregation is sporadic, though both of them wish it were more regular. Roger, especially, feels the need to connect with other men. Sometimes the influence of work and international connections causes him to doubt the validity of his Christian upbringing. He wonders if connecting to a small group of men might give him a place to work out his doubts. Most of Lisette's relational contact is electronically mediated: email, teleconferencing and Skype for work and Facebook for friendships. She longs for more face time with adults. She also wants to sense that she and Roger are building good family patterns that will encourage their children in matters of faith.

As a sociologist looking at the landscape of today's emerging adults, Christian Smith explains in his book *Lost in Transition:*

> Studies agree that the transition to adulthood today is even more complex, disjointed, and confusing than it was in past decades. The steps through schooling, a first real job, marriage, and parenthood are simply less well organized and coherent today than they were in the past. At the same time, these years are marked by a historically unparalleled freedom to roam, experiment, learn, move on, and try again.[18]

Smith comes to the conclusion that, "notwithstanding all that is genuinely good in emerging adulthood—emerging adult life in the United States today is beset with real problems, in some cases troubling and even heartbreaking problems."[19] The two mini-portraits we presented exemplify aspects of the emerging adult world that relate to two overarching themes: the instability of their world and the societal value shifts that affect their daily decisions.

Instability. Emerging adults today do more exploring than their predecessors. They travel, form relationships with people of other cultures which are sustained via the Internet, move back in with parents,[20] change jobs[21] and change churches[22] more than ever before. Arnett simply states, "Exploration and instability go hand in hand."[23] We will look briefly at three kinds of instability: career, relational and physical.

Career instability. The job market is less stable for emerging adults than it was for their parents because of high rates of turnover due to layoffs, a technological explosion that minimizes the number of workers needed and outsourcing that drains job opportunities. This is a common situation in many economically developed nations. As a result, emerging adults tend to expect it to take awhile to find the job they will eventually settle into.

Another result of an unstable job market is that young adults are pursuing more education (both to delay having to find a job and to ensure that they get a higher-paying one). In particular, an increasing number of women are pursuing education and are part of the workforce. Additionally, since the North American college system does not require students to specialize until they have had two years of college, going on for a master's degree gives them the option to change their focus again if they want to. Delaying marriage and parenthood provides young adults like Chanda with even more time to explore career options. Consequently, careers play an increasingly important role in the lives of emerging adults, such that they require that their eventual careers be an expression of their identity.[24]

Relational instability. Lisette and Roger are more likely to stick with the jobs they have because they have children to support. Though economic conditions may cause fear about losing their jobs, they are in the latter, more settled stage of emerging adulthood. That doesn't mean they don't experience instability at all, however. Like many emerging adults, they may, for example, still be figuring out how to relate to their parents. A semi-dependence on their parents for the twenty-six years before they married makes creating their own, independent home base challenging. They, similar to most young adults, search for how to transform family-of-origin relationships to reflect adult patterns without cutting off their parents altogether. Although this can be difficult for both genders, psychologist Daniel Levinson found that independence from parents might take five to ten years longer for young women.[25] So Lisette, in particular, might find *emotional* independence from her parents difficult, even while she's living in a self-sufficient home base.

Relational instability extends beyond parent-child relationships to *all* young-adult relationships. Erik Erikson identifies one stage of psychosocial development as isolation versus intimacy, in which the adult must figure out what it means to truly engage with others or else suffer isolation.[26] Thus, emerging adults like Lisette and Roger must navigate issues like their level of intimacy in marriage, as well as availability or unavailability to relationally connect with friends. They may find satisfaction or be disappointed with what relating to young children entails. For example, Lisette's desire to be more connected at church is stirred up by feelings of isolation from friends and a lack of meaningful interaction since, beyond work, her daily conversation partners are ages one and three.

In contrast to Roger and Lisette, Chanda's relationships are in danger of constantly changing because of potential relocation for new jobs or additional education. If she has the time and energy to keep up with old contacts, this relational uncertainty may not bother her. As she moves further into her twenties, however, and social circles—as well as her capacity to keep in touch with past friends—shrink, she may become more relationally frustrated.

Furthermore, since actively looking for a mate is still a cultural expectation in the twenties, Chanda experiences relational anxiety related to the delay of marriage and parenthood. Though emerging adults today typically marry four or five years later than their parents did,[27] entering the thirties without marrying would likely add to Chanda's sense of instability.

In addition to all this, the sometimes elusive goal of being financially independent (without the help of parents) is important to emerging adults,[28] so needing financial support could also increase Chanda's experience of relational instability. Her struggle to become independent might occasionally cause her to feel like a child in her parents' eyes.

Traditional markers of adulthood have faded over the past several decades (though some may still be prevalent in certain religious traditions). It used to be that the majority of men and women in their early twenties settled down, got married and began a family. When those markers were reached, they felt "adult." Among today's emerging adults, often there are less consistent markers, making "reaching adulthood" more confusing.

Physical instability. A subtle but very substantial physical transition begins in the latter half of emerging adulthood. You may have noticed the preponderance of twenty-eight- to thirty-five-year-olds at workout gyms. In contrast to many forty- or fifty-year olds who join gyms but never go, emerging adults actually seem to take advantage of their memberships! This is probably because they have begun to experience the downward turn of physical resiliency and energy. Weight gain is lost more slowly. Recovery from illness or injury takes longer. The realization that what they eat really does affect their energy level sinks in. Men and women ramp up their exercising to wage war against their aging body. The pressure for women in this area is particularly high. The media's infatuation with the physical and sexual freshness of the twenty-something body causes women to feel they are leaving their most attractive years behind. Single women wonder if men will still find them attractive; *Am I still marriageable?* they wonder. Married women wonder if they are losing their appeal to their husband. These physical, external changes can provoke a sense of internal instability.

Value shifts. The center of the contiguous United States is marked by a historical marker and a flag flying on a pole near Lebanon, Kansas. Well, not the actual center. Supposedly, that spot is about one-half to three-quarters of a mile down the road on a private farm—but the owner did not want tourists trampling his fields, so the markers were placed *as close as possible* to the spot.

Well, okay, that's not that bad, right? The plaque even acknowledges that it's a little bit off. It's within range. Close enough to be "reliable," yes?

Not exactly. In 1918 some folks at the U.S. Coast and Geodetic Survey determined the geographical center by—I can hardly write it—balancing a cardboard cutout of the lower forty-eight states on a single point! One article concludes that the true center could be twenty miles or more from the marker, but that it'd be hard to pinpoint exactly, "as an official measurement would have to be defined by an *agreed upon standard which does not exist.*"[29] In 1999, the senior mathematician for U.S. Coast and Geodetic Survey said of the situation, "There is no definite way to locate such a point," and "This may be a case in which all may differ but all be right."[30]

Huh? All may differ but all be *right?*

The instability of truth. This is how our society presently handles truth: with no "agreed upon standard." Increasingly, the cultural consensus is that truth cannot be located in one timeless reality. Truth is thus reframed as personal and shifting, changing as we go. Our interpretation of our experiences creates the standard, not God. The explosion of information and rise of globalization (our next two value shifts) have helped create the sense that the pool of truth is both larger than we once thought and dependent on our location and cultural upbringing.

This value shift creates instability in the convictions of the emerging adult, who are encouraged to construct their own "truths" according to their experience. They learn to settle for *information masquerading as truth,* or they give up on truth altogether, as it's confusing to make decisions in a culture in which there seems to be no solid guidelines to discern what is true, best or right.

Roger's convictions, for example, are impacted by interactions with fellow workers as well as business connections in other countries—especially as he personally interacts with a devout follower of a religious system that is vastly different from his. Younger adults steeped in a cultural perspective that views truth as unstable may not even be aware that there has been a shift. Indeed, most eighteen- to twenty-three-year-olds that Smith interviewed were "de facto doubtful that an identifiable, objective, shared reality might exist across and around all people that can serve as a reliable reference point for rational deliberation and argument." Their conclusions were formed not from a lack of intelligence but because they *couldn't even conceive of objective truth.* He concludes,

"What emerging adults take to be reality ultimately seems to consist of a multitude of subjective but ultimately autonomous experiences."[31]

Easy access to information. The Internet explosion has affected the type of information available as well as the way information is acquired. Emerging adults strongly prefer the Internet over print media as a means of finding out information. In this realm, ideas and opinions abound and are replaced by new information rapidly, creating the impression that information is impermanent.[32] When an encyclopedia can be amended or updated hourly by its users (Wikipedia), what value can be assigned to the entries? How should the emerging adult discern *which* update presents them with the truth? To them, the whole category of "truth" has been brought into question.

Global awareness and an embrace of diversity. This accessibility creates a greater diversity of information as well. The entire world seems within reach. This diversity is not just factual, religious or racial, though; it also includes images and sounds. Exposure to music and art are key factors in the young adult's world, as evidenced by the fact that, in the last three decades, the number of professional artists has tripled and the amount of money spent on music has doubled.[33]

While the Internet is a substantial factor in becoming internationally aware, it's not the only means emerging adults have of learning about the world. They travel, live among an increasing immigrant population, or have jobs that are globally connected or depend on global markets.[34] This means they generally exhibit a greater openness to and acceptance of others with different lifestyles and values. It also means they have become more approving of others' beliefs. To Smith, the consequence of embracing so much diversity is that "none of what is distinctive about any given religious tradition, history, worldview, worship style and so on matters all that much to emerging adults."[35] In other words, an inclusiveness that equally values diversity often ends up devaluing distinctions in a young adult's own faith system.

Provisional connections. Emerging-adult relationships and connections are taking on new forms. The roots they put down tend to be shallower than those of previous generations in order to keep options open, please employers by staying mobile,[36] and handle the increased number of times they move or change jobs. They therefore depend on social networking sites like Facebook and Google+ to keep in touch with friends over distances. Those interactions, however, must be followed up with other kinds of contact to be satisfactory. Wuthnow calls this being "psychologically mobile."[37] For Lisette, life circumstances make it difficult to follow up on her short Facebook conversations, which contributes to a sense that her relationships are provisional and shallow.

This temporary, conditional nature of relationships tends to affect the attendance of young adults in church (along with the decreasing rate of other factors that draw emerging adults back to church, such as being married and having children);[38] church hopping (visiting different congregations without an intention to choose one) and church shopping (a continual search for the "right" church) have become more common. If young adults cannot find what they want in one place (which is often the case), they may choose to worship at one church and attend another for social events.

Personalized spirituality. At one time in the United States it was common to speak about religion as personal or private. Today, though, the *personalization* of spirituality has less to do with being private and more to do with being individually *stylized.* Since emerging adults have difficulty conceptualizing an objective reality, dependence on themselves rather than on a traditional belief system makes sense to them. They "see it as their personal responsibility to develop a set of religious beliefs that is uniquely their own."[39] This kind of "pick and choose orthodoxy" is clearly revealed by one twentysomething interviewee in Wuthnow's book who grew up in an evangelical church but now uses her Bible time *to pick out the things she sees as truth.*[40] In one study, 42 percent of those who identified themselves as biblical literalists explained their view that Christianity was the best way to understand God by saying that it was best for them *personally* rather than that it was universally so.[41]

IS THIS A UNIVERSAL LANDSCAPE?

Let us emphasize that the above descriptions are generalizations. There are a number of factors that affect the way an emerging adult experiences the landscape we have described: socioeconomic factors, location (urban, rural, etc., as well as the country they live in), gender, education, and cultural or ethnic norms. Socioeconomic factors are particularly key in determining who can or cannot pursue higher education. In 2001 the U.S. Census Bureau found that 15 percent of adults in their early twenties lived below the poverty line—and that percentage was higher if they were African American (25%) or Hispanic (20%).[42] Similarly, a young adult living in a rural area is less likely to have the resources or opportunities that a young adult from an urban area would.[43] Thus, the delay of marriage and family due to further education is not as likely to happen in these subgroups.

In addition, different countries approach education in varying ways. In Europe, for example, students must commit to a course of study at a much younger age than eighteen or nineteen, as in the United States.[44] A career delay experienced by American youth because of their educational experience will not be felt as strongly by European youth because they are encouraged to set their career direction at a much earlier age. And while industrialized or postindustrial countries (including the West and some Asian countries like Japan and South Korea) are experiencing the effects of the emerging-adult landscape the most strongly, Arnett believes that emerging adulthood will be a normative experience in *all* countries by the end of the twenty-first century (though he acknowledges potential variations in length or specific content).[45]

Gender also influences a person's experience of emerging adulthood. Though men and women face a similar external landscape, different internal pressures may skew how they respond to the challenges of this life stage. Levinson suggests that both emerging males and emerging females are striving to construct an initial "flawed" adult life structure. A "flawed life structure" denotes an initial and usually imperfect attempt at creating patterns that will accommodate a new stage in a person's life. For the young adult, this structure—which determines how they relate to friends, career, family, etc.—only needs to facilitate their ability to establish themselves as adults. Once that has been achieved, a new life structure will most likely be needed. In the mind of a young adult, however, the choices being made at this stage—the structure they're developing—may look and feel as if they are permanent.

Young single women especially feel the pressure of the choices they make in this life stage. They can fall under the illusion that making the right choices and forming the right relationships now will "create a satisfactory life pattern that will last forever after."[46] Their temptation is to compare themselves with others who seem to have made the "right choices" in their lives. Decades ago, women were expected to accomplish everything they wanted to *after* they raised children; now they feel the pressure to do so *before* marriage and family. For example, as a young woman, my (Jana's) mom worked in radio broadcasting, but without much hesitation she gave that up to get married and have a family. It wasn't until after her children were on their own that she pursued a vocational passion for genealogical research. In contrast, Sarah (from our opening illustration) felt pressure as an emerging adult to pursue and find success in her career in acting and film *before* thinking about having children, since a single woman has more flexibility to entertain changes in direction or priority.

A young woman who is already married with children is not immune to the "right choices" illusion either, though. If she married and started a family early, she may wonder if she made the "right" choice when she compares her life to the seemingly carefree life of her single friends.

In the midst of feeling pressure to construct her ideal life, a young woman also faces the challenge of living wholly present to reality. The tendency to mentally construct a satisfying future or romanticize present circumstances is strong. So, for example, while her career or relationships can be *imagined* to be on a positive trajectory, in reality they might be stalled. Living in the imagined future can prevent her from enjoying the present or confronting the challenges that might facilitate a satisfying future. On the other hand, she may only be able to imagine a negative future. In either case, the net effect is that fear and anger replace trust and love in the heart of the follower of Christ.

Young men are not immune to this specific challenge, but for them, it's less a tendency to construct an ideal life and more a tendency to dream of a particular unattainable ideal. This becomes harmful if their picture of an ideal mate or an ideal job immobilizes them in relational or career pursuits, thereby delaying adulthood even further.

Levinson suggests young men have two major tasks to accomplish that are somewhat at odds with each other. The first is to explore options—to test a variety of relationships, careers and lifestyle choices. Commitments are therefore often kept tentative in order to keep exploring. The second task is to create a stable life structure—to make firm choices, define goals and lead an organized life.[47] How does a young man maintain equilibrium in the midst of these contradictory tasks? Fear of failure may keep him from defining goals or making strong choices. Anger at having given up options may prevent him from enjoying the choices he has made.

Additionally, young men often find themselves contending with the cultural mores handed down about what it means to "be a man." Dr. Alvin Baraff, in his book *Men Talk*, found that men are still very affected by past myths of manhood: "Men *do* feel they are *not* supposed to cry, they're not supposed to ask for help, they are supposed to *know* what to do, period."[48] Emerging adults can greatly benefit from a same-gender mentor who has already negotiated some of the specific challenges of becoming a godly man or a godly woman.

In addition to gender, *culture* is a key factor in the adult experience. I (Rick) spent four days in London immersed in the world of a local Anglican church, Holy Trinity of Brompton, and its partner ministry, St. Paul's Theological Centre. The church and the accredited equipping ministries of the Centre are primarily attended by emerging adults. Being a white-haired, fifty-year-old pastor of a church in Knoxville therefore made me a very conspicuous member of the minority. As I continue to reflect on my experience there, I'm comparing the spiritual journeys of these vibrant London emerging adults with those of young adults in churches and equipping ministries I have visited over the last eleven months in Poland, Uganda, Malawi, Zimbabwe and Mexico. While each context has much in common, each is deeply shaped by cultural variations such as gender-role expectations, the prioritization and availability of higher educational opportunities, the degree of global awareness and experience, leadership ethos as demonstrated in local churches, and expectations for the young-adult phase of life. Even within just Europe itself, the impact of different cultural contexts on emerging-adult attitudes, behaviors and expectations is clearly observable.

RESPONDING TO THE EMERGING ADULT'S CHALLENGES

"Do people really know when they're grown-ups? Do they wake up one morning and say, 'Yes! Now I'm grown'?"[49] This question, from a woman

nearing thirty, reveals the puzzle young adults are trying to solve. For believers, the question centers on what it means to be an adult follower of Christ. How does a wise disciplemaker walk with young adults in the midst of their questions? Foundationally, disciplemaking with emerging adults will focus on empowering them to discover their adult identity and their present purpose in the midst of God's larger story.

As emerging adults face the challenges of independence, they will be presented with the all-important tasks of learning dependence on the Father's wisdom and interdependence in the body of Christ. Developing intentional relationships with a community of believers and seeking to walk in Christ's ways *together* is therefore crucial for young adults, as it enables both singles and married couples to move toward an experiential answer to their relational questions. Authentic Christian community also provides a crucial link in learning about purpose and contribution. It is in the midst of these kinds of relationships that young adults will face immaturities that currently hinder them from relating in ways that are mutually satisfying and God-glorifying. The growth that results from learning in community will teach them humility and the skills required to love others proactively. And maturing in the capacity to trust the Father, surrender to his love and leadership as well as proactively enter into the center of his will prepares them to enter fully into God's mission for their lives.

A caring disciplemaker does not soothe the unpleasant aspects of this stage away. Instead, they value this God-given time of life as a way for the young adult to become more attuned to the work of becoming like Christ. Whether a young man struggles with passive tendencies or is overwhelmed by alternatives, his crisis, even if mild, creates a window for he and his mentor to address his unease in light of God's provision. Entering places of discomfort, disappointment, failure or disillusionment will lead to opportunities to revisit expectations about what it means to be a follower of Christ in the midst of imperfection. Similarly, a compassionate disciplemaker can walk with a disillusioned young woman as she discovers what it means to trust the Father's wisdom and fulfill God's will as a Christian adult in the reality of her world.

When the crisis of initiating a more stable phase of adulthood is purposefully navigated, young adults may be pleasantly surprised at what lies ahead.[50] Moving into greater maturity, many will discover that the feared aspects of functional adulthood (such as stability and decreased options) can actually create greater freedom to pursue purposeful goals. Fulfillment of the desire to love and be loved becomes even more possible. And an ability to see patterns in the work of the Father come into view more clearly because of a stronger sense of being rooted.

Emerging adults need spiritual caregivers who will prayerfully engage the disciple's maturation, steering them away from navigating these life-shaping years primarily based on their own personal or experiential truth. To reach full maturity and maximize potential impact, the emerging adult needs to be challenged and supported as they are awakened to the way, the truth and the life offered by the Father, discovered in the Son and imparted through the Spirit. Jesus said plainly that *he* is the way, the truth and the life (Jn 14:6) and prayed to the Father, "Sanctify them in the truth; your word is truth" (Jn 17:17). And he promised that he would send us a Counselor, "the Spirit of truth" (Jn 15:26; 16:13), to guide us in all reality. As disciplemakers of emerging adults, God has given us a stable "geographic center" based on the reality reflected in God's Word and represented by his Son. The next chapter will explore ways we must shift our thinking in order to breathe new life into disciplemaking in this new territory.

PART ONE

Simplifying Our Vision

Life-Giving Rhythms
for Spiritual Transformation

BREATHING NEW LIFE
INTO DISCIPLEMAKING

"BUT YOU'RE NOT ACTING like a leader."
I (Rick) still remember the weight with which those words landed on my heart. I was in the process of dealing with a potential change of roles in my job. The new role required a much higher degree of leadership commitment and acumen. I felt ready for the challenge, but the seasoned leader sitting across the table from me was not so sure. In fact, he was uncertain as to whether I was a leader at all, much less whether I was prepared for the challenges that lay ahead with this new role. When I asked him what he meant by his statement, he contrasted the way I was responding to difficult issues with how a leader would respond. The examples he gave illustrated for me how I was approaching several situations with a view toward minimizing conflicts rather than pursuing solutions. "If you are going to lead," he shared abruptly, "then you are going to have to start thinking and acting like a leader."

On that day I committed myself to making several dramatic shifts: I would no longer ignore my leadership instincts, even if they were going to increase rather than diminish current conflicts. I also decided to stop calculating my actions based on my perception of how others would respond to me. I would choose, rather, to act according to the vision and purpose that God had planted in my heart. These shifts were not easy, simple, one-time decisions, but they were absolutely necessary if I was going to fulfill the leadership calling I sensed that God had placed in my heart.

I am so thankful for the honesty of that veteran leader who named what needed to change in my leadership. I am even more thankful for the grace and patience God showed me in walking me out of several deeply ingrained patterns of thought and action that were hindering my leadership responses to mission-critical challenges that lay before me.

Similar to my experience, fulfilling the mission-critical challenges of shepherding and equipping emerging-adult disciples of Christ will require several significant shifts within the fabric of the church in this century. Each of the following five shifts represents a movement away from entrenched, established patterns that have dominated the Western evangelical church for at least a generation, if not longer. Making these shifts will be neither quick nor painless—but make them we must.

SHIFT 1: FROM TWENTIETH-CENTURY THINKING TO TWENTY-FIRST-CENTURY THINKING

Robert Quinn, in his provocative leadership book *Deep Change*, contrasts technical change with transformational change. Technical change, essentially, is adapting how we do things in order to do them more efficiently. Transformational change, in contrast, is rethinking the present, reimagining the future, and revolutionizing everything for the sake of meeting new challenges and fulfilling new vision.[1] The time is well past for the church, particularly the Western church, to rethink and reimagine what it means to be the church in the twenty-first century.

Rethinking and reimagining are not easy, and should not be entered into casually. Lots of preparation and guidance are required along with many risks. Often there's no certainty of success. Not replacing twentieth-century thinking with twenty-first-century thinking is, however, certain death to the influence and impact of the church on the next generation. Brett McCracken, in a *Wall Street Journal* article, references a gushing oil well in the Gulf of Mexico in his urgent cry for new thinking about the church:

> "How can we stop the oil gusher?" may have been the question of the summer for most Americans. Yet for many evangelical pastors and leaders, the leaking well is nothing compared to the threat posed by an ongoing gusher of a different sort: Young people pouring out of their churches, never to return.[2]

McCracken continues by pleading with the church not to simply attempt to be "cool" or "shocking" in order to get the attention of this generation. "Cool" and "shocking" responses materialize and vaporize as quickly as the attention span of the culture changes. The amount of energy and level of resources invested in these reactionary responses often represent an overshift on the part of the church. The presence of this overshift exists largely as a carryover from the successes of the late-twentieth-century megachurches in America. Desiring to reach an increasingly secularized culture, church leadership focused more and more of their energies on answering the question "How do we get people to come to our church?" The twenty-first-century church must not ignore this relevant question but must demote it to its rightful place in our twenty-first-century conceptualization of the church.

The twenty-first-century church must focus more of its energy and resources on answering a different question: "How do we take the people God has brought to our church and empower and equip them to go into the world as disciplemakers who will lead others to know and follow Christ?" Alan Hirsch, a pioneer in the shift to twenty-first-century concepts of the church, and a plethora of others have used the term "missional church" to describe the movement from a preoccupation with attracting people to a broader vision of empowering and equipping people for service.[3] What is thus needed is a shift to thinking in twenty-first-century cultural terms regarding how the gospel and Jesus shape the church as Christ's presence in the world.

The longing for such transformation can be seen in the hunger the next generation has for the leadership of pastors like Francis Chan and David Platt. Chan's *Crazy Love* and Platt's *Radical* represent twenty-first-century rethinking and reimagining of the "why?" and "what?" of the church. They bash "thinking outside the box" over the head by rejecting "the box" itself and calling for revolutionary living of the gospel in the 101st generation of the church since Christ's resurrection and ascension.

The nature of emerging adulthood, more than any other life stage, provides great capacity to make bold moves in response to a rethinking of convictions and commitments. Adult thinking processes are well-developed. A plethora of yet-to-be-determined major life decisions and commitments lie directly ahead. Therefore, experimental risk-taking is not only possible but even desirable; the emerging adult wants to be challenged, supported and empowered. The church that attempts to cater to them, then, by trying harder and harder to attract them, will ultimately drive them away.

Jesus' lifestyle was unconventional, and he was significantly predisposed against catering to the crowd. Emerging adults want to know who this authentic, biblical Jesus really was and is. They want a Messiah to whom they can wholly commit their mysteriously unfolding lives. Getting stuck in twentieth-century conceptions of "what works" relationally and structurally in the church renders our presentation of Christ not only irrelevant, but—and this is much, much worse—inauthentic.

SHIFT 2: FROM DISCIPLEMAKING FORMULAS TO DISCIPLEMAKING RELATIONSHIPS

I (Jana) was participating in a small group discussion with ministers on the importance of disciplemaking. My intense interest in this subject had me listening carefully. At one point, the discussion focused in on how essential it is for disciplemakers to spend time with those they are mentoring—life on life—really getting to know their strengths and life challenges. I was nodding my head in enthusiastic approval. Nicolás, a bivocational minister, mentioned his struggle with a colleague's suggestion that spending ten to fifteen hours a week for each disciple was key. We began to discuss the reasonability of that for his circumstances and helped him redefine what life-on-life ministry might look like in his context.

Then one of the veteran full-time pastors—in an effort to make discipleship a more manageable task, I think—suggested a book that explores twelve characteristics of a disciple. He triumphantly suggested to Nicolás, "There's your curriculum! You could cover one characteristic a week for three months or one every two weeks for six months." The implication seemed to be that once these twelve areas were covered you would have a fully formed disciple. My head responded internally this time—not up and down in agreement but back and forth in dismay.

I recently perused a book on discipleship that covered thirteen distinguishing marks of a disciple, five environmental conditions to create, eight steps to take with the disciple, a fourfold model of Jesus to follow, three principles for spiritual transformation, five models of effective disciplemaking and much, much more in its nine-page table of contents. We seem to have this tendency to want to make things simple with formulas—and yet our formulas consistently make them more complex. As A. W. Tozer points out, "Right now we are in an age of religious complexity. The simplicity which is in Christ is rarely found among us."[4]

I later pondered what I wished I had said to Nicolás about disciplemaking. I think I would have told him that, instead of focusing on outward actions, disciplemaking could be approached from the inside by exploring the attitudes that drive the character and behaviors of the disciple. And I would have encouraged him to focus not on the hours that need to be spent but on the rhythms of disciplemaking that would enable him to be responsive to God's agenda in order to journey most effectively alongside the disciple.

SHIFT 3: FROM "THE GREAT UNTRUTH" TO GRACE AND TRUTH

Bernice Gallego had a decision to make. Should she list the well-worn, obscure baseball card on eBay for ten dollars or fifteen dollars? A fifteen-dollar listing would cost an additional twenty cents. Unfamiliar with baseball, much less baseball memorabilia, the seventy-two-year-old veteran antique trader questioned whether she could even give the card away. What possible value could there be in possessing a faded, wrinkled baseball card featuring the Red Stocking B. B. Club of Cincinnati? Not fifteen dollars' worth, Bernice reasoned. So, she set the bar low and saved twenty cents. The card was listed at a ten-dollar minimum bid.

A few hours later, Bernice had reason to rethink her decision. Potential buyers were assigning a higher value to the card than she had. Realizing that the card was more valuable than she had originally imagined, Bernice began to dream of selling it for as much as fifty dollars, or even one hundred dollars. Her good friend George Huddleston advised her to cancel the auction and investigate the true value of the card. This would turn out to be the best advice anyone ever gave her.

Bernice casually placed the card in a sandwich bag and pinned it to the wall in her laundry room. She then contacted Rick Mirigian. Mirigian, like Bernice, lived in the Fresno, California, area. But unlike Bernice, Rick Mirigian traded in baseball cards—including the rare ones.

Bernice's card, she would soon learn, was 139 years old and featured the first professional baseball team, the 1869 Red Stocking B. B. Club of Cincinnati. Mike Osegueda, a reporter for the *Fresno Bee*, recounts Mirigian's reaction to seeing the card for the first time: "When I came to meet her and she took it out of a sandwich Baggie and she was smoking a cigarette, I almost fainted," Mirigian says. "They've uncovered a piece of history that few people will ever be able to imagine or comprehend. And it comes out of Fresno," he says. "That card is history. It's like unearthing a Mona Lisa or a Picasso."[5]

From the 1869 Red Stockings' seemingly insignificant beginnings as a traveling all-star baseball team would emerge the first ever professional sports team and the first ever professional sports league. The ten men in knee-high socks staring back at Bernice were the "Adams" of professional sports as we know them today. The card is not just rare; it is *extremely* rare. Bernice's card, once not considered worthy of risking twenty cents to auction at the fifteen-dollar level, eventually sold for over seventy-five thousand dollars. Bernice thought she had a nearly worthless piece of paper when in fact she possessed a nearly priceless piece of history.

Bernice's story encapsulates what I (Rick) have continually confronted in my ministry in the last decade as it's been centered on walking men, young and old, into a new vision for their lives as relational disciplemakers. I call it "the Great Untruth," and it seems to be almost universally believed among the seemingly ordinary, common people like me who comprise the kingdom of Christ. Simply worded, the great lie is this: *my life really does not have much to offer—I am simply inadequate when it comes to making a difference in the life of an emerging adult.* People see themselves as ten-dollar trinkets when in fact they are treasures worth well over seventy-five thousand dollars. We have millions of men and women walking the halls of our churches who have the potential to invest powerfully in the life of a young adult but aren't doing it because they consider themselves inadequate and unqualified.

Evidently, the Great Untruth did not originate in our generation or even in the one immediately before us. Paul wrote these encouraging words to a Corinthian church that was struggling to find its identity and purpose in the kingdom:

For God, who said, "Let light shine out of darkness," has shone in our hearts to give the light of the knowledge of the glory of God in the face of Jesus Christ.

But we have this treasure in jars of clay, to show that the surpassing power belongs to God and not to us. (2 Cor 4:6-7)

"The light of the knowledge of the glory of God in the face of Jesus Christ" (2 Cor 4:6) dwells within the hearts of Christ's body, the church. Wrinkled with human weakness and faded from the effects of sin, we tend to miss the surpassing glorious power that dwells within us as his disciples. But by his grace and through his Spirit, we possess hearts of immeasurable, eternal value. There lies within each of Christ's "jars of clay" the limitless power of God to transform our common, worn lives into the exalted likeness of Christ and then to use us to influence others toward that same glorious change. Reflecting on this power, Paul prayed over the local church at Ephesus:

> Now to him who is able to do immeasurably more than all we ask or imagine, according to his power that is at work within us, to him be glory in the church and in Christ Jesus throughout all generations, for ever and ever! Amen. (Eph 3:20-21 NIV)

What a tragedy it is when this power to transform common human lives into indescribable self-portraits of Christ is undervalued and thus left in a sandwich baggie tacked to a wall. By doing so we cut off the flow of Christ's life from one generation to the next. The net effect is a "clogging of the spiritual arteries" and an impairment of function within the body of Christ.

The Great Untruth must therefore be replaced with this spiritual reality: *The presence of the power of Christ transforms every believer into a relational vessel whose heart can be used by God to connect the hearts of others to his grace, truth and love.* That connection, made through relationships rooted in the radical grace and truth of Jesus Christ, is what we mean when we use the term *disciplemaking.* The power of Christ is what allows us to make an impact in the life of an emerging adult. And the relational nature of the gospel and of Christ's disciplemaking strategy does not merely suggest but rather fully demands that we invest ourselves to "make disciples" who will "make disciples." Emerging adults are, therefore, not simply containers *into* which the life of Christ is poured. They are designed by their Creator and Redeemer to be vessels *through* which the life of Christ is poured. A failure to invest in them as such only serves to reinforce negative cultural pressures that, as we examined in chapter one, tend to postpone maturity and hinder deep connectedness to a spiritual community.

SHIFT 4: FROM CASUAL COMPLACENCY TO PASSIONATE URGENCY

Leaders who are able to provide vision and inspire courage in times of crisis are often quoted for their brave and wise words. I (Rick) recently visited Winston Churchill's underground war rooms in the heart of London and was amazed by the proliferation of quotes covering the displays throughout the tour. In contrast, General John Sedgwick—a brave and effective leader for the Union during the crisis of the American Civil War—is not remembered for words of bravery and wisdom. Rather, he is remembered for his casual response to a dangerous situation that led to a fatal miscalculation of the enemy's position and potential. Calmly looking over the scene of the impending battle with the Confederates at Spotsylvania, Virginia, Sedgwick's last words were, "They couldn't hit an elephant from that dist-"

Leaders of God's people who approach the challenges facing the next generation of the church with a casual complacency, rather than a passionate urgency, greatly miscalculate the dangers that lurk ahead. I (Rick) live in the Bible belt; we still pray to Jesus at all of our football games (which are, in the South, often hard to distinguish from religious events anyway!). Several of my children's public school teachers have been openly professing disciples of Jesus, and throughout Knox County we have several megachurches as well as several hundred smaller ones. Even here, though, where church remains central to the cultural ethos, an estimated 40 percent of our county's population either claims no religious affiliation whatsoever or claims an affiliation with a faith not recognized as Christian.[6] Moreover, in a recent church-planting workshop hosted at my church, the presenter suggested that as much as 80 percent of our county live their lives fundamentally disconnected from any spiritual community.[7] Times have changed—those committed to the community and cause of Christ may be a declining minority from a cultural standpoint.

The proper response of a declining minority cannot be calm, casual complacency, as the story of Dr. LeRoy Carhart dramatically illustrates.

In 2009, the August 24 edition of *Newsweek* carried Dr. Carhart's story. This sixty-seven-year-old doctor from Omaha, Nebraska, belongs to a dying breed of doctors in our country—and he feels it. Especially since his friend Dr. Tiller was fatally shot in nearby Wichita—expressly because he was a part of this declining minority—while handing out bulletins for Sunday morning services at his Lutheran church. There are only a handful of doctors in America who perform late-term or partial-birth abortions for women who want them, and Dr. Carhart is one of them. That a woman can obtain an abortion for an unborn child as late as twenty-four weeks (six months) into her pregnancy is not well received by many. (We—Rick and Jana—are among those who grieve deeply about this reality.) With Dr. Tiller gone, LeRoy understands that he is the *only* doctor in his area of the country willing to do so. He said, "I think the only thing I can do . . . is just train as many doctors as I can *to go out on their own and provide abortions* and get enough people providing them." *Newsweek* adds, "LeRoy Carhart is determined to train as many late-term-abortion providers as possible—or the practice just might die with him."[8] There is a palpable sense of urgency in the article. Carhart knows that he won't live forever and that he cannot ensure the continuation of this practice on his own. He knows what his task has to be.

Given the intent of Dr. Carhart's "disciplemaking," his story unnerves us. We want the practice of late-term abortions to die with him—but it won't, because when it comes to passing on values and skills to the next generation *he gets it*. He feels and understands something we desperately need to get as Christians. We stumble or sail along in our own stories, consumed with our blessings or our challenges, forgetting that we are part of a grander story that needs to be passed on, and passed on to the point where others can go out on their own. If we don't pass the story on, authentic engagement in walking out the Christlife could die out with us, with our generation. Dr. Carhart is dedicated, determined and urgently working to pass on a practice that *ends* life while we sit on our hands, half-heartedly passing on that which *brings life*—life abundant and eternal. How much more important is it for us to take up our calling with urgency?

SHIFT 5: FROM CRUISE SHIPS TO BEACHHEAD LANDING SHIPS

Consider the difference between being a passenger on a cruise ship and being a soldier on a landing vessel designed to deploy troops and supplies on a beachhead. Imagine for a moment the contrasting thoughts and emotions that would be present while boarding a cruise ship headed for the Caribbean and boarding a landing ship aimed at the beaches of Normandy.

Table 2.1.

	CRUISE SHIP	LANDING SHIP
Purpose	Provide leisure	Launch missions
Mission	Attract consumers	Prepare conquerors
Strategy	Meet needs	Empower for the mission
Roles of Leaders	The crew serves the passengers	Everyone is the crew and everyone has a mission-critical role

The gospel in the words of Jesus and the lives of the apostles throughout the early church make it inescapably clear which of these metaphors best fits Jesus' intention for the church. Actually leading with a landing-ship mentality can be hard to do, however. I (Rick) am the lead pastor of what is commonly referred to as a megachurch. In the midst of evaluating our present and future as a church in 2008, our associate lead pastor, Kevin Huggins, made this profound statement: "If we don't do something soon we are going to drift irreversibly into a consumer-based mentality." I left our conversation shaken. Kevin was right. As I prayed and reflected more thoroughly on his words, I realized that we were on the verge of buckling under the expectations of the consuming public who wanted us to look like a cruise ship. From that day forward I resolved in my heart to teach, lead and live in such a way as to repurpose our "cruise ship" into a community that would launch spiritual landing ships to infiltrate our world with Jesus' grace, truth, love and service.

The landing-ship mentality seeks to fulfill the shift to twenty-first-century "missional church" thinking described earlier in shift one. Note that this is a mentality, not a model. There are no clearly defined "one size fits all" models for doing this. Rather, leaders committed to a missional vision simply, creatively build their churches by investing resources toward eventual deployment of emerging adults for kingdom service. Leading a landing-ship church in the twenty-first century thus requires continual corrections away from the strong currents of both consumerism and institutionalization. Leadership must have an unrelenting commitment to make disciples and build teams of disciplemakers to be sent into the world outside the church as specialized ministry teams, missional communities and church plants.

When questioned about what leadership training should look like in the twenty-first century, Chris Wright provided a concise, distinct description of the shift that's required. Wright challenged, "I wouldn't start out with training leaders, I'd start out with making disciples."[9] Wright's thoughts are as ancient as they are simple. Two thousand years ago, faced with the improbable task of preparing a rag-tag group of men for the spiritual transformation of the world, Jesus committed himself to one specific task: making disciples. Three years later, when the Holy Spirit entered the hearts of his disciples, they were launched as conquerors to Jerusalem, Judea, Samaria and the uttermost parts of the earth (Acts 1:8).

MAKING THE SHIFTS

What Jesus modeled in the Gospels, what twenty-seven-year-old Megan expressed a longing for in her email, what a world drowning in spiritual hopelessness so desperately needs is a courageous, faithful church fully engaged in making these shifts. Providentially, the people most qualified to lead these urgently needed shifts will be found in the one-hundred-and-first generation of Spirit-empowered adult disciples emerging on the twenty-first-century horizon. We are therefore going to turn our minds and hearts toward fulfilling our calling to name, call out and empower the presence and power of Christ in their lives. To paraphrase the prayer of Paul in Ephesians 3:20-21 (NIV), we pray expectantly:

> Now to him who is able to do immeasurably more than all we in this generation could ask or imagine, *according to his power that is at work within us and in the next generation of disciplemakers*, to him be glory in the church and in Christ Jesus throughout all generations, forever and ever!

RHYTHMS FOR LIVING THE CHRISTLIFE

Trust, Submission and Love

TODAY, TWO THOUSAND YEARS and one hundred generations after Christ walked on earth, his simple, final command to "make disciples" remains unchanged. The task is perhaps even more urgent in this new era the church is in, resulting from such diverse contextual factors as

- the rise of terrorism
- the explosive expansion of the Internet
- the emergence of an intimately interdependent global economy
- the growing concerns regarding global environmental crises
- the shifting of world power from West to East
- the easy access to nuclear weaponry
- the millions of children born daily into hopeless poverty
- foundational changes globally in philosophical thought and cultural values
- the "shrinking" of distance due to advances in technology and travel

The global cultural context in the twenty-first century is simply not the same as it was in the twentieth century. Previously unimagined opportunities and challenges face Christ's twenty-first-century disciples, disciples whose role it will now be to "make disciples" to lead the one-hundred-and-first generation of the church.

Beyond all these factors, next-generation young adults in the culture of the United States are the first generation of adults in their country to be raised with a pervasively negative view toward Christianity's exclusive claims. Far from being trusted and revered as a foundation for society, Christianity is often distrusted and reviled. David Kinnaman and Gabe Lyons, authors of *unChristian,* write,

> To outsiders the word *Christian* has more in common with a brand than a faith. This shift of meaning in recent decades has been magnified by an increasing use of the term *Christian* to label music, clothes, schools, political action groups, and more. In the middle of a culture where Christianity has come to represent hypocrisy, judgmentalism, anti-intellectualism, insensitivity, and bigotry, it's easy to see why the next generation wants nothing to do with it.[1]

As discussed in the previous chapter, the time has come for a shift in our approaches to making disciples of young adults. Given the extent and the depth of rapid, cataclysmic change, failing to enter into a radical shift in thinking by the one-hundredth generation of the church can only lead to catastrophic results in the one-hundred-and-first generation of the church.

BEYOND "FADS AND FOOLISHNESS"

During the current period of great cultural upheaval, disciplemakers continuously confront the temptation to react with "fads and foolishness." Faddish discipleship techniques are rooted in the false, foolish belief that if we can find the newest, greatest method that's working for someone else, we can make it work for our setting. The pattern has become fairly predictable. A church in America experiences God's favor and grows by the thousands in a short period of time. Ministry leaders, assuming that the fast-growing church must be "doing it right," flock from all over the country to discover what is working. Rather than asking for God to use this exposure to his work to stir their own creativity, they (falsely) assume that if they just follow the same steps, they will get the same results ("Mimic the methodology, follow the fad—life change guaranteed!").

While learning from the experiences of others and exposing our mind and heart to new ways of doing things can have great value, following the latest discipleship fad more often than not does not produce the same dramatic results as the model "successful" church. Disheartened leaders are left wondering: Why are we not growing fast? Is it me—am I really that inadequate as a leader? Is it them—are my church members just stubborn sheep who will never get it? Foolishness breeds foolishness as leaders unconsciously embrace the seductive assumption that numerical participation equals deep life change. Truth be told, many of these frustrated leaders soon began fantasizing about being somewhere else—somewhere where these ideas would work and they could be "successful."

Faddishness eventually leads to new levels of foolishness—ones that corrupt vision and compromise the very types of relationships that actually build mature disciples. Emerging adults of the early twenty-first-century church clearly want no part in this unhelpful progression:

> If the evangelical Christian leadership thinks that "cool Christianity" is a sustainable path forward, they are severely mistaken. As a twentysomething, I can say with confidence that when it comes to church, we don't want cool as much as we want real.
>
> If we are interested in Christianity in any sort of serious way, it is not because it's easy or trendy or popular. It's because Jesus himself is appealing, and what he says rings true. It's because the world we inhabit is utterly phony, ephemeral, narcissistic, image-obsessed and sex-drenched—and we want an alternative. It's not because we want more of the same.[2]

The stakes for disciplemaking in this generation are too high to allow fads and foolishness to dilute Jesus' vision for disciplemaking relationships. Fads must be replaced by simple *faithfulness* to the gospel and to the strategic command of Jesus Christ: "make disciples."

Let's face reality: There are no programmatic shortcuts to effective disciplemaking. There is no "easy button." Disciplemaking is about relationships. Relationships are inefficient. Disciplemaking is about life change. Life change is messy. Disciplemaking is centered in the person of Jesus Christ. Jesus Christ allows no pretense. Disciplemaking is unpredictable. Unpredictability requires risk. Disciplemaking is unique to each person, each generation, each cultural context. Uniqueness eliminates the possibility of universally applied "paint by the numbers" disciplemaking relationships.

Therefore, we firmly believe two things are essential for moving confidently into the relationships our Lord calls all disciples in every generation to pursue:

1. a simple vision for what a mature disciple of Jesus Christ looks like

2. an authentic understanding of relationships that will facilitate, encourage, challenge, support and lead young adults in this generation to become mature disciples of Jesus Christ

Simplicity and authenticity. Nothing so complex that only a seminary-trained professional can really understand it or so complicated that only wealthy churches can afford to sustain it. Nothing so difficult that only a few highly gifted people could ever hope to be effective at it or so demanding that only a few uniquely positioned people could ever set aside the time to participate in it. No mechanical five-step strategies for life change, clever methodologies to mimic or ultra-cool programs to apply. Just inefficient, messy, unpretentious, unpredictable, risky relationships with no "paint by the numbers" answers on how to proceed. Just you, the young adults you are investing in and Jesus. Nothing more—but so much more than enough.

The rest of this chapter will address these two necessary foundations for life transformation among this generation. Chapters four, five and six then offer life-giving rhythms for building disciplemaking relationships that faithfully fulfill Christ's strategic command to "make disciples."

A SIMPLE VISION FOR MATURITY

Imagine attending a concert to hear your local symphony orchestra. Now imagine someone asking you to identify which members of the brass section are disciples of Christ, based on your observation of the concert alone. Absurd? Absolutely. Christian trumpet players and non-Christian trumpet players cannot be identified based on how well they play their instruments. Indeed, it would be ridiculous to think that being a Christian makes you a better (or worse) trumpet player.

Some of the ways in which we tend to "measure" spiritual maturity, however, are equally absurd. Each of us, over the course of our three decades as disciples and disciplemakers, has been exposed to a lot of absurd ideas about what marks a person as spiritually mature. *Theological intellectualism* was one form of measurement we heard, but we know that the Christlife cannot be defined or evaluated simply by right answers on the "church quiz." Life in Christ *includes* knowledge of the truth, of course, but it's more than just what we know. It is all too possible, for example, to have a head for Christian theology partnered with a heart that is sealed off from relationship with Christ.

Emotionalism was another category we'd see people use to measure spiritual maturity. While the Christlife does include emotion and passion, it cannot be defined simply by religious experiences. Many people say they "feel close to God" even as their lives reflect a total disregard for his commands and boundaries. The Christlife must be more than what we feel.

We also knew that the way to measure spiritual maturity was not *legalism*. The Christlife we were called to could never be defined by a simple set of rules that were to be externally followed. Though the Christlife does consist of concrete actions, it cannot just be reduced to what we do. Lots of religions practice the moral and ethical behaviors that Christians uphold apart from any knowledge of or relationship with Christ. Thus, when we began to wrestle with the all-important foundational question *What does spiritual maturity look like in a disciple?* we knew what it does *not* look like long before we knew what it does.

The life Christ intended for us to live is *his* life. To understand how to evaluate our spiritual progress therefore requires a framework for understanding the essential characteristics of Christ's spiritual journey with his Father. The "marks of maturity" must be fashioned in the image of Christ's spiritual life if they're to be helpful to us as we invest in the spiritual journeys of young adults.

An irreducible core. What then are the essential marks of a mature Christlife? And how can these marks be understood when faith includes knowing his truth *and* experiencing his life *and* choosing to live in his love? Ultimately the quest led us to examine the irreducible core of Christ's life as the God-man. While there are many ways to organize the core characteristics of Christ's life, the following seemed to capture for us the essence of what set him apart from all other men and women, religious and irreligious, of the day.

1. *Perfect trust: Christ's confidence in the Father's wisdom.* Christ always sought the Father's truth and guidance; he listened to the Father in all things and deferred his knowledge to the Father's wisdom. And his obedience grew out of a deep root of trust in that wisdom. We need look no further than the temptation of Christ by Satan to see that Christ surrendered himself faithfully to the truth of the Father's wisdom. As a result, Jesus' teaching consistently amazed the disciples with its absolute authority.

2. *Perfect submission: Christ's humility in response to the Father's heart and leadership.* Christ humbly and passionately looked to the Father as the source of life in all things and exhibited a heart that was continually surrendered to the Father. That surrender fueled perfect submission to his Father's heart and leadership. He considered the Father's affirmation, affection and glory to be greater than any earthly pleasure, comfort, achievement or possession. He relied fully on the Father's provision and considered anything that minimized the Father as the eternal source to be idolatrous. Asked to teach his disciples how to pray, he responded with a simple prayer that reflected his vision that they too would fully embrace the Father as the source of all true life.

> Our Father in heaven, hallowed be your name.
> Your kingdom come, your will be done,
>   on earth as it is in heaven.
> Give us this day our daily bread, and forgive us our debts,
>   as we also have forgiven our debtors.
> And lead us not into temptation,
>   but deliver us from evil. (Mt 6:9-13)

3. *Perfect love: Christ's fulfillment of the Father's will.* Christ flawlessly pursued the hearts of sinful humanity, lovingly displaying the Father's agape love as a light shining into a graceless world darkened by sin. Christ's deep love for sinful human beings was like a river of life-giving water that flowed directly from the gracious, pure heart of the Father.

Christ pursued the hearts of the lost and the hearts of the disciples according to the Father's will, even though it would mean pouring himself out in a sacrificial death. The "verse of all verses," John 3:16, demonstrates Jesus' understanding that his ultimate act of love originated in the heart of the Father. Likewise, when he taught the disciples to love, he taught them that authentic love toward one another and the world was the ultimate expression of relationship with the Father. He thus led them not only to pray for the Father's will to be done but also to initiate their role in becoming a part of his answer to that prayer.

All three of these characteristics of Jesus are summarized in a hymn about him from the first-century church, one Paul included in the book of Philippians:

> Though he was in the form of God, [Jesus] did not count equality with God a thing to be grasped, but made himself nothing, taking the form of a servant, being born in the likeness of men. And being found in human form, he humbled himself by becoming obedient to the point of death, even death on a cross. (Phil 2:6-8)

Christ's *perfect trust* of his Father's wisdom led him through a life of perfect obedience born from a deep trust of the Father as the Holy God of all truth. And Christ's *perfect submission* to his Father's heart and leadership demonstrated that his obedience flowed from an intimate Father-Son relationship—not from fear or legalistic duty—as he humbly sought the Father as the Holy God of all of life. Christ's trust and surrender found their full expression when he, as a sacrifice for sin, acted out of *perfect love* in fulfillment of the Father's will. He chose a perfect obedience that would display the glory of the Father as the Holy God of all grace and love. The irreducible core of Christ's uniqueness, then, is *perfect obedience in relationship with his Father as Holy God*. In simple terms, Christ wholly obeyed his Holy Father. This is therefore the essential marker of the Christlife.

The indisputable mandate. Given this understanding, the meaning of Matthew 28:19-20 is much richer than what has been commonly taught and understood in twentieth-century fads of disciplemaking:

> Go therefore and make disciples of all nations, baptizing them in the name of the Father and of the Son and of the Holy Spirit, *teaching them to observe all that I have commanded you*. And behold, I am with you always, to the end of the age. (emphasis ours)

Christ commanded his disciples to build relationships that would teach a new generation of disciples how to wholly obey their Holy Father. His vision for disciplemaking centered on encouraging, challenging, supporting, coaching and equipping individuals to increasingly wholly obey his Father by means of the life that Christ himself provided.

Wholly obeying must not be limited, therefore, to a set of things to memorize or a type of experience to pursue or even a list of rules to follow. To approach spiritual maturity in these ways is to attempt to externalize and quantify spiritual growth, with spiritual depth existing as "something out there" that must be pursued according to prescribed religious activities. To wholly obey the Father as Christ obeyed him, however, is to build a relationship of *trust, submission* and *love*. Spiritual maturity is thus a relational reality to be cultivated from the inside out through an ever-deepening relationship with Christ in the midst of the daily rhythms of life.

Amazingly (to our way of thinking), Jesus gave this challenge in Matthew 28 to a rag-tag group of disciples who had consistently had a very difficult time being obedient *themselves*—even with Jesus right beside them for three years! Essentially, Jesus was asking them to teach to others after he was gone what they could not get right while in his presence.

We imagine the disciples were thinking something along the lines of, *You're leaving us—and this is the plan? You've got to be kidding! What makes you think we can do this?* It was not like people were flocking from all over the country to see how amazing Jesus' disciples were and how successful his ministry plan had been, so the disciples can't really be blamed if they did, in fact, panic at the thought of attempting anything like "making disciples" in Jesus' absence. Yet, in generation one of the church, this was precisely Jesus' plan. And the disciples would soon learn that they were not being left alone, that they did not have to do this without him. "I am with you always," Jesus had told them, and he kept good on his promise. Wholly obeying the Holy Father happens as an active response to Christ in us; through his Spirit he was present to empower them to lead new disciples who in turn became the second generation of the church. Ninety-nine generations later, the plan has not changed. Neither has the need for his presence through his Spirit—nor the reality of it: he is still here with us through the Holy Spirit.

SPIRITUAL HYDRATION: A METAPHOR FOR DISCIPLEMAKING

I (Rick) am not a runner. In fact, I may be the anti-runner. Years of running as a form of discipline in basketball practices combined with major back surgery created in me a great aversion to "pounding the pavement." My son Zach, however, is a cross-country runner. He runs multiple miles, day after day. I love that he does this—and I love that I do not.

Through Zach's experience I'm learning more about what running requires; hydration is at the top of the list. A runner must hydrate well the day before a race and the morning of the race, as well as immediately after the race. Hydration is key to racing well and recovering well. In fact, I'm told (I'm sure I'll never learn this by experience!) that if you're running a marathon and you wait until you're thirsty to drink, it will be too late. Running yourself to dehydration cannot be quickly solved with a cup of water or a sports drink.

The presence of Christ through the Holy Spirit is the source of spiritual hydration for all disciples. Christ's trust, submission and love dwell within each of his disciples through his Spirit and by his grace. Perpetually "hydrating" by connecting with Christ relationally is a non-negotiable essential for growing as a disciple. Tapping into the stream of his life is also the non-negotiable source of spiritual vitality in disciplemaking relationships; they simply cannot flourish without the "spiritual hydration" of the presence of Jesus.

Becoming dehydrated while investing in another disciple's life can have devastating effects on the disciplemaking relationship. The dehydrated disciplemaker risks avoiding confrontation; settling for an impersonal, clichéd approach to faith; seeking affirmation or acceptance from one another instead of from the Father; allowing busy schedules to choke out a shared intentional pursuit of maturity in Christ; exposing personal vulnerabilities to sin's seductive lure. . . . The list goes on and on.

The apostle Paul revealed his absolute dependence on Christ as his "spiritual hydration" repeatedly throughout his writings. Nowhere is this stated more clearly than Paul's previously mentioned prayer for the young disciple Timothy and the church he shepherded at Ephesus:

Now to him who is able to do immeasurably more than all we ask or imagine, according to *his power that is at work within us,* to Him be the glory in the church and in Christ Jesus throughout all generations, forever and ever! Amen. (Eph 3:20-21 NIV)

The first generation of disciples became, sometimes reluctantly, the original group of disciplemakers. They knew beyond any shadow of a doubt that they were absolutely dependent on Christ's presence and power. And so are we, as is the one-hundred-and-first generation of disciples as well as those who will follow after. Thankfully, he will be with them—always. He is the source of all they will need, and he is all that they will have to give.

Disciplemaking can thus be described simply as *building a relationship with another person that encourages, challenges, coaches and equips that person to more deeply connect to the trust, submission and love of Christ that dwells within by the power of his Spirit.* Once this is understood at both the head and heart level, the disciplemaker is well on his or her way to building a relationship that will make all the difference in a young adult's spiritual journey to maturity.

AN AUTHENTIC UNDERSTANDING OF DISCIPLEMAKING RELATIONSHIPS

Before exploring how such relationships are nurtured by disciplemakers, two critical observations need to be made. Each observation correlates to a common misunderstanding about the nature of authentic disciplemaking relationships. The first critical observation is that *disciplemaking relationships can take multiple forms, varying in style and approach according to the personalities involved.* Some are highly structured. Others, more informal and spontaneous. Some are very attentive to the intellectual component of faith, while others focus more on the service component. Many disciplemaking relationships are between peers, often in a group of men or women who become the fulfillment of "iron sharpening iron." A large number also form around intergenerational relationships of "spiritual fathers" and "spiritual mothers." In addition, disciplemaking relationships can be intensive, short-term relationships of a year or less or they can be lifelong relationships that last two or three decades or more!

Attempting to create a disciplemaking relationship by merely copying someone else results in hollow, dissatisfying interpersonal relationships. We can definitely learn a great deal from reading about, observing and especially experiencing disciplemaking relationships. However, a relationship must be unique to the individuals in it; the Christlife cannot be shared authentically if the relationship is formed artificially.

Jennifer, a thirty-five-year-old systems analyst, has a ministry discipling recent college graduates, mostly single women from twenty-two to thirty. She invests in them for an entire year—leading Bible study and prayer, spending time in informal settings individually and with the whole group, speaking the truth while communicating care to challenge the women's hearts toward reproducing her relationship with them in the life of another young woman. Using Scripture and prayer in the context of relationship, she leads these young women to identify obstacles that keep them from fully participating in the call to be disciplemakers. She also stands with them as they "reposition" their minds and hearts to experience the flow of Christ's grace and truth in previously barren places of insecurity and immaturity. As these women move into being "Jennifers" in the lives of others, Jennifer continues to come alongside them, guiding them in continuing to reposition their minds and hearts to live in the flow of Christ's life within.

A very different, more community-based portrait of disciplemaking can be found in John and Cindy's missional community of emerging adults. The parents of three emerging adults themselves, John and Cindy recognized a significant gap in the disciplemaking of the next generation of my (Rick's) church. Hundreds of college students attended the church, and multiple opportunities were provided to reach them for Christ, strengthen their faith and disciple them into a full engagement of the world with the gospel. Postgraduates, however, were not receiving the same level of intentionality from the church's leadership.

John and Cindy gathered together a leadership team of twentysomethings and immediately began to equip and empower them to lead. Soon their community, The Grove, began growing—in number and in impact. Acting as spiritual mentors of the leadership team, they are now seeing young-adult leaders take full responsibility and ownership of key aspects of the group's mission. Having noticed the spiritual vitality in the hearts of these emerging adults, John and Cindy's peers in a community called The Launching Years have now approached them about forming new intergenerational disciplemaking relationships between the two groups. The fruit from The Grove has not only expanded well beyond the walls of the church but also across what is often an even greater chasm: the disconnected generations in the church. All of this has resulted from a sense of calling in the hearts of John and Cindy to prepare a handful of emerging adults to lead their peers in the mission of living and sharing the gospel.

The second critical observation for disciplemaking is that, while the form may vary, *the non-negotiable center of a disciplemaking relationship is learning from Christ in a manner that leads to a deepening relational connection to him and his trust, submission and love.* Hanging out with other Christians is a great expression of Christian fellowship. Indeed, such fellowship is an indispensable component of a disciplemaking community. Thinking that this kind of hanging out in Christian fellowship is substantive enough to be called disciplemaking, however, is a misconception. Unless there is an intentional commitment and active pursuit of learning more of Christ and his gospel, relationships among Christians do not in themselves constitute disciplemaking relationships. To quote Kinnaman and Lyons once again, "Being a Christian is hard work."[3] Naturally, so is Christian disciplemaking.

Paul and Timothy: A closer look. The apostle Paul's letters to Timothy give us an intriguing, instructive case study in disciplemaking. We know that they spent a lot of time together, traveling and serving. And Paul clearly loved Timothy dearly, even coming to the point of tears as he sat in his prison cell thinking of him. What made this a disciplemaking relationship, however, was the commitment Paul made to invest intentionally in Timothy so that Timothy could then do the same for others. No doubt they hung out at times, simply sharing fellowship together and with others such as Luke. But woven through all their time together was Paul's persistent effort to call Timothy to live the Christlife of trust, submission and love.

Paul recognized that young Timothy had a lot to learn. And, with Timothy having been thrust into the role of point leader for the church in Ephesus, Paul knew that the sooner the learning occurred, the better.

Ephesus was like a spiritual bonfire where the wood had been stacked, kerosene had been lavishly poured onto the wood, and the air was extremely dry and hot. All it lacked was a match. Paul and Timothy both knew that preaching the gospel was like throwing a torch into the mix.

Paul's self-described role in each letter to Timothy is therefore that of a spiritual father. The depth of Paul's relational intentionality offers an astoundingly vivid portrait of a disciplemaker and his young-adult disciple learning to "hydrate" their minds and hearts in Christ as they ran their leadership races for him. Paul nurtured a life-encompassing relationship with Timothy as mentor, missionary partner, pastoral supervisor and spiritual companion. He was a coach and a teacher. He was a father and a friend. He saw the best in Timothy without ignoring Timothy's weaknesses. He called Timothy out, but he also walked beside him. As Timothy cautiously took his first unsteady, hesitant steps to obey the Father as a leader, Paul was there to catch him when he fell and to challenge him when he did not want to get up again.

Their relationship provides a compelling picture of how to build an authentic relationship that will facilitate, encourage, challenge, support and lead young adults in this generation to become mature disciples of Jesus Christ. While our own disciplemaking relationships rarely match the breadth of Paul and Timothy's, the essence of their relationship reveals profound truths regarding what it takes to lead well as a disciplemaker. Together they learned to trust in the Father's wisdom, to humbly embrace the Father's heart and to fulfill the Father's will through love.

Learning to trust in the Father's wisdom. Paul always understood his spiritual journey as an expression of the Christ who dwelt within him. He wrote to the Galatians:

> I have been crucified with Christ. It is no longer I who live, but Christ who lives in me. And the life I now live in the flesh I live by faith in the Son of God, who loved me and gave himself for me. (Gal 2:20)

Christ had given himself for Paul. Now Paul was giving himself for Christ. The Christlife, including the presence of Christ's trust in the Father's wisdom, gave Paul the confidence to yield all to the wisdom of the Father's will. Paul would repeatedly risk his life in order to follow God's leading.

Trusting the Father's wisdom drove Paul straight into the arms of Christ and directly into the path of young Timothy. And Paul, in turn, invested the trust of the Father he learned from Christ deeply into the life of Timothy. At a time when Timothy was clearly being challenged to remain firm in his belief in the authenticity and authority of the teachings of Scripture, Paul wrote to Timothy:

> Do your best to present yourself to God as one approved, a worker who has no need to be ashamed, rightly handling the word of truth. . . .
>
> Continue in what you have learned and have firmly believed, knowing from whom you learned it and how from childhood you have been acquainted with the sacred writings, which are able to make you wise for salvation through faith in Christ Jesus. (2 Timothy 2:15; 3:14-15)

Paul's trustful surrender to the wisdom of the Father provided a secure foothold on which Timothy could stand as he grew in his relationship with Christ and Scripture. When the pagan philosophers of Ephesus and even those within his own congregation challenged Timothy's authority and teaching, Timothy could remind himself of the words of Paul, his spiritual father:

> All Scripture is breathed out by God and profitable for teaching, for reproof, for correction, and for training in righteousness, that the man of God may be competent, equipped for every good work. (2 Tim 3:16-17)

"Son, you can trust his Word," we can almost hear Paul saying. "Be shaped by it. Surrender to the wisdom of God it contains. Teach others to do the same." Disciplemakers continually surrender their minds and hearts to the wisdom of the Father's truth. As they do so, they come alongside another disciple to assist them in building that same confidence through the presence and power of Christ within their minds and hearts.

Learning submission as a response of humility toward the Father's heart. As my (Rick's) kids have gotten older, one of the things I miss most are the "snuggle" times that little children value so much. Whether we were in a restaurant or at a ball game or sitting by the pool, my son Zach would always ask, "Can I sit in your lap?" Honestly, I can remember thinking, *I'll be glad when he outgrows this and doesn't always want to sit on my lap.* Now, of course, I regret those thoughts. I miss being the father of a young child. I miss the simplicity of the tender moments of just having my son on my lap. (Fortunately, my twenty-year-old daughter still loves to curl up close and get her "daddy fix." Thank God for daughters!)

As we grow older, our relationships with our parents change. We become more independent and less inclined to draw close on a regular basis. Of course, this is healthy. If my sixteen-year-old still constantly asked to sit in my lap, I would be strongly suggesting that he move on to a new stage of life! With our Father God, however, the expectation is actually the reverse; the longer we walk with Christ the more we learn to share his longing for the Father's embrace. Spiritual maturity is more like returning to the embrace of the Father you have been missing than growing out of the need for your father's presence and touch. Our posture toward God the Father is to be that of Christ in us: increasingly, simply and humbly seeking to embrace him for all of who he is and to allow his heart to reform our hearts with his love.

Paul's humble embrace of the Father's love is evidenced in this portion of his prayer from Ephesians 3:

> For this reason I bow my knees before the Father, from whom every family in heaven and on earth is named, that according to the riches of his glory he may grant you to be strengthened with power through his Spirit in your inner being, so that Christ may dwell in your hearts through faith—that you, being rooted and grounded in love, may have strength to comprehend with all the saints what is the breadth and length and height and depth, and to know the love of Christ that surpasses knowledge, that you may be filled with all the fullness of God. (Eph 3:14-19)

The Father's heart was Paul's prize. Humbly living in the lordship of Christ who had fully embraced the heart of the Father provided the path to the Father's heart and the hydration needed for the journey. Paul modeled this for Timothy. But Paul did something else in the relationship that powerfully shaped Timothy's heart toward the Father. Paul begins 2 Timothy with these words of fatherly affection:

> To Timothy, my beloved child:
>
> Grace, mercy, and peace from God the Father and Christ Jesus our Lord.
>
> I thank God whom I serve, as did my ancestors, with a clear con-

science, as I remember you constantly in my prayers night and day. As I remember your tears, I long to see you, that I may be filled with joy. (2 Tim 1:2-4)

Timothy was not a "project" for Paul; he was not assigned to Paul as one of many tasks on a checklist. Rather, Paul called Timothy to the heart of the Father by offering the heart of the Father in their relationship through direct affirmation.

Furthermore, as Timothy's disciplemaker Paul bragged about Timothy to others. One of our favorite portraits of Paul and Timothy's relationship is found in 1 Corinthians 4, where Paul is instructing the Corinthians on how to act (from the letters written to the church in Corinth, it's clear that they needed a lot of help regarding how to act!). Notice Paul's "bragging" on his spiritual son, Timothy:

I urge you, then, be imitators of me. That is why I sent you Timothy, my beloved and faithful child in the Lord, to remind you of my ways in Christ, as I teach them everywhere in every church. (1 Cor 4:16-17)

We learn in 2 Timothy that Timothy's spiritual heritage came from his mother and grandmother. On the one hand, their mentoring and nurturing were evidently very effective in preparing him to be both a disciple and a disciplemaker; having a father or grandfather to lead him was therefore not essential in order for him to follow Christ wholeheartedly. Yet every young man possesses a God created longing to be called out and sent out by another man whose strength and courage can be trusted. No male spiritual ancestor is listed in Scripture as playing this role for Timothy. Imagine then what these words must have meant to Timothy, along with the fact that he, the next-generation apprentice of the great apostle Paul, had been entrusted with carrying this extraordinarily important message to the church at Corinth.

When Timothy arrived, the Corinthians likely regarded him respectfully as Paul's trustworthy courier; they had probably heard of Timothy and knew he was a solid young man. It's unlikely, though, that they regarded him as more than that. But when they opened the letter and came to the words, "That is why I sent you Timothy," they must have looked toward Timothy, first with a slight warmth in their faces and then with approving nods. Timothy would have recognized the new approval and respect written on their faces and maybe sat up straighter as a result, recognizing his place as one of them. He might have been a *young* man of God, but he was a man of God nevertheless.

How immeasurable is the impact of Timothy's affectionate spiritual father! Paul's words created a longing in a young man to be more than he was. To pursue Christ with greater fervor, to know more of what it is like to be secure in the Father's heart. All of this occurred as Paul submitted to the Father's heart with affectionate humility and then offered that heart to Timothy. As Timothy learned through Paul's influence to connect to the presence and power of Christ within to humbly embrace the heart of God as his Father, he, in turn, grew in courage and strength. History tells us that Timothy would remain in the midst of the storm in Ephesus, faithfully serving the God who loved him, until he was martyred for his faith late in the first century.

Learning love that fulfills the Father's will. Consistently rehydrating in the Christlife produces a resolve that goes beyond determination, persistence or "doing what is right." That resolve can only be described by one word: *love.* Love is more than believing in or even having feelings for God and others. It completes the journey of surrendering to his wisdom and embracing his heart. Love is Christ forsaking all for the sake of the Father's will—in the desert, in the garden of Gethsemane, on the cross. And love is Christ in us forsaking all for the sake of the Father's will, through our battles with temptation, our most fearful challenges and our most difficult relationships. Love is choosing him. Simply. Authentically. Exclusively. Wholeheartedly.

Paul clearly revealed his love for the Father and for others in all of his life. With humble confidence he wrote to Timothy,

> You, however, have followed my teaching, my conduct, my aim in life, my faith, my patience, my love, my steadfastness, my persecutions and sufferings that happened to me at Antioch, at Iconium, and at Lystra— which persecutions I endured; yet from them all the Lord rescued me. (2 Tim 3:10-11)

Paul's teaching and conduct, faith and patience, persecutions and sufferings—all chosen for Christ. All experienced with Christ. Paul loved Christ and the Father, and he lavished on others, especially Timothy, the love with which he had been loved. Faithfully setting his mind and heart to demonstrate this love in all circumstances, including martyrdom, he mentored Timothy to do the same. "As for you," he instructed Timothy, "always be sober-minded, endure suffering, do the work of an evangelist, fulfill your ministry" (2 Tim 4:5).

In all of life, under great duress and even impending death, in discipling young Timothy and in entrusting the gospel to Timothy for the next generation, Paul always had only one life goal in mind for himself and for Timothy: "The aim of our charge is love that issues from a pure heart and a good conscience and a sincere faith" (1 Tim 1:5).

The aim, the goal, the destination was always *love*. Not humanly manufactured love. Not religiously mimicked love. Real love. The kind of love that can only be formed by a pure heart—one that's continually being filled with the grace and truth of the Savior. The kind of love that can only be formed by a mind that's positioned spiritually to be shaped by the life of Christ. A good conscience and a sincere faith. Loving as Christ loved. Living as Christ lived. Giving as Christ gave. This was Paul's life. Through a disciplemaking relationship in which Paul shared the Christlife within himself, this also became Timothy's life.

By God's grace, this becomes your life if you are willing to live with an open heart toward the Father. And, as the presence and power of Christ in you is invested in others in authentic disciplemaking relationships, this becomes true of the next generation as well.

TURNING POTENTIAL INTO IMPACT:
STRENGTHENING RELATIONAL SKILLS

According to Paul, Christ in a disciple reveals to the world "the hope of glory" (Col 1:27). Each disciple therefore carries in them the potential for being a disciplemaker. The vision is simple. The power is present. The nurturing of authentic relationships, however, requires practical skills that must be learned over time.

My (Rick's) son Ben plays a variety of positions on his football team. Ben's favorite position is linebacker. The role is very straightforward: be fast, be powerful and run people over. The critical athletic qualities for these positions are therefore speed, strength and an unflinching desire for full-speed collisions. Ben has learned, however, through hours and hours of coaching, that his speed, strength and desire can be quickly neutralized by poor technique. Much effort is required to turn potential into impact. Skills must be developed and practiced, and then real-game situations create opportunities to highlight progress and expose weaknesses. Thus, Ben—and each person on the team, no matter how clear and straightforward their role is—must strengthen the habits and techniques that produce impact.

Paul and Timothy's relationship demonstrates the straightforward nature of the role of a disciplemaker: simply learn to live in the hydrating flow of the Christlife and authentically enter into relationships where an overflow of the Christlife is poured into another person's journey with Christ. Live it and give it in the midst of the daily patterns of life.

Potential for this impact dwells within every disciple. Turning potential into impact, however, requires disciplemakers to strengthen their aptitude for nurturing disciplemaking relationships. A person's unwavering trust in God's wisdom, humble submission in embracing God's heart, and love that pursues God and others with selfless generosity can all be rendered ineffective and unproductive by relational incompetence in the disciplemaking journey. Without intentionally developing the kinds of rhythms for restoring life that we will turn to next, disciplemaking relationships—even ones with clear disciplemaking vision—can actually deteriorate over time, so that what is intended to become a life-producing relationship instead becomes, at best, disappointingly shallow and, at worst, unhealthily controlling.

Thankfully, the ability to restore life in our relationships with emerging adults can be learned, practiced and improved. This is the hope that lies ahead. And thankfully, having a heart and mind *willing* to move from potential to impact in the Christlife will take us most of the way. What we can be most thankful for, though, is that Jesus is with us—always.

LIFE-RESTORING RHYTHM 1

Discernment

ENDURANCE WAS RUNNING LOW. The smaller children were hoisted onto our backs. Confused by unreadable trail markers, we were traveling in circles; our only progress was into deeper frustration. Our initial excitement for hiking up the mountain trail to a rocky fossil field had all but evaporated. Laura, Scott and I (Jana)—and their four children, who ranged in age from ten months to six years—had been wandering around the wilderness of the Talkeetna Mountains in Alaska for about two hours, but we were not much closer to our destination than when we had begun.

We had decided on an early afternoon hike, asked about appropriate trails and sought out advice. The guy who gave us directions genuinely tried to be helpful by taking us part of the way to the trailhead and furnishing us with a small map. The map, however, had been carried away in the wind when six year-old Colton wanted to see if it would fly. (It might not have helped much anyway, though; it was extremely general—a few barely identifiable colored squiggly lines.) We tried to stay on the red trail, but the plastic marker ribbons were few and far between, and when we did see one it was hard to tell if it was red, faded red, orange or faded brown. At one point Scott finally spotted a rocky expanse, which we headed to with renewed fervor, but it was only a steep and somewhat treacherous hill of falling rock.

After stumbling around a bit more, we decided we should head back. Two-year-old Isaac fell asleep on Scott's shoulders, and we arrived back at the car with aching feet and without having found the fossil field. The hike wasn't a complete disaster; we had fun, saw a lot of beauty, slid down some rocks and got some great exercise. But at times it was also frustrating, disappointing and exhausting, and ultimately, we were deflated at not having found our way.

Two days later, we left the boys at a friend's house, laced up our hiking shoes again and headed up to the abandoned-copper-mill town of Kennecott. Our guide, Rebekah, met us there, fitted us with crampons (spikes for our shoes), explained what we would be doing, asked us some questions and visited with us a bit. She then led us through the ghost town, highlighting points of historical interest as we walked. Next we hiked two miles through the mountain scenery and over a rushing stream toward a massive glacier. Rebekah paced with us patiently, never seeming like she was in a hurry, slowing when she saw one of us lagging, pausing to share an interesting geological fact. When the time was right to put on the crampons, she taught us how to navigate steep inclines on the ice, locked arms with us if we looked a bit unsteady and led the way over an icy landscape that looked like the surface of the moon. This hike was exhilarating! We played, explored and stood in awe together as we gazed down ice cracks filled with bright aqua water rushing and sparkling in the sunlight.

When we returned to Kennecott, tired but excited, Rebekah ate dinner with us, listening as we reflected on the day's journey. We were sorry to say goodbye. Yet we also still felt the glow of accomplishment from successfully navigating previously unexplored ground.

Both hikes were physically challenging, but we came back from one deflated and the other exhilarated. What made the difference? Was it just that we reached our destination on one and not the other? Yes and no. Reaching the destination *was* exhilarating. Our increased joy, however, came from *how we got there*. It made such a difference to have a guide who paced with us well and who was intentional about steering us in ways that led to a rewarding and rich new experience. It did not make our journey easy or pain free—in fact, on the glacier hike there were some scary moments traversing the ice when we stumbled from the fatigue of lifting our feet high and then stamping them down to engage the crampons over a sustained period of time. But Rebekah's thoughtful guidance, generosity and selfless service enabled us to take our mishaps in stride and move forward with purposefulness in the midst of community.

A spiritual guide's work is much the same as Rebekah's. Unfortunately, many would-be spiritual influencers stop short of fruitful disciplemaking, merely pointing the way, offering the Bible or a book as a map, and standing way off to the side, as our first "guide" did when we were looking for the fossil field. In contrast, effective spiritual guides for emerging adults spend time building spiritual friendships and discerning appropriate direction and then move in caring, responsive, intentional ways to help others navigate the uncharted waters of their faith journey. They hike alongside others in suffering, celebration and all that lies between, helping to identify the work of the Holy Spirit in the ups and downs of everyday circumstances and decisions. Effective disciplemakers also purposefully explore the deep truths of the faith *with* emerging adults rather than *parallel* to them. Finally, an effective spiritual caregiver takes time to reflect and reevaluate as the path unwinds.

Participating in God's glorious work of spiritual transformation in his body can be a freeing experience as we follow the intertwined rhythms of *discernment, intentionality* and *reflection* that make up the disciplemaker's overall rhythm. *Discernment* affects how we choose to be *intentional,* while *reflection* creates space for us to contemplate what occurred as we acted in discernment. Finding these rhythms and learning to live in harmony with them will breathe life and beauty into disciplemaking relationships, as each rhythm assists the disciplemaker in approaching relationships through the postures of the Christlife. This first rhythm encourages disciplemakers to trust the Father for wisdom as they move into the life of an emerging adult.

UNDERSTANDING DISCERNMENT

What is your reaction to the following intentional strategies from everyday life?

- A coach of a T-ball team spends practice time with his four- to seven-year-olds working on hitting home runs rather than the basics.

- A middle-school teacher starts each week by reviewing the ABC's with her class.

- A couple uses their family meetings to discuss the importance of doing chores on time even though the kids are experiencing deep sadness after the sudden death of two well-loved family pets.

A lack of discernment causes the T-ball coach to aim too high, the middle-school teacher to aim too low and the couple to miss the mark completely with their family. These extreme scenarios are examples of a denial of the obvious.

In contrast, discernment would have led to the appropriate response in each case. It enables us to go beyond, to see or understand things that are not immediately clear or obvious. Along with this, discernment asks us to pace with God and with the emerging adult to receive vision and valuable information in order to truly serve another. It typically takes time, prayer, waiting, watching and listening to meaningfully respond to someone in the tender or hardened places of their life.

It is important to note our particular use of the term *discernment* here. In the midst of a list of spiritual gifts given to followers of Christ, 1 Corinthians 12:10 includes "discerning of spirits" (KJV). This gift is often explained as the ability to discern between good and evil (Heb 5:14) or to distinguish when a prophecy is truly from God (1 Cor 12:3). We, however, are using *discernment* in its broader sense—as when Solomon asked for a wise and discerning mind to govern the people of Israel or when Paul prayed that the Philippians would be able to discern what is best. In Scripture, the word *understanding* is often used for this type of discernment, as in Proverbs 16:21: "The wise are known for their *understanding,* and pleasant words are persuasive" (NLT, emphasis ours). Proverbs 3:5 also uses the word *understanding,* reminding us to depend on God rather than ourselves for it.

Discernment allows the disciplemaker to respond in a more relevant way. Isaiah 50 declares of the Lord's servant:

> The Sovereign Lord has given me his words of wisdom,
>   *so that I know how to comfort* the weary.
> Morning by morning he wakens me
>   and opens my *understanding* to his will.
> The Sovereign Lord has spoken to me,
>   and *I have listened.* (vv. 4-5 NLT, emphasis ours).

As the Lord's servants, discernment calls for us to listen carefully so that we might know how to respond to weary emerging adults, whether worn by the challenges they face, the tempo of living life at a breakneck speed or even the sustained excitement of the adventures they pursue.

WHY PRACTICE DISCERNMENT?

When I (Jana), as a young adult myself, mentored a young woman named Julie, I was guilty of approaching her with an agenda—one that didn't really have much to do with her—rather than exploring her questions. I volunteered as a mentor simply because I was wanting to take a more active role in my church. This was not a *bad* aim, but becoming acquainted with God's reasons for making disciples, or understanding the needs of the person I was about to pour into, were not factors. I was serving me, first and foremost; my desire was to do things that would propel my growth as a Christian. If you asked me, I would have *said* that I wanted to serve Julie and God—but my actions betrayed that my focus was on how *I* was going to accomplish that. Julie and God were almost completely left out of the equation.

I was also serving a method. The discipleship book that was placed in my hands became *the way* to serve her. Ironically, I ended up serving the book more than I served Julie. When we got together, we talked about the assigned chapter and then I left. I'm sure its wisdom had important things to add to her life, but since I didn't take any time to discern where Julie needed to be strengthened—and because I didn't pause to ask God which content areas needed to be highlighted for her—the book was just a book. God's leading could have made it an inspired tool in my inexperienced hands. It could have been the stimulus for life-giving conversation. Instead, it hung between us like a film that I could barely see her through, and our discussions fell flat.

Another problem was that, as a new disciplemaker, I wanted to impress the ministry leader (who placed both the book and responsibility in my hands) with my willingness and ability. I looked up to her and wanted to show my respect by following her lead. My desire to please was misdirected, though. She may have sensed this and probably tried to redirect me to pleasing Christ (I don't remember), but I failed to translate that into depending on the Lord to energize my discernment so that my service to Julie could be more Christ-centered.

Setting aside time to listen for God's direction for others helps us learn to surrender to the will of the Father and deepens our ability to approach and respond to those we're discipling with wisdom. It also facilitates our own growth as disciplemakers in living the Christlife by inviting us to come to disciplemaking as Christ did—not pursuing our own agenda, but fulfilling the agenda of the Father. In addition, exercising discernment deepens our humility, because it requires that we choose to move toward another person with self-control and patience. We must be willing to wait and to admit our need for direction from the Father so that we can say with Christ, "I can do nothing by myself; I do only what I see the Father doing" (see Jn 5:19). Ultimately, practicing discernment is an opportunity to love as Jesus loved by providing space to exercise selfless generosity. We consider the true needs of others *before* and *as* we act on their behalf. It is the place where we acquire God's heart for others.[1]

In Matthew 4, Satan tries desperately to redirect Jesus from this kind of trust and selfless generosity. He tempts Jesus by essentially saying, "Here are some good things you can do: prove your own power and ability to create for positive ends [turn these stones into bread], see if God will really fulfill his promise to protect you and make *your* life good [jump off the temple], and take the world and all its glory from my hand [just worship me]." But Jesus does not waver. He understood something we desperately need to understand: being directed by the Father, letting him set your agenda and obeying his purposes—this is where life is found. Loving emerging adults from a place of listening discernment brings life to the process of disciplemaking.

Practically speaking, discernment encourages the disciplemaker to ascertain the spiritual condition of the disciple. When an emerging adult expresses a desire for a mentor, it can be tempting to think they are "empty vessels" and we are the "filler of the void." But whether they've been Christ-followers for a few years or many, young adults have plenty to bring to the experience. They may, for example, come painfully aware of the "requirements" of living by Christian standards, so they don't need to be met with a Christian "to do" list; rather, they're probably craving the assistance of someone who will help them explore their ability to respond to the list already in their head. They may also need help getting perspective on whether their "list" is actually what God is asking of them. They might wonder, *Is this standard realistic in my present circumstances? Why should I want to do this in the midst of the pressures I daily face? Is this really what God is asking of me or do I have a culturally skewed perspective of it? Do I want to do this as a means of worship or is it about accomplishment?*

It can, of course, be intimidating to mentor a young adult who appears to know more than you do about living the Christlife. Be assured, however, that an emerging adult generally expresses a desire to grow because he or she feels deficient somewhere—though the "deficiency" may just be lack of support from an established adult. Discernment helps us determine where those deficiencies are and how to best engage them so that we're not held captive by preconceived assumptions that create fear and insecurity. Accurate discernment actually empowers us in our disciplemaking to humbly and truly serve the other.

Discernment is therefore crucial because it positions disciplemakers in a genuinely God-empowered process rather than a purely human one. At this point in my (Jana's) life, the temptation to think I'm the one in charge of the disciplemaking process is stronger than it has ever been. Because I have been a disciplemaker for many years, mentoring hundreds of women (as well as some men) and leading countless fruitful small groups, I can start to feel pretty confident in my abilities as I see my life impact others. I *cannot,* however, be sure that I am making a *spiritual* impact that will truly lead someone to Christ-filled abundance or that my efforts on their behalf will stand the test of time. I cannot be sure that I'm helping someone truly become a disciple of Christ and not merely *my* disciple. I'm glad Paul acknowledges this mixed bag of human motives amidst spiritual aims in 2 Corinthians 10:2-5:

> I am begging you now so that when I come I won't have to be bold with those who think we act from human motives.
>
> *We are human, but we don't wage war as humans do.* We use God's mighty weapons, not worldly weapons, to knock down the strongholds of human reasoning and to destroy false arguments. We destroy every proud obstacle that keeps people from knowing God. We capture their rebellious thoughts and teach them to obey Christ. (NLT, emphasis ours)

As humans, our default mode and burden is an inability to act without some measure of our fallen nature factoring into what we do, yet we know we can go beyond our humanness through *his* wisdom, love and power. God's mighty weapons can cut through human ignorance, arrogance and defiance. Making a commitment to practice discernment moves the disciplemaker closer to entering into someone's life in the places where God is already at work. In other words, it provides a space to consider how to join in with what God is doing rather than to forge ahead in our frailty and with the burden of making an impact on our own. Discerning and joining God's work in a person's life brings about a spiritual energy and joy at seeing God-induced growth (1 Cor 3:6). That energy, in turn, fuels perseverance for the long haul when the disciplemaker is walking alongside someone in a season of resistance.

STRATEGIES FOR DISCERNMENT

Discernment involves pacing, identifying growth potential and listening for God's wisdom.

Pacing. Slowing down to match the stride of another is the first step of loving discernment for effective disciplemaking. It requires us to see beyond words and behaviors and listen to the heart of the disciple. It also requires time and the attentiveness to go beyond a surface conversation and enter into the experiences of the emerging adult. Pacing is costly but reaps significant relational and spiritual rewards. For one thing, going at another's pace builds trust. Trust produces relationship, and relationship, in turn, gives birth to spiritual life exchanges. Such exchanges are sacred places where the Holy Spirit reaches with transformative nurture through the life of a disciplemaker into the life of the young adult seeking to grow.[2]

Pacing is a *prerequisite* commitment that must be made in order to discern wisely. Unfortunately, it's often skipped because the journey from external assumptions about another person's life to actually seeing and sensing his or her true personal reality is never easy or quick. It may involve working through layers of self-protective barriers built up because of disappointing relationships. Interpersonal demands and busy schedules on the part of both adults can likewise slow the tempo of pacing to that of a snail's gait. Given these challenges, it's no wonder that many well-intentioned disciplemakers default to *telling* instead of *pacing*.

Resisting the urge to tell. Telling puts intentionality before discernment. Telling can be distinguished from pacing in the ways outlined in table 4.1.:

Table 4.1.

Telling . . .	Pacing for discernment . . .
enters the relationship with a prepackaged agenda	has the agenda of understanding the young adult's thoughts, feelings and circumstances
emphasizes teaching and advice-giving abilities	emphasizes listening and care-giving abilities
emphasizes the disciplemaker's expertise and knowledge about God's will for the other person's life	emphasizes the disciplemaker's willingness to listen *with* the other person for what God is doing in his or her life
focuses on getting the disciple to agree to the disciplemaker's goals for their growth	focuses on the initial goal of creating space for the disciple to relate authentically to the disciplemaker and to God and then adopts God's goals for the emerging adult

Relationally, instructing someone is less costly, easier to control and more efficient than pacing. But effective discernment and the ability to be relationally and spiritually intentional hinge on the disciplemaker's willingness to pace.[3] Pacing encourages the spiritual caregiver to ponder a person's emotional, relational and spiritual condition with questions like

- How does she presently perceive God in her life?
- How is he experiencing God in the midst of recent challenges?
- How does she deal with decisions about the future?

These kinds of questions and others (see the "pacing questions" in chapters seven through eleven) help disciplemakers learn about the people they're serving in order to best lead them toward God in a holistic, transformational way right in the midst of real life. Effective pacing precedes and helps facilitate effective intentionality in disciplemaking.

Identifying growth potential. Authors Keith Anderson and Randy Reese have written, "Mentoring is deeply relational, wisely alert to the movement of God in the dailyness of life and anchored in the passionate love for God and for the growth of the mentoree."[4] Becoming "wisely alert" to areas where the "dailyness of life" is meeting the movement of God is the next step in practicing discernment. This is best done by working to identify obvious growth areas, hidden growth areas and/or debilitating growth obstacles.

Obvious growth areas. The easiest area to discern will be growth frontiers—obvious places that need attention, exploration or expansion. These areas may jump out at you as you observe or interact with the young adult you're mentoring. For example, you may both be aware that his next step needs to be learning to control his tongue in his interactions with others. Or she may come right out and *tell you* that she wants to grow in self-discipline because she has already identified it as an area of weakness. He may identify that his next step in maturity needs to be developing compassion or becoming more involved in serving the underprivileged. The disciples themselves may make the area that needs to be the focus of your intentional growth times with them clear.

Hidden growth areas. When someone comes to us having already identified an area where they want to grow, we almost always start there. However, sometimes a growth frontier is a veneer for something beneath the surface. A model of interpersonal awareness called the Johari Window explains that each of us operates in the midst of four levels of awareness.[5] The adaptation of the Johari Window in figure 4.2 helps us understand how growth areas may be hidden.[6]

Table 4.2.

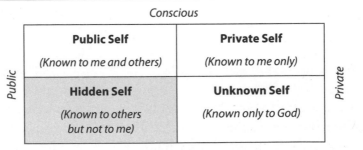

	Conscious		
	Public Self	**Private Self**	
Public	*(Known to me and others)*	*(Known to me only)*	*Private*
	Hidden Self	**Unknown Self**	
	(Known to others but not to me)	*(Known only to God)*	
	Unconscious		

The *public self* of the emerging adult will be known to us. They may reveal the *private self* to us over time. A *hidden* growth area is a place in the young adult's life that they're unaware of. A healthy, meaningful relationship with a disciplemaker who is discerning provides an outstanding opportunity for the disciple to become consciously aware of these hidden areas. She may not be aware of how she resists relationships. He may not know that his sarcasm affects others. The last space is the *unknown self*, which is known only to God. For his glory as well as for an individual's benefit, however, the Holy Spirit may choose to reveal parts of the unknown self to the disciplemaker or to the emerging adult, thereby presenting the disciple with unexpected areas for growth.

Hidden growth areas are often multilayered. Motivations, ingrained patterns, deeply established lies, worldviews, assumptions, behavioral or character issues, or deep-seated fears can be potential culprits. Discernment can occur by noticing patterns emerging over time or sensing a common root for multiple issues. Probing questions like the following (this is not an exhaustive list) can help you discern areas that may be in need of transformation:

- What do you think your reasons behind that choice are?

- What scares you most about this situation?

- When have you sensed (or faced, acted like, felt or chosen like) that in the past?

- What kinds of assumptions about God might be leading you to that conclusion?

- How do you think your perspective on this matches up with God's Big Story?

Special growth obstacles. Be alert to obstacles that hold the disciple of Christ back from enjoying and flourishing in the Christlife. Growth obstacles are particularly troublesome habits or hurts that clog the inflow of grace—the connection to God as a life-giving source—in a disciple's life. They're debilitating to the disciple's sense of spiritual well-being, and may take the form of addiction, idolatry, misplaced dependence or pain. Because a sense of shame may accompany growth obstacles, it can take a long time for disciples to admit their struggle. They may, for example, feel embarrassed to admit their inability to conquer a habitual sin, or humiliated at the thought of sharing about the pain of abuse. Sometimes a young adult may actually seek out a disciplemaking relationship *because* of their growth obstacle, but this is not what usually happens. If it does, be aware that an aspect of discernment in this category may be distinguishing whether a supportive disciplemaking relationship can help or whether professional counseling is needed.

Learning to attentively pace and become aware of potential growth areas (obvious, hidden and special obstacles) are two legs of a three-legged stool that's completed by one more aspect of discernment.

Listening to God for others. The most sacred and perhaps the most important part of discipleship to pursue is listening for God's direction and wisdom in preparation for and in the midst of spiritual life exchanges.

Half listening versus dual listening. Discernment encourages us to focus on God *and* the disciple simultaneously, but not with the distracted kind of listening that Dietrich Bonhoeffer calls "half listening":

> There is a kind of listening with half an ear that presumes to already know what the other person has to say. It is an impatient, inattentive listening that despises the brother and is only waiting for a chance to speak and thus get rid of the other person.[7]

No, discernment requires the ultra-focused kind where you are listening with equal intensity to two things at once, like the way you would listen to the breathing *and* the last words of a dying loved one. Listening for the Lord *while* you listen to the disciple is discernment *alongside* the other. And we actually already possess this skill. We listen to music in our cars while we are talking to our spouse, attend to our children's demands while we are on the phone with a friend, or catch the news on TV while reading an email. Though some of us are better at it than others, we all do it. We can take this innate tendency for dual listening and develop it to its fullest advantage in the disciplemaking context, paying attention to the lives and stories of emerging adults while listening for God's whisper even as they're speaking.

Listening for God's "consent." We also need to practice discernment *for* the other by listening to God apart from them. Hosea 8 emphasizes the necessity of consulting God. Picture Hosea, the only prophet from the rebellious northern kingdom, standing among the tribes with his dark predictions and warnings trying to get their attention. Next to the smaller, more organized tribes of Judah, Israel was a mess—an unruly conglomerate of people lacking a governmental or religious center. The challenge of securing an attentive audience must have been overwhelming for Hosea, but his message from God for the people of Israel had to be communicated, as it was urgent and immensely important:

> Sound the alarm!
>   The enemy descends like an eagle on the people of the LORD,
> for they have broken my covenant
>   and revolted against my law.
> Now Israel pleads with me,
>   "Help us, for you are our God!"
> But it is too late! (vv. 1-3 NLT)

Sound the alarm! It's too late to plead for help! Why? What is causing this panicky prediction? The second half of verse 3 explains: *"The people of Israel have rejected what is good, and now their enemies will chase after them"* (NLT, emphasis ours). No wonder they're in trouble. They've rejected what is good. And what, specifically, is the good they've rejected? Hosea's message from the Lord answers that too:

> The people have appointed kings *without my consent,*
>   and princes without my knowledge.
> By making idols for themselves from their silver and gold,
>   they have brought about their own destruction. (v. 4, emphasis ours)

"Without my consent." These simple words leap off the page and press deeply into us. They cause us to ask ourselves, *How often have I been guilty of rejecting the same good that Israel did—moving ahead, doing the "Lord's work" without ever consulting the Lord on it? How often do I make an idol of my own ideas or the practiced or published ideas of another instead of humbling myself at the feet of the Lord? Do I forget that he is the one who made the person I'm hoping the Lord will use me to impact?*

Seeking God's consent in disciplemaking consists of a willingness to listen for the Lord and to be surprised by how he might choose to work or direct us. After all, we consult with the same God who used a donkey to confront Balaam (Num 22:28), a dream to direct Peter to eat what had been forbidden (Acts 10), and a whale, the hot sun and a plant to rebuke Jonah. Practically, this means we need to bring the young adult we're discipling before the Lord in prayer and then wait, watch and listen for his response, however he chooses to communicate it to us—through a Scripture verse, an impression or insight, sensing some redirection in our ideas or plans, experiencing peace about the direction of our meeting, or some other way.

NAVIGATING WITH WISDOM

Moving into rich, transformational relationships with emerging adults becomes much more likely when we take time to practice discernment. Discovering appropriate inroads for spiritual growth that will truly allow us to travel alongside young adults with intentionality as they navigate uncharted territory depends on our ability and willingness to take our cues from the Father's wisdom rather than our prior experiences. Pausing to realign ourselves with the Master Disciplemaker frees us to journey with others in the midst of their uncertainty with more than a book or a method. And we will find joy as we accompany them in exploring how to live the Christlife in the midst of the new opportunities and challenges they face.

LIFE-RESTORING RHYTHM 2

Intentionality

STEVE WANTED HIS SPIRITUAL friendship with twenty-one-year-old Joe to be comfortable. When they met together to discuss Joe's life, Steve listened attentively and accurately reflected back to Joe what he heard him saying. I (Jana) was therefore quite surprised when Joe asked me if I would consider mentoring him.

"I thought you and Steve were meeting. Isn't that going well?" I queried.

"Oh, it's going fine. I love Steve. He's a great guy and I know that he really cares about me." I waited. "It's just that . . . well, I don't ever feel like I'm getting anywhere. I really want to grow. I guess I think you'll be able to help me move forward," Joe explained.

I asked him if he had communicated to Steve what he needed. He assured me he had but that Steve responded with, "That's just not my style."

Steve would probably say he was following the example of Jesus, who just "hung out" with his disciples. That misunderstanding of Jesus' relational style makes me cringe! Yes, Jesus hung out with his disciples and they lived life together. But he also challenged them with words and experiences, imparted vision to them, exposed them to important truths, taught them, delegated roles, created learning experiences for them, sent them out for mission, and debriefed with them. He was intentional and proactive in how he related to them.

Joe knew that hanging out was only the *beginning* of a good spiritual friendship; he wanted to experience the next step in discipleship. Steve took the first step of discernment by pacing with Joe but neglected the second discernment step of helping Joe identify areas of growth potential. This neglect compromised Steve's ability to be intentional in the relationship, which left Joe with a sense of being cared for *but without a sense of movement toward life transformation*. I agreed to mentor Joe and we spent an extremely fruitful year together exploring truth, listening for the Lord's voice in his life, sharpening his skills and delving into the areas where he felt stuck. Listening together for how the Lord was working in the midst of Joe's heart, struggles and goals allowed me to be responsive in a personal and dynamic way.

This second rhythm of intentionality directs the disciplemaker to engage the third posture of the Christlife—fulfilling the Father's will through loving others proactively. It calls us to approach our disciplemaking relationships with purpose in order to move the disciple toward life transformation in becoming like Christ.

UNDERSTANDING INTENTIONALITY

The rich young ruler's heart was sold out to his accumulated wealth. The woman at the well had a heart burned out by her lost loves. How did Jesus meet them in their stubbornness and pain? He actively loved others as he discerned their hearts and then endeavored to intentionally connect them with truth that would be meaningful for their particular spiritual condition. To the young man Jesus spoke in terms of commandments and action, pointing out that the upwardly mobile heart must bow in submission to Christ's kingship. To the woman Jesus spoke in terms of relationships, ultimately drawing her to the heartbeat of the Father, with whom she was not a social outcast.

A young man's heart is captured by the fear that he will never find the right job or be able to support himself because of a crippled economy. A young woman struggles to commit to a relationship because she's afraid she won't be able to do the deep work of relating. As we, like Jesus, take time to discern what captures or immobilizes the hearts of emerging adults, we can begin to relate to them in intentional ways, considering not only what needs to be said but also how to communicate it in a way that will be understood. Intentionality calls us to not only pass on the truth we've learned but also do it in a way that is relevant to the emerging adult's world. Truth telling is primarily concerned with the question, "Did I communicate truth?" *Intentionality* adds: "Did I communicate truth *meaningfully?*"[1] Asking both these questions together allows the disciplemaker to explore how to say the right things for *that person's* heart in their particular stage of life or circumstances. Speaking or pointing to truth in a way that is personally meaningful is the fruit of Spirit-directed discernment that's responded to with intentionality.

Characteristics of intentionality. What does it mean to move into a relationship with intentionality? Different personalities or experiences may cause us to come up with various answers to that question, but there are a few key aspects of intentionality that we need to be aware of before we can practice it in our relationships with emerging adults.

Intentionality is not "natural." Choosing to love through intentionality may come naturally to type-A, action-oriented personalities, but many of us would rather believe that disciplemaking relationships become productive on their own—*naturally.* An aversion to anything that feels scripted is understandable; being intentional *can* take on an organic feel, though, when it is in response to discernment. Ephesians 5:15-17 exhorts us, "So be careful how you live. Don't live like fools, but like those who are wise. *Make the most of every opportunity* in these evil days. Don't act *thoughtlessly,* but understand what the Lord wants you to do" (NLT, emphasis ours). Discernment teaches us to be thoughtful about our encounters with others. Intentionality teaches us to make the most of every opportunity. Intentional disciplemaking capitalizes on the opportunities that present themselves through discernment and seeks to partner with the Lord in taking action for the good of the other.

Intentionality produces positive spiritual tension. Being proactive about responding to the work of the Spirit—instead of choosing the path of least resistance, which is our natural tendency—may cause tension. An experienced disciplemaker learns to not only embrace tension but also to lead others toward healthy tensions that can facilitate spiritual growth. Disciplemaking that avoids tension may actually nurture the emerging adult's flesh. Think again about the components of the Christlife: self-surrendered trust, submission through humility and genuine love expressed as an act of selfless generosity. Which of these comes naturally for any of us? Consider these examples:

> You sense the Lord asking you to humble yourself before an arrogant co-worker. "But Lord," you protest, "won't he take advantage of me if I do

that? You want me to set myself up?" Surrendering to the Father's wisdom when he prompts us to do something is in conflict with our tendency to want to protect ourselves.

You really want to have that new _____ (insert the appropriate noun here: intriguing electronic toy, beautiful dress, chocolate toffee cheesecake). In fact, you feel that you need it: "God, do I really need to think through this purchase with your mindset? Can't I just buy it?" Believing that God knows our needs better than we do feels less comfortable than believing that things are the source of our satisfaction.

The contents of the garbage can are spilling all over the garage floor. You know you weren't the last one to put garbage in it, so you reason, "Why should I clean it up? So what if that other person is carrying a heavy load right now. That person was responsible." Living in selfless generosity by thinking of others first pulls against our inclination to want to defend our right to be served.

Annie Dillard wrote, "How you spend your days is, of course, how you spend your life."[2] Acting with the mind, heart and will of Christ in the small nooks and crannies of our days will be in tension with the path of least resistance our flesh wants to take. Helping others become like Christ in those everyday moments provides an important arena for life-giving transformation. The fact that we and those we disciple are given grace to enter into the Christlife does not mean we can sit back and coast. Grace and effort are not opposites; they are companions. Grace energizes effort. Grace *and* effort are needed for intentionality to take place. Intentionality in our spiritual friendships allows us to restore the flow of life-giving grace and truth into areas of spiritual disconnection.[3] But assisting someone in trusting the Father's wisdom, humbly submitting in response to the Father's heart and leadership, or fulfilling the Father's will in love may require us to

- offer correction
- confront untruths
- call out their potential
- help them redefine their reality
- assist them in recasting their vision for their life
- train them in certain skills

- pursue truth with them

- celebrate victories with them

These are intentional actions for loving others as God loves us.

Keeping our focus on the goal. Actions like those listed above can never become our goal, or a checklist of discipling steps. Skills and tasks are merely *tools* that are available as needed on the disciplemaking journey.

I (Jana) love to fix stuff around the house. My roommate laughs at me because I'll spend five hours trying to fix something rather than call a professional who could accomplish the same task in an hour. I am not an expert by any means, but I own a few tools and have developed some skills. Even those with no experience, though, know one of the most basic principles of repair: different repairs require different tools. Being required to use a hammer for every repair, for example, would be extremely frustrating and inefficient. In any given project I'm working on, I use the tools that will be most helpful for the job and save my other tools for different projects. Whether it's unclogging a sink or fixing a broken screen door, using tools is clearly not the goal; fixing the (sometimes costly!) problem is.

In a similar way, focusing on the goal of developing the postures of the Christlife as disciplemakers leaves us free to pick up or discard a tool according to its usefulness to the relationship. Discipleship relationships rarely go "according to plan," so we need to be flexible and purposeful; indeed, the spiritual journey, with its spiritual battles, requires intentionality that transcends checklists and "paint by number" formulas. I have often pressed into disciplemaking relationships with one set of assumptions about how to best connect a person to Christ only to discover a new set of issues that shifts my approach. Again, Jesus came not to accomplish a long checklist of actions but to accomplish the will of his Father. Following Jesus as our model, then, means that we must focus on the goal—developing the Christlife postures of trust, submission and love and helping others do the same. Continually refocusing on this goal positions our encounters toward true transformation.

STRATEGIES FOR INTENTIONAL DISCIPLEMAKING

What does it look like to focus on trusting the Father's wisdom, submitting to the Father's heart in humility and fulfilling the Father's will in love within a spiritual friendship? How are fear, pride and anger truly replaced with Christ? The following are some specific strategies for refocusing the emerging adult: envisioning potential, encouraging trust, enabling submission and empowering love.

Envisioning potential. Seeing another person with God's eyes sets the stage for transformative growth in that person's life. A disciplemaker's ability to envision the potential of Christ living through the unique personality of another profoundly affects that person's ability to envision it for him- or herself. Sociological studies have consistently shown that when people are subjected to low expectations they have a tendency to underachieve. Envisioning potential in positive terms has the opposite effect.[4] Even as a young adult, our ability to succeed in life may be strongly affected by our internalization of the potential others have reflected to us. An important tool for a disciplemaker is the ability to mirror a godly vision of potential. For example, when I (Jana) was nineteen years old, a disciplemaker in my life (Karen) helped me see budding capabilities I had for training and empowering others for leadership. It was news to me! She pointed out ways that God was already using me in that capacity and gave me a vision for how God might want me to participate in building his kingdom. I will always treasure the gift she gave me in doing so. It led me toward a lifelong trajectory that has been both fruitful and fulfilling.

Such envisioning reflects the Father's approach to his people. Deuteronomy 7:6 says, "For you are a holy people, who belong to the LORD your God. Of all the people on earth, the LORD your God has chosen you to be his own special treasure" (NLT). In Matthew 5:14, Jesus tells his followers, "You are the light of the world." We are a holy people—God's treasure. We belong to the Lord. We are the light of the world. We can give light to others. Imagine the impact we could all have if disciplemakers not only believed this about themselves but also learned to impart the Father's vision to those whom they disciple.

As citizens in God's kingdom our potential is boundless, but only, we must remember, because of our capacity in Christ. Disciples can make progress in living the Christlife because Christ lives his life through us. As disciplemakers, then, we can help emerging adults turn their attention from failures to the hope of Christ who is able to "make all things new." Connect them with a positive vision for their life in Christ—grounded in the truths of Scripture, enhanced by an understanding of how God uniquely created them to function in the body of Christ and sealed by the transforming work of the Holy Spirit.

Encouraging trust: Surrendering to the Father's wisdom. Paul exhorts his readers, "Let God transform you into a new person by changing the way you think. Then you will learn to know God's will for you, which is good and pleasing and perfect" (Rom 12:2 NLT). Changing the way we think is essential to living the Christlife. We must learn to think with the mind of Christ even while we're surrounded by a culture that often pushes our minds in an opposite direction from his. We desperately need to connect ourselves and the emerging adult to a stable touchstone of truth—the truth and wisdom that come from above.

To lead someone from the foolishness of this world toward trusting God's wisdom may require tools like confrontation, correction, speaking truth, championing them, or helping them see the truth in God's Word or his world. Again, the purpose of using tools like these is to encourage trust and surrender. Keep the purpose at the forefront so that you'll be open to discovering other tools as well. We offer explanations and examples of these tools in chapters seven through eleven.

Ultimately, lives are transformed as disciples grow in their ability to see and trust the wisdom of the Father over their own. Self-surrendering obedience to the Father out of love, not law, positions the disciple to allow the Lord Jesus to live through them. The net result is not only joy but also fruitful witness to others, as Jesus promised: "When you obey my commandments, you remain in my love, just as I obey my Father's commandments and remain in his love. I have told you these things so that you will be filled with my joy. Yes, your joy will overflow!" (Jn 15:10-11 NLT). We have the privilege of walking with emerging adults into this joy as they learn to trust God's wisdom instead of their own.

Enabling submission: Humbly embracing the Father's heart and leadership. Fully embracing the Father's love for us—choosing to respond vulnerably with an open heart—is humbling. It means being willing to find our ultimate satisfaction in his all-embracing affection and care for us. It also means choosing to believe, with the simplicity of a baby dependent on his or her mother for sustenance, that he has our best interests in mind. The disciplemaker, then, might need to help young adults turn from a prideful, controlling or fearful independence to a humble dependence on God and interdependence with his people. Or they might need to journey with emerging adults as they take intentional next steps in looking to God for his leadership in their lives and following wherever he might lead.

All of us struggle to keep soft hearts in a world that rushes in with harsh realities. Sometimes it can feel like we're standing in a batting cage without a bat while a relentless machine throws distractions, temptations, lies and challenges at us with alarming speed. I may dodge the balls the best I can, but once I've been hit several times, I begin to harden myself against further damage. Our tendency to self-protect turns us away from the shelter of the Father and causes us to develop survival strategies like relational and emotional distance, self-focus, self-sufficiency, self-justification, self-gratification, denial, and using or blaming others. These strategies pull us away from drinking deeply from the well of living water that promises to nourish our hearts and souls—and allows us to stand calm amidst an unwelcome torrent. Jeremiah recognized these twin tendencies long ago in the Israelites; they, like us, were not leaning on the Father and instead were relying on faulty strategies (cracked cisterns): "For my people have committed two evils: they have forsaken me, the fountain of living waters, and hewed out cisterns for themselves, broken cisterns that can hold no water" (Jer 2:13).

Wise disciplemakers are intentional about unearthing faulty strategies and connecting young adults to the reality of their choices. And they reveal the alternative opportunity: embracing love, protection and the fulfillment found in Christ, our living water.

Only in the light of God's all-encompassing love can we release the nagging needs of "self" and find our true needs met. Right before John the Baptist said a somewhat self-effacing-sounding statement ("He must become greater and greater, and I must become less and less"), he revealed how humility flows from a loving relationship with Jesus: "It is the bridegroom who marries the bride, and the best man is simply glad to stand with him and hear his vows. Therefore, I am filled with joy at his success" (Jn 3:29-30 NLT). His posture of humbly receiving all God had given him from heaven allowed him to be "simply glad to stand with him." As a disciplemaker, it is a joy to encourage intentional movement in an emerging adult's life and see him or her progress from standing apart from God to submitting to him, glad to merely stand in his presence.

Empowering love: Fulfilling the Father's will. Simply put, "Jesus calls us into intimacy with Him and then imitation of Him."[5] Fulfilling the Father's will through loving others flows from the intimate connection found in the first two purposes: trusting the Father's wisdom and submitting to his leadership and heart. These are what move us pro-actively into the lives of others. Those who surrender to the Father's wisdom understand that it is God's will for them to live in selfless generosity, lovingly pursuing those on whom God places such a high value. And those who live within the embrace of the Father's heart will find their hearts beginning to beat in cadence with his. As disciplemakers, we can help empower emerging adults toward this, guiding them to fulfill God's will by pursuing godly relationships with an engaged heart.

It is so easy to embrace this value, but often so difficult to live it out. Thirty-one-year-old Emily, for example, was great at using a combination of media (Facebook, texting, etc.) and face-to-face encounters to show interest and connect with others as she built relationships; engaging others through both words and appropriate affection was definitely a strength of hers. However, she had never learned skills that would help her navigate difficult relational encounters and hang in there until they were resolved. She needed to be taught how to practically persevere in relationships. If young-adult disciples are not actively loving those around them, we need to be intentional by challenging unawareness, confronting unwillingness, exploring wounded areas or teaching relational skills that will help draw the disciple toward this important posture of fulfilling God's will. Again, you'll find examples of tools for intentional disciplemaking in chapters seven through eleven.

Empowering emerging adults who are intent on living the Christlife means helping them embrace an ethic of involvement in the lives of others and learn to love the things that God loves from a place of selfless generosity. These will come from an overflow of Christ's wisdom and heart in the disciple.

INTENT ON GROWTH

Becoming like Christ does not happen for emerging adults through merely "hanging out" with someone older or wiser than them. It must be an intentional pursuit. For the past five years, twenty-eight-year-old Kristin has served the Lord in Thailand by teaching elementary-school children who have never heard of Christ. Knowing the challenges she would face, she deliberately stayed connected to other Christians and looked for mentors. With great relief and even greater excitement, she recently told me (Jana) that she finally found a couple willing to proactively speak into her life. Their readiness to pursue her with Christ-focused intentionality is making a huge difference in her ability to grow in the midst of the challenges she faces as an emerging adult and vocational missionary.

While much can be accomplished through discernment and intentionality, the next rhythm we will explore *maximizes* our impact in the lives of others.

LIFE-RESTORING RHYTHM 3

Reflection

EVERY YEAR ALL TEMP HEATING calls me (Jana) with a discounted offer to tune up my furnace. And every year I hesitate. After all, when they call, I'm not having any noticeable problems with my heating. Experts tell me, however, that getting a tune-up will save money, increase efficiency and prevent unexpected breakdowns. Over time (I'm now on my third furnace) I've become convinced that practicing the habit of regular maintenance is worthwhile even though it feels like a nuisance.

Setting aside the time required to practice reflection in a disciplemaking relationship can also feel like an unnecessary inconvenience, especially if things are going well. Why scrutinize something that's already functional? Why not leave well enough alone? Proverbs 24:30-31 gives us an answer:

> I passed by the field of a sluggard,
>   by the vineyard of a man lacking sense,
> and behold, it was all overgrown with thorns;
>   the ground was covered with nettles,
>   and its stone wall was broken down.

Without attention, almost anything—whether a machine, a garden or a relationship—is vulnerable to decay. The rhythm of reflection asks us to live in submission to the Father's heart and leadership by pausing to contemplate with him the fruit of the first two rhythms—both in our life and in the lives of emerging adults. We can then submit to his leadership as he redirects us or submit to his encouragement as he allows us to see how we have been in cooperation with the good that he is accomplishing.

UNDERSTANDING REFLECTION

Reflection keeps the discipleship process healthy and growing. Keith Anderson and Randy Reese call this kind of reflection "adaptable discernment."[1] The major difference between the rhythm of discernment and the rhythm of reflection is that reflection focuses on *refining the process* of disciplemaking. In contrast, discernment focuses on *creating* the context for meaningful spiritual interaction. They are like two sides of a coin, similar in essence but different in purpose. Discernment is a pre-activity used to determine what intentional actions would be most helpful in moving the emerging adult toward life-restoring connection with God and others. Reflection looks at what is occurring or has just occurred in order to determine if effective movement is happening.

The book of Haggai opens with a call to be reflective:

> This is what the Lord of Heaven's Armies says: *Look at what's happening to you!* You have planted much but harvest little. You eat but are not satisfied. You drink but are still thirsty. You put on clothes but cannot keep warm. Your wages disappear as though you were putting them in pockets filled with holes! "This is what the Lord of Heaven's Armies says: *Look at what's happening to you!*" (Hag 1:5-7 NLT, emphasis ours)

The prophet calls the people to see the reality of their present condition. We too must look at what is happening in our disciplemaking relationships in order to see and attend to the places that need recalibration or adjustment. Sometimes the news is good! Other times reflection reveals minor areas for adjustment. Or we may become aware of areas that need a complete overhaul.

WHY REFLECT?

The discipline of reflection creates space for celebration, for wisdom regarding redirection and repair, and for cooperation with the Holy Spirit, all of which helps us refine and enrich the mentoring process.

Celebration of movement. I (Jana) have a small vegetable garden in my backyard. If someone inquired about it and I said, "It's terrific! I'm getting juicy red tomatoes, large carrots, crisp cucumbers and tasty peppers, and the weed barrier I laid down last month is working," there would be cause for celebration! But my ability to celebrate is dependent on my having actively observed and assessed my garden.

Our fast-paced world presses us to move on to the next thing. Noise, busyness and activities in our lives do not facilitate looking back to see where we have been. Moreover, growth is incremental. Intentional steps are often small, so change is often gradual. It's easy to miss the progress we've made. One of the most important things we might discover in the process of reflection, however, is that things are going well; God *has* been working. The acknowledgment and celebration of movement are needed to gain perspective and facilitate further movement. Celebration also leads us to give honor to the Lord in the midst of disciplemaking relationships. Reconnecting with *his* part in changing and growing his disciples is vitally important. When we celebrate movement, we celebrate his power in our lives.

In addition, reflection helps us connect to the story that is being acted out in the lives of others—the grander, multidimensional, multigenerational story of God's work in sanctifying his church. This brings hope and energy to both us as disciplemakers and the young adults we're journeying alongside. We can celebrate *with* them, facilitating their own ability to recognize God in their midst. Our role is similar to that of a spiritual director as described by Thomas Merton in *Spiritual Direction and Meditation:* "A spiritual director is, then, one who helps another to recognize and to follow the inspirations of grace in his life, in order to arrive at the end to which God is leading him."[2] These "inspirations of grace" can best be recognized through celebration in the midst of reflection. Acknowledging God's good in our lives, in turn, brings a renewed ability to trust and surrender to the Father's wisdom and leadership.

Redirection. During a recent trip to England, I (Jana) rented a car because I was staying in a rural area without much public transportation. Consequently, I found myself sitting on the right (not the left) side of the vehicle to drive, using a stick shift that was (to me) backwards and driving on the opposite side of the road than I'm used to. I quickly learned about the power of established patterns in my life. I kept looking the wrong way at intersections, reaching my right hand instead of my left to shift the car and stepping on the brake when I meant to engage the clutch. Driving at home is fairly effortless. It's easier to function in established patterns; ruts are comfortable, and routines are safe. While driving in England, however, I had to stop often and reflect on what I needed to do differently from my routine responses.

In a similar way, reflection in disciplemaking forces us to stop and think about what we are doing instead of moving ahead in an established routine. Routines are not necessarily bad, but sometimes we need to step back and make sure that the routine we have developed is still functional and productive.

For the past seven years I (Jana) have met with a small group of emerging-adult women (they all just reached their thirties within the last two years). They have named our group the "BSGE" (Best Small Group Ever), which I love! About every six months we evaluate the patterns we have developed over the past year. Is the design of our group still facilitating spiritual growth? Is it appropriate to our present level of relationship and relevant to identified areas for growth? Last summer we sat on my front porch for our mini-overhaul and came up with a new plan designed to challenge us in ways that would truly push us forward. Granted, we *could* have kept on with the established routine and still seen some growth. But stopping to reflect helped us to optimize future meetings for the benefit of all.

Besides looking at overall spiritual growth patterns, reflection enables us to think about areas where the emerging adult might be personally stuck. Problem solving is part of most disciplemaking relationships, but problems do not always respond to the solutions we recommend. What then? Reflection with the Lord and the young adult can move us past set patterns or assumptions and bring new life.

Insight for repairing damage. Dealing with areas of immaturity or woundedness can be tricky. Leaving those areas unaddressed can stunt an emerging adult's maturation process spiritually and relationally, and even affect their career path. Past wounds might hinder the disciplemaking relationship from being fruitful. Entering into a time of reflection that includes waiting on the Lord for insight, talking with another disciplemaker for ideas on how to help others with their wounds and looking to Scripture for understanding about what wholeness looks like can bring fresh insight in journeying with someone toward healing. And times of reflection *with* emerging adults about an area where they need restoration can be a respectful way to engage them in seeking the Lord for wisdom in their own healing process.

Cooperation with the Holy Spirit. In her book *Community That Is Christian*, Julie Gorman says,

> We . . . work with the Spirit to do whatever is necessary to prepare the way for his arrival. This is our ministry—creating conditions receptive to his working among us. These conditions do not cause the actual transformation in themselves but rather create an environment that helps put us in a place where God can move among us and shape us to reflect more fully his image.[3]

If we believe this is true—that God is the one who transforms both the disciplemaker and the emerging adult—then we ought to take time to reflect on how well we are cooperating with him in the process. Yes, he uses us—our willingness, our gifts and abilities, our care—but *he* is the agent of transformation.

God is always at work in his children. He cares very much about *completing* the work of conforming us into the image of his Son (see Phil 1:6). As disciplemakers, are we moving with him, in spite of him or against him? Sometimes we can get so focused on what *we* think needs to happen to create growth in another's life that we forget to consider God's movement.

As you reflect, then, seek first what God is doing and then examine how well or poorly both you and the emerging adult are cooperating with his Spirit. Jesus appeals to us to seek the kingdom of God *above all else* (see Mt 6:33). While celebrating movement, redirecting areas that have fallen into unproductive ruts and seeking insight for areas that need repair are all important, assessing our cooperation with the Holy Spirit is essential. God's children are transformed into the likeness of his Son through the pathway of receptivity to the Spirit. Reflecting helps both us and the young adults we're discipling keep in step with him and remain open to his work.

STRATEGIES FOR EFFECTIVE REFLECTION

In the passage from Haggai we explored earlier, it is intriguing that the Hebrews are hungry, thirsty, poorly clothed and poorly paid but somehow *unaware* of this to the extent that the Lord has to prompt them to consider their state of affairs. A similar message is given to the church of Laodicea in Revelation 3:17: "You say, I am rich, I have prospered, and I need nothing, not realizing that you are wretched, pitiable, poor, blind, and naked." It's like what my (Jana's) family calls "the pee pee dance," when a young child's body is urgently calling them to visit the bathroom. If you point this out by saying, "Dana, do you need to go to the bathroom?" they stare at you with an incredulous look that says, "Huh? What a ridiculous thing to suggest," because they're still learning to pay attention to the signals of their body. The passages in Haggai and Revelation suggest that we, too, need to learn to pay attention. We need to find ways to practice reflection until it becomes a regular part of our ministry rhythms. Here are six practical strategies to get you started in learning the art of reflection. (Specific examples and helpful illustrations of these strategies will be developed throughout chapters seven through eleven.)

Talk less, pause more. Pausing requires us to stop talking and leave space to hear God's "still small voice" in our own spirits, to consider others' responses or even to let young adults think before they answer our questions. Using fewer words and pausing more is also a way to demonstrate our own trust in the Father's wisdom. As the apostle Paul wrote, "The Kingdom of God is not just a lot of talk; it is living by God's power" (1 Cor 4:20 NLT).

Develop reflection questions. A basic reflection tool is a set of two-to-five overall assessment questions that can be revisited at regular intervals. Ignatius suggested that believers practice a daily examen, a discipline that involves asking ourselves a few specific reflection questions that help us detect God's presence and discern his further direction. Similarly, we suggest keeping your set of questions to a manageable number so you can take time to answer them deeply. You may want to choose questions that will specifically help you celebrate, redirect, repair or cooperate with the Holy Spirit. Or you may want to explore a version of the examen[4] and personalize those questions to fit you as a disiplemaker as well as the relationship or context you are working within.

Journal. Recording thoughts about your interactions with the young adult you're discipling can help you slow down and process the relationship as a whole as well as specific times together. It also provides space where we can invite God to give us perspective, direction, correction or encouragement.

Seek multifaceted feedback. Living in such an individualistic culture might cause us to think of the practice of reflection as a purely individual adventure, but it need not be. In fact, Proverbs 15:22 tells us, "Without counsel plans fail, but with many advisers they succeed." Because we're part of the disciplemaking process, looking at the relationship by ourselves to see what God is up to may be difficult. The reflections of the young adult, the Holy Spirit and trusted others can function as "many counselors."

Map patterns and movement. Create something visual that portrays how God has been at work. You can map progress through a timeline or map patterns with a diagram. It's a highly structured way to look at how transformation is occurring over time.

Fast. The practice of reflection can be intensified with the spiritual discipline of fasting. In fasting, we set aside a distraction—such as food, television or music—to clear the way for the Lord to speak to us and for us to hear his wisdom.

A CONTINUING, LIFE-GIVING RHYTHM

The Old Testament is full of admonitions to practice a "holy pause." In the book of Habakkuk, for example, the prophet asks the Lord a series of questions regarding his work and plans and then says, "I will climb up to my watchtower. . . . There I will wait to see what the LORD says and how he will answer" (2:1 NLT). Habakkuk understood the necessity of reflection in moving forward in God's purposes. Reflection is not an end in itself. It unearths areas where we need more discernment and helps us choose more effective ways to love with intentionality. These rhythms are employed in a cyclical way by an effective disciplemaker to keep the pursuit of the Christlife fresh and vibrant and to strengthen the disciplemaking relationship in significant ways.

Like the blatant difference between the frustration of a hike to nowhere and a satisfying trek with a generous and attentive guide like Rebekah from chapter four, discernment, intentionality and reflection in disciplemaking make the difference between stagnant, disappointing spiritual relationships and life-giving, purposeful ones. A year after that hike on Root Glacier in Alaska, I (Jana) am still showing pictures and telling stories. And even though my stories are not usually focused directly on Rebekah, I'm aware that she was a key factor in my experience that day. In a similar way, by focusing on connecting emerging adults to Christ in such a way that they can trust the Father's wisdom, submit in humility to his heart and leadership, and fulfill his will by loving proactively, Christ—not us—takes center stage. The experience the emerging adult is having with *God* is our focus.

Rebekah had hiked that glacier before. Instead of fulfilling her own needs and desires, however, she focused on designing an encounter that met us where we were at and yet also challenged us to go beyond our present abilities. She understood how to lead us in the midst of journeying with us. As spiritual guides helping emerging adults navigate through the issues discussed in the following chapters, may we all be as discerning, intentional and reflective as Rebekah!

PART TWO

Applying Life-Giving

Rhythms to the Challenges

of Early Adulthood

RESTORING LIFE IN THE EMERGING ADULT'S SENSE OF IDENTITY AND PURPOSE

SO MANY UNANSWERED QUESTIONS.
What color is his birth mom's hair? Is his personality more like his birth mom or his birth dad? Who does he look like? Adopted when he was an infant, Cody had learned to live with the unknown. Now, at the age of thirty, he was about to come face to face with some of the answers. With his newly pregnant wife beside him, he prayed for strength. His hands shook as he opened the five-page letter from his birth mom—the first contact he had ever had with her.

So many emotions. Cody drank in the words his birth mom had written, marveling that pen, ink and paper could produce such an effect on him. Finding out that she's a Christian and that she had prayed for him filled him with wonder. Learning about his heritage and his mom's personality and preferences as well as the circumstances surrounding his birth gave him answers to questions he never knew existed. The differences that made him stand out in his adoptive family seemed to be familiar territory in his birth family. For Cody, a three-decades-old mystery was suddenly being solved.

When he reached the fifth page, a photograph fell out. He couldn't stop staring at it. There was his birth mom, sitting between her brother and sister. He had waited his whole life to see a face where he could glimpse some family resemblance and see traces of himself. To finally see that face was a beautiful and profound experience.

That began a year of important "firsts" for Cody. His first letter from his birth mom, the first time knowing her voice, their first meeting . . . and eventually the first time meeting the rest of his relatives. Later, his first child was born to the delight of not two but three sets of grandparents. It was a time of enlightenment and blessing that would be hard to surpass.

Cody's search for his birth mom may not, in its particular details, exemplify the journey of the "typical" young adult. What *is* universally characteristic, however, is the desire to look more deeply into questions surrounding the adult self. Though it takes a lifetime to completely answer the "Who am I?" question, there is a drive in young adulthood to discover some of the puzzle pieces that will help clarify the emerging-adult identity. As part of this process, those in their twenties and early thirties often find themselves examining "family resemblances" to discern what they want to embrace and what they want to change. This is different from the important but more reactive "differentiation from parents" phase often associated with adolescence. It is more like a long hard look in the mirror to see what may need to be dealt with in order to become the kind of person they want to be and create the kind of life they want to live.

This chapter and the four following will explore some of the places where emerging adulthood becomes particularly complicated or confusing. In each chapter we'll explore some general contours of the issue and then present a vision of what it would look like for an emerging adult to live out the Christlife in the midst of that issue. We'll also give specific examples of how the disciplemaker can be discerning, intentional and reflective as they walk through these issues with young adults.

IDENTIFYING CHALLENGES IN IDENTITY AND PURPOSE

In *Emerging Adulthood,* Jeffrey Arnett identifies three pillars of identity formation: love, work and ideology.[1] A young adult desiring to walk the Christlife may experience struggle in any one of those areas—or, like Janine, all three at once. Janine turned thirty two days ago. She is still crying off and on. Her birthday seemed to her to be a marker highlighting all the dreams that still eluded her grasp. She moaned, "I'm in a career I trained for, but I'm not sure I really like it anymore. I feel like I'm responsible with my finances and doing fine on my own but my parents still treat me like I'm fifteen years old. I think it's because I'm not married yet"—something that was also on her dream list. Janine has observed that there seems to be about ten unmarried women for every godly unmarried man at church. She said she feels a strange mixture of being more secure and competent as an adult and yet still somehow feeling like she has failed. The most difficult part of this for her is how it all has affected her image of God as her provider. *If he is my provider,* she wonders, *then why doesn't he do a better job of providing?* The sum of a somewhat unsatisfying job and the lack of a life partner have made it seem as though he is giving her second best. Let's look closer at her struggles with her relational, vocational and ideological identity.

Who am I? Relationships. Janine is experiencing a mild sense of panic because her ideal identity included being married, having a family and, at the very least, being respected as an adult by her parents. Since none of these critical expectations has been met at this significant life juncture, she wonders if the current state of her life is how it will be from now on. Chapter nine specifically explores the issue of relationships in emerging adulthood, but it's important to briefly consider here the effects of relational connectedness and love on the way young adults define themselves.

Initially, one of the young adult's most defining relationships is with their parents. Karen Fingerman, a developmental psychologist at Purdue University, asked parents of grown children how much assistance they provided to their sons or daughters. In 2008, 86 percent of parents had given their adult children advice (in contrast to less than 50 percent who did so in 1988), and two out of three gave practical help—in everyday tasks or financially—versus one in three in 1988.[2] Forging an identity of competency and independence in the midst of the prevalence of help from well-meaning parents may be more of a challenge for this generation than it's been for other ones. Therefore, in adult-sized hardships, the emerging adult's journey of identifying themselves as independent from parents while at the same time becoming more dependent on the Lord and community can be bumpy and complex.

In regard to marital status, emerging adults may feel parents and older generations define them as "incomplete" or "unadult" if they are not married or having children. Peers, however, may send signals that marrying too early is overly conventional or will keep them from finding out who they really are. In religious circles, they may get the impression that it's important for them to marry while young (to avoid sexual temptation) and begin a family (to support family values in society). Indeed, one source reports that women who are religious are most likely to bear children after age twenty-four. In contrast, those who don't consider themselves religious are "more likely to have unplanned births or remain childless into middle age."[3]

Redefining relationships can be scary—especially with one's family of origin. During these times of transition, continuity is replaced with disruption, which can produce anxiety and self-protecting reactionary responses. Small conflicts may quickly escalate and unmet expectations may erode trust. Disciplemakers' reassurance, wisdom and consistent relational presence provide a secure place for young adults to begin to differentiate themselves from their family of origin as fully functioning adults. The relationship also provides a healthy context for exploring how to renegotiate expectations for themselves and their family. Shared times of examining the Scriptures and prayer can provide Janine with the connection to Christ she needs to define a vision for her relationships as a young adult. What has the potential to be a threatening task can become a very creative, redemptive process—one that coincides with two more components critical to answering the question "Who am I?"

Who am I? Vocation. Studies conducted by Arnett and Christian Smith provide hopeful pictures for the emerging adult's vocational identity. Arnett finds that "most young people manage by their late twenties to find a job that they enjoy, that provides a decent income, and that provides a reasonably satisfying fit with their identities."[4] In addition, Smith's research gives the good news that emerging adults who are devoted in their faith have a greater sense of purpose and therefore greater life satisfaction than nominally religious or secular peers. They are less likely to feel that they're wandering aimlessly or lacking clear goals or direction.[5]

Still, the majority of emerging adults are sorting out purpose and life devotion at this stage. Those who attend college may have had an idea of what they wanted their career to be upon entering but in the midst of taking courses found out that they did not want to go in that direction after all. Similarly, when emerging adults acquire jobs in their intended career, they may discover that it doesn't actually fit them well. Like Janine, this may produce questions about whether their career really connects with how they see themselves. An unstable economy plus difficulty in finding the "right" job means that the typical young adult in the United States holds an average of eight different jobs between the ages of eighteen and thirty.[6] In a good news/bad news kind of way, Arnett concludes, "The road to that job [one that fits their identity] is long and winding for most emerging adults, with many obstacles and detours along the way, but more often than not it ends with a reasonable degree of success."[7] Jennifer Lynn Tanner, a developmental psychologist at Rutgers University, describes it this way:

> You get on a pathway, and pathways have momentum. In emerging adulthood, if you spend this time exploring and you get yourself on *a pathway that really fits you*, then there's going to be this snowball effect of finding the right fit, the right partner, the right job, the right place to live.[8] (emphasis ours)

When emerging adults get on a pathway that doesn't fit their identity or that clashes with their faith, disciplemakers can enter the struggle to help refocus, redirect or reenergize them for the journey.

Who am I? Ideology. Janine has funneled her fears into an angry questioning of God and his will for her life: *Haven't I been following God? Is this really the life he has planned for me? Why hasn't he blessed me with the desires of my heart? Can I be at peace with how my life is going or would it be better to take matters into my own hands?* Her crisis has propelled her into a time of critical spiritual reflection. She may begin to question beliefs related to what it means to find her identity in Christ. For example, if she feels she *is* "finding her identity in Christ" and yet it seems like God does not want to give her marriage or a family, does she need to redefine herself as having the "gift of celibacy"? Additionally, did God want her to pursue the career path she did? If so, is there a "godly" purpose for her job that she needs to stick around for, even though she isn't crazy about the job itself? She may wonder how her desires and choices fit with God's sovereignty. Does being "in Christ" mean sacrificing her identity and her desires?

Left alone, Janine will struggle mightily to gain a vision for her life beyond her current fears and confusion. Like the Bill Murray comedy *Groundhog Day,* she will consistently make what seems like incremental progress only to find herself back where she started. Thus, like all of her peers—and the generations of the church who have gone before—she needs the challenge and support of a disciplemaker who will coach her in developing the postures of the Christlife as she seeks to step toward Christ and his will for her life.

THE CHRISTLIFE IN IDENTITY AND PURPOSE

Coaching gives me (Rick) multiple opportunities to cast vision. At times this means focusing on an individual's development. As a coach of middle-school boys I can often see the high-school player "inside" the early adolescent body. I will communicate to a player, "You let me correct your shot and a year from now you'll be a scorer. Don't worry whether or not the ball goes in the basket. Just learn the mechanics of an excellent jump shot and the points will come." What a sense of satisfaction when, after hours of instruction, correction and repetition, it all comes together!

Coaching also means explaining to a player what his role is on the team. In order to maximize their unique abilities, players must learn from experience and feedback where they fit best on a team. For example, we don't encourage our 6'3", thirteen-year-old post player to dribble the ball up the court on a fast break. (With kids who've grown that fast, we just hope they can learn to dribble!) Likewise, we don't spend hours working with our super-quick, outside-shooting point guards on how to rebound under the basket. They are not made for it—and we want to take full advantage of their best strengths. Part of learning the game of basketball is learning your strengths, weaknesses and role on the team.

In one sense a Christian emerging adult's core identity is *in* Christ. In another sense, he or she has a unique identity and purpose specifically crafted for the purpose of bringing glory to Christ. Discovering that identity and clarifying that purpose involve learning what their strengths, weaknesses and role in the body of Christ are. 1 Corinthians 12:4-7 instructs the church regarding the role of each member of Christ's body:

> Now there are varieties of gifts, but the same Spirit; and there are varieties of service, but the same Lord; and there are varieties of activities, but it is the same God who empowers them all in everyone. To each is given the manifestation of the Spirit for the common good.

Completing the process of fully becoming who we are—for the glory of Christ, for the benefit of his body and for the sake of the world—requires all aspects of the Christlife: trust, submission and love.

For Cody, for example, trusting the Father's wisdom is a reminder that God has formed him in his image and adopted him into his family as a beloved son. Humility that embraces and submits to the Father's heart leads Cody to accept the person God made him to be as a gift— a gift to Cody and to those in whom Cody invests the Father's love. When Jesus was baptized, the Spirit descended on Jesus in the water and the Father audibly spoke, "This is my beloved Son, in whom I am well pleased." These words precede all of Jesus' miracles, his teaching ministry, his leadership of the disciples and his obedient sacrifice. The Father deeply loved and rejoiced in the Son because of who he was, not what he had done. This biblical vision for the Father's love establishes in Cody's heart an assurance that, above all, he is a deeply loved adopted son of God.

Knowing these truths about himself allowed Cody to draw a tremendous amount of courage from Christ when he approached his birth mom. Nothing about that first contact was for the faint of heart. Whatever Cody discovered about his family of origin and how those family members responded to him had the power to encourage or discourage, to energize or frustrate in significant ways. Note, however, that whatever Cody discovered did not have the power to *define* him.

Imagine if Cody had determined in his heart, *I'm only worthy of love if I discover that my birth mom really loved and wanted me.* Or if Cody had reasoned, *This is a test of my value in life. If my birth mom refuses to connect with me it will mean that I must be a person of little value.* The error of such thinking is evident. *Emotionally,* Cody certainly would have been deeply affected by his birth mother's rejection, and may indeed have wrestled with feelings of worthiness or unworthiness. However, feeling something and being defined by those feelings are two different things. Cody's identity is rooted in the unique person God has made him to be.

Disciplemakers, like coaches, provide an up-close "feedback loop" that (1) helps emerging adults discover their unique design, talents, spiritual gifts and role in the kingdom; (2) reminds emerging adults of their uniqueness; and (3) encourages and challenges emerging adults to keep maturing in their uniqueness with full security in the love of the Father.

The process of discovering and learning to live in our uniqueness is far from tame, as Janine well knows. When she compared the reality of her life script at age thirty with her ideal, deep disappointment led to a pervading sense of loss of God as her Father. Janine needs the firm, gentle coaching of a disciplemaker to redirect her heart toward a Father who can be trusted in his wisdom and humbly invited in with his heart, and who has deeply meaningful intentions for his love to be expressed through her life. Beyond this, Janine needs to learn to walk in the freedom of the life that she has been given. The disappointments in her life were never meant by God to destroy her. Rather, these disappointments have been sovereignly given for the purpose of deepening her relationship with Christ and, consequently, empowering her unique contribution to the world.

The ability to approach disappointments, challenges and obstacles in healthy ways has much to do with how emerging adults experience their spiritual journeys. In *The Peacemaker*, Ken Sande casts vision for how hard places help mature us.

> In 1986 I was hiking with three friends in the Beartooth Mountains in southern Montana. It was early in the summer, and the streams were still swollen from melting snow. Ten miles into the mountains, we came to a stream where the bridge had been washed away. The water was deep and icy cold. There was one place where we might have been able to cross by leaping from rock to rock, but it would have meant risking a fall into the rapids.
>
> As we stood there trying to decide what to do, three different perspectives surfaced. One person saw the stream as a dangerous obstacle. Afraid that one of us might fall in and be swept away, he wanted to turn back and look for another trail. Another friend saw the stream as a means to

show how tough he was. He wanted to wade straight across, even if it meant we would be wet and cold for a few hours. But two of us saw the stream as an interesting challenge. We studied the rocks leading to the other side and determined where we would need additional footing. [9]

Reflecting on this experience, Sande adds,

I have found that people look at conflict in much the same way that my friends and I viewed that stream. To some conflict is a hazard that threatens to sweep them off their feet and leave them bruised and hurting. To others, it is an obstacle that they should conquer quickly and firmly. But a few people have learned that conflict is an opportunity to solve problems in a way that honors God and offers benefits to those involved.[10]

Perspective gained from growth in the Christlife enables emerging adults to recognize potentially identity-shaking disappointments, challenges, obstacles and even relational conflicts as *gifts* rather than *threats*. Trust in God's wisdom breeds hope that good will be found through even the most painful experiences. Humble submission that embraces the Father's heart breeds worship that eliminates a fear-based need for control. Love that seeks to follow after him in the midst of opposition breeds passion and resolve. Our identities and purposes as believers are thus restored not by the changing of external circumstances but by the transformation of the heart, mind and soul through Christ's life in us.

Emerging adults therefore require coaching on (1) how to trust the Father's wisdom in how they were created—their unique design of personality, talents and motivations; (2) how to humbly receive his goodness and submit to his grace in the midst of circumstances that seem more like threats than gifts; and (3) how to choose to act in confidence by moving toward Christ no matter where their lives seem headed (or not headed) at the moment.

SHEPHERDING WITH DISCERNMENT, INTENTIONALITY AND REFLECTION

Case study: Lee (23) and Jim (41). Lee grew up in a household with a father who was harsh, distant and dismissive. In the midst of that environment, his Asian background taught him to keep his emotions hidden. His ability to trust God with his fear, sadness or tender emotions suffered. When he approached the Lord, he always felt like he needed to be strong and in control. His cultural identity was running contrary to his ability to adopt the postures of the Christlife. He wanted to embrace and be embraced by the heart of the Father, but prior wounds kept him from being vulnerable.

Lee got paired up with Jim in a mentoring program at the church they both attended. Jim used the skills of discernment, intentionality and reflection to shepherd Lee in powerful ways.

Discernment. Jim was determined to approach his relationship with Lee through a spiritual lens. He began to pray for Lee and their times together, seeking the Lord's wisdom for how he might interact meaningfully with him. For eight months, they spent time getting to know each other as they worked through a book that they had chosen together. Jim used the book discussions to create space to share stories and hear about various struggles Lee experienced. This time of pacing intentionality revealed Lee's struggle to see himself as a person who could be vulnerable with the Lord. Though dealing with areas of immaturity or woundedness can be difficult, Jim knew that leaving these areas unaddressed would keep Lee from locating his identity in Christ, so he began to press into this area of Lee's life.

Intentional strategy 1. The first thing Jim focused on was being a "champion" in Lee's life. He took time to communicate the Father's heart through attentiveness in identifying Lee's strengths and weaknesses, gifts and gaps. This allowed Jim to convincingly communicate his confidence and belief in Lee and point out ways he saw the Lord working in Lee's life. Jim encouraged Lee every chance he could and began to see some evidence that Lee was on firmer ground as he gained confidence in the way God had designed him.

Reflection/discernment. This relational foundation created a better environment for Lee to talk about wounded areas, but his emotional distance with God remained. Since Jim journaled to reflect on his times with Lee, he began to see how often he was stumped by how to help Lee move forward. Jim therefore enriched his reflection practices by seeking out multifaceted feedback, first through prayer and God's Word. As he sought the Lord for insight, Jim was led to several Scripture passages that gave him a clearer picture of the Father's heart for Lee and Lee's place as God's deeply loved child. Jim also sought feedback from Lee himself. Since some of Lee's issues stemmed from his cultural identity, Jim asked him questions about the messages he had received growing up as a second-generation Asian American. (Sometimes we forget that young adults can offer us valuable perspective on how to help them if we just ask them for it!) Finally, Jim received feedback from two other disciplemakers whom he approached for ideas (initially leaving out Lee's name to protect his privacy). One had also come from an Asian American background and was able to give Jim a clearer understanding of some cultural nuances. The other was a believer who had had similar struggles in his relationship with the Lord.

Intentional strategy 2. Jim shared with Lee the Scripture the Lord had revealed to him to help Lee get a clearer picture of himself as a beloved son with a caring Father. Together they brought cultural messages from Lee's upbringing before the Lord. Jim listened, shared and prayed over Lee. He also asked Lee for permission to connect him with the two men he had consulted.

Reflection/thanksgiving. At some point after these steps, Jim sat down to journal about the last few months with Lee. He lifted up a prayer of thanksgiving as he reflected on the healing that had begun in Lee's heart. In their last meeting, Lee had shared with him how the insight and compassion of one of the other believers Jim had connected him to had helped him identify a key blind spot. As they prayed about that together, Lee was noticeably more vulnerable in his prayers before the Father. His identity was not suddenly changed, of course, but Jim sensed that Lee was unstuck and headed in a healthy direction, which was allowing Lee to see himself in a new way as a treasured and welcomed son. Out of that, Lee was much more able to surrender to the Father's wisdom for his future. And Jim was rejoicing.

MORE DISCERNMENT, INTENTIONALITY AND REFLECTION IDEAS

The case study about Lee and Jim gives only a small slice of one disciplemaking relationship. Here are a few more options related to shepherding the emerging adult in identity and purpose.

Discernment

- *Think about how adulthood is being defined.* The absence of traditional markers provides disciplemakers with the opportunity to explore a spiritual definition of adulthood. Take time to search for *biblical* markers of maturity. Differentiate between childlike faith and childishness. Look for Scripture that expresses growth in terms of spiritual wisdom, responsiveness and love. Grapple together with the concepts of dependence, independence and interdependence within the family of origin and the body of Christ. Potential passages to look at include Proverbs, Ephesians 4, Hebrews 5:14 and 1 John 2. You may also want to take time to explore how the young adult is defining adulthood for themselves.

- *Ask pacing questions.* These are questions regarding the young adult's journey that you can ponder as well as questions you may want to actually ask them, such as, How does the disciple see herself in relation to God? What is his present sense of God's purpose for his life? And how does he live out that purpose in the midst of a job or present relationships? What present circumstances make it difficult for her to trust how God designed her?

Intentionality

- *Provide correction that helps emerging adults trust God's wisdom regarding identity.* A woman in my (Jana's) small group was convinced that God was only interested in using her as a tool for the sake of others. She did not see God as a Father who valued her as his precious daughter whether or not she did something for him. Change began to come as, over time, others in the small group repeatedly corrected her false view of God and her worth to him. Correction is important when someone is believing lies about God, or is misinformed about how to live out a calling to be like Christ. Jim might have used this strategy with Lee as he confronted various untruths about how God viewed him.

- *Challenge unawareness about the importance of doing the Father's will in discovering purpose.* Emerging adults may not understand that God has given them a spiritual gift to use as an expression of love within the body of Christ. But the apostle Peter says this is "most important of all":

> Most important of all, continue to *show deep love for each other,* for love covers a multitude of sins. Cheerfully share your home with those who need a meal or a place to stay.
>
> God has given each of you a gift from his great variety of spiritual gifts. Use them well to serve one another. Do you have the gift of speaking? Then speak as though God himself were speaking through you. Do you have the gift of helping others? Do it with all the strength and energy that God supplies. Then everything you do will bring glory to God through Jesus Christ. All glory and power to him forever and ever! Amen. (1 Pet 4:8-11 NLT)

These gifts were given to us as a means of loving. We are told to manage them well in order to be a conduit of God's generosity, love and wisdom. This implies two things: first, we must help emerging adults discover their areas of giftedness, and second, we must help them understand how to engage these gifts as a loving outflow of God's generosity and an expression of kingdom purpose rather than as a legalistic requirement to fulfill.

Recently, as I (Jana) interacted with two different groups of emerging to established adult leaders, I asked them to take a test to determine their spiritual gifts.[11] For many of them, this was still an area of discovery. We cannot assume that the person we're working with knows how God has supernaturally equipped them to lovingly engage in the body of Christ. Even if we're working with emerging adults who know their spiritual gift, we still may need to help them understand it as an expression of purpose and overflow instead of obligation.

- *Encourage trust in the Father's wisdom in making life decisions.* It can be frustrating to journey alongside an indecisive young adult. Prodding her to make a choice or pushing him to act on a decision may produce compliance instead of responsible action. Helping a young adult develop a pattern of reliance on the Father for wisdom as they make decisions or for the power to act is therefore essential. Exercise caution here, though. As fallen creatures, we all are imperfect in discerning wisdom and in carrying out his will. Encourage humility when poor choices are made and an acceptance of life circumstances; this can help relieve the pressure young adults might feel to be perfect. And no matter what the outcome, reinforce the truth that God is *for* them and accompanies them on this journey.

• *Explore vocational and relational identity questions.* Adults in their late twenties and early thirties may think they should have it all figured out by now. Singleness or a career choice that turns out to be unsatisfactory may feel like a setback for them. Help them find ways to grow in trust and lean into the Father's embrace in the midst of their questions. The ability to love and be loved is achievable no matter what one's marital status. And the potential for living purposefully exists within and outside of one's job.

• *Encourage proactive contentment in present life situations.* Older emerging adults are in the midst of making a transition to a more concrete identity and a more settled lifestyle. They need to know that they aren't necessarily as constrained by their circumstances as they may feel. If they're not yet in a career that they think meshes completely with their sense of identity, help them listen for God's call about whether they should stay in their current job for a time or move on. Then encourage contentment in following the Father's will and relying on his wisdom, like Paul expresses in Philippians 4:11-13. Helping disciples see the hand of their Father in present circumstances can encourage them to learn the embrace of the Father as they experience the different stages of emerging adulthood.

Reflection

• *Chart patterns to gain a clearer sense of calling.* This can be a helpful reflection exercise for the both the disciplemaker and the young adult. I (Jana) did this with Susanne when I was discipling her. For several weeks, every time Susanne and I met, we created a timeline that highlighted the ways God had moved in her life up to the present day. Seeing his past work in her life then helped us discern how he was presently working. For example, we noted how God seemed to bring new personal growth each time she exposed herself to an experience that forced her out of her comfort zone. In addition, insights about her gifts and abilities created new understandings for us about how God had wired her as well as his purposes for her life.

- *Reflect on what it means live into God's Story.* Emerging adults may hesitate to commit to a direction with their life or career out of a desire to first figure out who they are or find a specific fit. In the midst of their waiting, help them understand that the story that God is writing through their life is the story they are living *now.* He is not waiting for them to find the perfect job, relationships or role in the church in order to use them mightily. Review the ways God is working in their present relationships and circumstances in order to help them sense purpose.

- *Reflect with them on the difference between constructing an imaginary future and living with vision.* In *Facing 30,* Lauren Dockett and Kristin Beck write, "How we deal with aging in large part depends on how well we deal with the age-appropriate task of accepting reality."[12] An imagination submitted to the Lord can be a wonderful asset. To have vision for our future or even to set our minds and hearts on heavenly things (Col 3:1-2) requires some amount of imagination. Living with our own fantasized idea of the future, however, creates specific expectations in our hearts that often lead to disappointment.

  God calls us to live with expectancy—to trust that he is at work and will continue to write his story through our lives. To live with expectancy (instead of self-created expectations) creates a hopeful vision. In John 8:32, Jesus proclaims that knowing and living in truth will bring freedom to us and he clearly reveals that *he* is the truth (Jn 14:6) and that the Holy Spirit will guide us into truth (Jn 14:17; 15:26; 16:13). Learning to stay connected with reality involves being dependent on the Holy Spirit and staying rooted in the perspectives and truths of Christ. That, along with openness to the insights and feedback of other adults, can help emerging adults exchange the temporary comfort of living in a daydream for the freedom of living with vision.

- *Help them see the "thirties crisis" as an opportunity.* Young adults can use the angst they feel as a motivator to take stock of their life and press toward new growth. They may need to revisit prior expectations for this stage of life and grieve over unmet goals or desires. When emotions have been acknowledged and expressed, the focus can turn toward developing a vision for the next stage of life. Areas of dysfunction and patterns that are no longer appropriate can be examined. New goals for growth can be established. Disciplemakers can help the disciple celebrate this stage as one that can be spiritually rich in its challenges and opportunities for growth.

THE COURAGE TO BE

Alan Deutschman opens his inspiring business leadership book *Walk the Walk* with a gripping story from the life of Dr. Martin Luther King Jr. At the close of the 1962 annual national meeting of the Southern Leadership Conference, Dr. King delivered a characteristically moving speech filled with morally rich content, emotionally captivating cadence and an irresistibly compelling call to action. In the midst of the passionate delegates at this convention that spearheaded the call for the southern civil rights movement sat Roy James. James was known to the FBI as "a member of the American Nazi Party. He was there in Birmingham on a mission."[13] All of a sudden, the raging bitterness and hate of James's heart exploded into violent action. Deutschman describes the scene that unfolded:

> James leaped from his seat, vaulted on the stage, and curled the fingers of his right hand into a fist. He punched King on the left cheek. The blow struck so hard and landed so cleanly that it made a loud noise. The historian Taylor Branch writes in *Parting the Waters* that King "staggered backward and spun half around" while "the entire crowd observed in silent, addled awe."[14]

James repeatedly pursued and struck Dr. King. Deutschman gives this vivid description of what the audience observed in horror: "At six feet two inches and two hundred pounds, tall and lean and powerful, the Nazi youth towered over the stocky five-foot-seven-inch preacher, who had already suffered bruises to his jaw, face, ear, and neck."[15]

Dr. King's response to the violent, rage-filled assault reveals what it looks like for a person to be fully rooted in their spiritual identity and purpose:

> Dr. King finally managed to turn and face his assailant. And then King showed the stuff of truly great leadership: he dropped his hands and re-

fused to fight back. He was "turning the other cheek." He was *walking the walk.*[16]

In extreme circumstances with no time to think about how to respond, Dr. King lived the reality of nonviolent protest, modeling a phrase from Paul Tillich: he had "the courage to be."[17] His identity and purpose were determined not by the heat of the moment but by his relationship to his Creator and his understanding of his role in the body of Christ. He walked the walk.

Weary from multiple incidents of public disgrace involving professing Christian leaders and demotivated by the gap they've seen and experienced between the "talk" and the "walk" in their own generation, emerging-adult disciples crave meaning, purpose and integrity. They long for "the courage to be." In search of this courage, they pursue faith in something lasting and deep—something that will so profoundly shape them that, if forced to respond in a moment, they would walk the walk of their faith. Achieving this place of authenticity and maturity requires cultivating an identity and purpose in Christ. And the courage that comes from an identity rooted in him is, in this generation as in every generation, guaranteed to not only leave a lasting impression but also make an eternal impact.

RESTORING LIFE IN THE EMERGING ADULT'S SPIRITUALITY

GRANT IS TWENTY-TWO and in his senior year at a state university. Though he has been involved in a Christian campus ministry during his time in college, he has his share of spiritual doubts. After graduation he is planning to get an apartment with two friends in a nearby town. All three of them are going to keep the jobs they've held during school while they search for better employment. Grant wonders if he should go through the trouble of finding a church to attend; he thinks it might be better to take some time off in light of his doubts. One of his new roommates is into Zen and the other one feels he can "practice his spirituality" without being connected to any organized religion. Added to all this is the feeling Grant experienced when he attended church back home. It seemed out of touch with the multiethnic, religiously diverse world he had been immersed in at college. He can have Christian community by simply keeping up with Christian friends online, he reasons. He also knows of a few websites where he can get the podcasts of sermons that he knows he'll enjoy.

Kara and Michaela are both twenty-nine, single and sold out for God. They met each other at the Mercy International Conference put on by YWAM. Interacting with Michaela, however, has made Kara wonder if she really is "sold out" for the Lord. Michaela is obviously in love with Jesus and Scripture and is able to draw deeply from the Bible when she prays. She also seems to know God's leading for her life and is pursuing an advanced degree in counseling to augment her ministry of speaking, training and praying for young people as she travels internationally.

Kara, on the other hand, feels unsure about what the Lord's call on her life is, especially compared to Michaela. Though she has a rich mentoring ministry, works for a church, and does some writing and teaching when the occasion presents itself, Kara is extremely aware, with her thirtieth birthday approaching, that the path she had thought she would walk (which included marriage by this age) is not in God's immediate plans. Kara is still trying to figure out her place in the larger story of God's mission.

Both Kara and Grant are experiencing spiritual challenges related to their life stage, but the challenges are very different from each other. Grant falls into a class of emerging adults who tend to approach religion pragmatically, nondoctrinally and moralistically. Penny Edgell, the director of graduate studies at University of Minnesota, describes this group as having "what some would call a therapeutic orientation, a sense that religious involvement is a good thing to do if it makes you feel good about yourself or if it expresses an important part of your individual (not group-based) identity—spiritually speaking, if it feels good, do it."[1] Kara is grounded in faith practices and doctrine but is caught in an unsettling spiritual identity crisis as she faces some transitions in the latter half of young adulthood. Though different, neither Grant's nor Kara's struggle is uncommon for their life stage. Looking at several key characteristics of the spiritual journeys of emerging adults will help us as disciplemakers effectively walk alongside them as they struggle to make sense of their faith and God's call on their life.

CULTURAL CHALLENGES: SPIRITUAL EROSION

In his lifelong work with Christian young adults, a colleague of Jana's developed an unpublished list of factors—three external ones, two internal ones and a supernatural one—that he believes contribute to spiritual erosion among this generation:

1. friends not committed to Christ

2. disappointment with ecclesiastical machinery

3. inconsistent mentors

4. unresolved doubts/personal fragmentation

5. poor personal choices with ongoing impact

6. spiritual sabotage from the enemy of our souls[2]

All six factors touch Grant's story in some way. Both of his closest friends are "spiritual" but not committed to Christ (1). He is disappointed with how his home church operates (2). The only students who received mentoring in his campus ministry were leaders, so his doubts were not personally addressed. The one conversation he did have with a campus ministry leader about his faith questions was never followed up on (3 and 4). Since he made the choice to connect only with a parachurch ministry at college, he does not belong to a church body that could encourage him in his faith as he makes the transition from college to postcollege life (5). His decisions to not get involved in a local church and to spend most of his time with friends who do not share his faith will continue to impact his spiritual life until they are rectified (5). And any—or all—of these aspects could be attributed to (or a tool of) the enemy (6).

Grant's choices may seem minor compared to the potentially devastating, identity-shaping moral choices of other students such as sexual experimentation through hooking up (serial noncommittal sexual relationships) or same-sex experiences; drug or alcohol abuse that leads to addiction; abortion and its aftereffects; gaming, pornography or gambling activity and addiction. But no matter what a young adult is struggling with—whether guilt, addiction or shame—they're likely to do one of three things: fragment their identity ("This is where my identity fits with Christianity" and "This is where my identity fits with what it means to be a young adult living in this culture"), redefine how a Christian acts and believes, or put their religious identity "away" for a time intending to "take it up" later. Tim Clydesdale used the term "lockboxing" in his book *The First Year Out* to describe the latter phenomenon—an increasingly common practice in which young adults put their "religious" identity in "storage" during college in order to explore the parts of their identity that fit the American mainstream.[3]

More broadly, the pool of emerging adults (ages eighteen to twenty-nine) who choose to identify themselves as belonging to a faith tradition is shrinking. In table 8.1, note that the percentage of nonreligious emerging adults is significantly larger than the percentage for the average adult population.[4]

Table 8.1.

Faith & Spirituality	All Adults	Emerging Adults
Do not belong to a religious tradition (any type)	14%	Over 20%
Are not members of a church, synagogue or mosque	19%	35%
Identify themselves as "secular" or "somewhat secular"	15% ages 35–64, 10% of those over 64	23% (ages 18-29)

In reporting this data in her essay "Faith and Spirituality Among Emerging Adults," Penny Edgell is not necessarily bothered by these numbers. She thinks it's too early to tell whether religious commitment levels are actually declining or whether emerging adults are merely taking a longer route on their way to participation in congregations.[5] Having children has often been the impetus that gets young adults who dropped church in college to return to it. With emerging adults today delaying marriage and children, it's hard to know if this pattern will continue or if they'll choose not to return at all, even once they have kids.

The statistics do, however, show that young Christian adults have less access to supportive peer fellowship. From a survey of eighteen- to twenty-three-year-olds, sociologist Christian Smith identified six religious types.[6] Up to 55 percent of these emerging adults could not identify with the type of faith commitment Grant entered college with, which means that, potentially, only 15 percent of Grant's fellow students would have shared his faith commitment.

Table 8.2.

Self-Identification of Emerging Adults	Description	Percentage
Committed Traditionalists	Embrace a strong religious identity, know doctrine, practice regularly	15%
Selective Adherents	Adopt *some* beliefs and practices	30%

Table 8.2. continued

Self-Identification of Emerging Adults	Description	Percentage
Spiritually Open	Not committed but open to the idea	15%
Religiously Indifferent	Not invested; unconcerned with matters of faith	25%
Religiously Disconnected	Little exposure; uninterested	5%
Irreligious	Skeptical and/or critical	10%

The spiritual erosion found in today's society may be contributing to the difficulty young adults are having connecting to the one place that should be a refuge in the midst of a confusing spiritual landscape. Even if they do find a way to connect to the life-giving body of Christ, however, they may struggle to find their place within it.

DEVELOPMENTAL CHALLENGES: FINDING A PLACE IN GOD'S STORY

Our first chapter mentioned two critical developmental transitions: a transition to functional adulthood and a transition to clarity regarding personal impact within functional adulthood. Kara is struggling with the latter. Her focus has shifted from the need to establish herself financially and make independent decisions to making sure the trajectory of her life is headed in a purposeful direction. For Kara, that means heading in a direction that allows her to follow the Lord's calling for her life. This brings some troubling questions to the forefront. Has she understood correctly what God might be asking of her? Did she miss an opportunity or misunderstand his voice? Even as she serves in her church, she wonders if she's living up to her full potential. She also wonders if the church's leaders underestimate her ability as a young single adult to contribute to the church, as some churches hesitate to give emerging adults responsibility because of the unsettled, transitional nature of their season of life.

In contrast to Kara, other emerging adults—both churched and dechurched (those disillusioned with their church experience growing up)—might *not* feel ready to play a consistent role in their churches, especially those in the earlier stages of adulthood. As they struggle to handle the transitional challenges of becoming functionally responsible, they may church hop as they look for a spiritual home that seems to express their identity or that will assist them in the myriad decisions that loom before them.

Of those who identified themselves as religious in Smith's study (the devoted, the regulars, the sporadic and the disengaged), young people in the first two categories were the most likely to participate in face to face organized activities (like church activities) and the least likely to spend a lot of time on social networking sites (like Grant does for his Christian fellowship).[7] The "nondevoted" may struggle in relating to the local church as they contrast it with a more global Christian community. They might also downplay the importance of being physically present with local believers when they can be conveniently and virtually connected elsewhere. Wuthnow found that although regular attendance at religious services was quite low for twentysomething adults, they were the most likely out of all adult age groups to have conversations about religion with friends.[8] Social networking sites like Facebook may be providing for emerging adults a sense of being religiously connected even if they are not entering the actual doors of a church.

The lack of vital connection to a local body of believers, coupled with the identity formation still taking place in this stage, also increases the tendency for young adults to explore different aspects of themselves religiously and individually stylize their faith. Social networking sites, blogs and webpages give them the opportunity to *create* their religious persona. As one emerging adult admitted, "My Facebook is more me. My self on MySpace is, um, probably more religious [looking] than I really am."[9] Spiritually speaking, creating different personas online can be confusing. Is *looking like* a Christian the same thing as *being* a Christian? Can a young adult have a Christian persona and a non-Christian persona?

In all this, however, whether the emerging adult is confronting spiritual erosion or dealing with developmental factors, there is hope.

THE CHRISTLIFE AND SPIRITUAL LIFE

The opening scenarios about Grant and Kara gave us a picture of two emerging adults struggling through a season of deepening spiritual disconnect. Grant's disconnection seems rooted in both personal doubts and his *disillusionment* with a perceived narrowness in Christian thought and faith. Kara experiences disconnection as she recounts her *disappointment* with what God has done with the life she entrusted to him. Both expected to "get more" out of their spiritual journeys as Christians. Deeper disconnection could easily lead to profound discouragement and even despair in relationship to God.

Expectations are critical in every relationship, including a relationship with Christ. If Grant had the expectation (as a carryover from youth group?) that a relationship with Christ would be simple and doubt-free, then pulling away from his faith is a natural reaction to the emergence of adult doubts. If Kara formed the expectation that a life entrusted to Christ was bound to head in the direction of marriage and vocational clarity, then the absence of these would naturally leave her feeling abandoned and alone. Doubt, disillusionment and disappointment may surface in the emerging adult's relationship with Christ as more experiences highlight the reality that the Christian life is not a guarantee of ease or success. Indeed, Paul assures us that part of identifying with Christ is learning what it means to suffer with him (Phil 3:10). Developing the ability to pursue the Christlife in the midst of these challenging places is critical.

Christ's first disciples faced similar challenges. James and John just wanted to be important: "Can we sit at your right and left hand in the kingdom?" (Mk 10:37). Philip just wanted to know that he knew what was going on: "Show us the Father and we will be satisfied" (Jn 14:18). Peter had lots of expectations. For the most part, Peter just wanted to get it right: "How many times do I have to forgive someone? Seven?" (Mt 18:21). In each case, Christ led them to a very different place than they had imagined. They wanted a sense of importance, personal satisfaction and religious success. Christ wanted them to be transformed— a much riskier, scarier and more challenging process than they originally signed up for.

Once they had a deeper, Spirit-empowered understanding of Christ, however, their expectations and lives changed dramatically. James was martyred by Herod's sword. John lived a long life, writing a Gospel, three epistles and finally Revelation during his exile on Patmos. Philip showed Samaritans and Africans the way to the Father by showing them

The Way, Jesus Christ. Peter found himself partnered with Paul, the man who, according to Acts 8:3, had *ravaged the church* before his conversion. How many times did Peter have to forgive the man who murdered his spiritual brothers and sisters?

Grant and Kara need to be encouraged to embrace the reality that they have come face to face with the end of themselves and their faith, and to see it as a good thing. The journey of the Christlife involves continually finding ourselves unable to obey and unable to respond as we know we should. The journey of the Christlife is all about realizing that our wisdom is insufficient; we need God's Spirit to teach us to trust as Christ trusted the Father's wisdom. The journey of the Christlife is all about confronting our arrogant expectations of control and importance and satisfaction and success; we need God's Spirit to lead us to the sub missive humility of Christ that ceases to work harder and simply surrenders to the Father's embrace of grace. The journey of the Christlife is all about acknowledging that we have run out of love—for ourselves, for others and for God himself; we need God's Spirit to birth within us the love of Christ that fulfills the Father's will.

In Grant's case, then, trusting the Father's wisdom means accepting the teaching of Hebrews 10:23-25: "Let us hold fast the confession of our hope without wavering, for he who promised is faithful. And let us consider how to stir up one another to love and good works, not neglecting to meet together, as is the habit of some, but encouraging one another, and all the more as you see the Day drawing near." Opting out of Christian community does not so much *create* Grant's disconnect as it *reveals* his disconnect. The Spirit of God moves us toward community. Our resistance often exposes the unwillingness to trust the Father's wisdom that resides in our hearts. Grant's choices are not simply about preference; actions reveal the heart.

In Kara's scenario, trusting the Father's wisdom requires embracing Paul's exhortation to the church at Ephesus: "For we are his workmanship, created in Christ Jesus for good works, which God prepared beforehand, that we should walk in them" (Eph 2:10). Kara's obedience to the Father is not wasted, even when her circumstances fail to turn out as she had planned; her life has been designed by God to be a product of his grace and a tribute to his glory. Kara's disappointment reveals her heart's expectation of being treated "fairly" by God. In other words, Kara, like all of us, has bargained with Christ to follow him according to her plan, reasoning, *If I do my part according to God's expectations, then he should do his part according to my expectations.* But, in the same way God loves all of us, he loves Kara too much to allow her to settle for a short-sighted, small-minded vision for her life. Her deep disappointment can therefore become the avenue for breaking out of her heart's demand for "fairness" and moving into a life of "living sacrifice," where she worships Christ for his worthiness, not for the bargains he provides.

Because of his goodness. By his grace. For his glory. The never easy, always worthwhile worship of the Savior King. Such is the nature of the Christlife for the emerging-adult journey.

SHEPHERDING WITH DISCERNMENT, INTENTIONALITY AND REFLECTION

Case study: Kaelee (20), Heather (21) and Lynn (50). Heather and Kaelee attended a Christian college and took Bible classes there. Separately they came to Lynn expressing a hunger to grow in their understanding of the purpose and scope of the Old Testament and of the coherent themes woven throughout Scripture. This was their growth frontier—the place they knew they needed to explore in order to move forward.

Initial discernment. Lynn listened carefully and asked questions. What did they understand from their prior study of the Old Testament? What was their current understanding of how God's story unfolded in the Old Testament? What did they wish they understood? What gaps did they sense in their knowledge? And what did they envision it would look like for those gaps to be filled successfully? Kaelee and Heather explained to her that although they understood individual stories in the Old Testament, they didn't see how those stories fit together or what they had to do with the New Testament. The wealth of information they had learned left them struggling to see the cohesive whole and relate it to the bigger story of God. All three of them prayed for direction.

Intentional strategy 1. Since Kaelee and Heather already had a level of spiritual maturity and biblical knowledge, Lynn decided they should be involved in researching the grander themes of the Old Testament rather than simply being recipients of her own knowledge on the matter. The first week, then, each of them took responsibility for one third of Genesis. And each week thereafter they covered three books at a time, with each person looking for themes in the book they chose and then reporting back. Then they worked on discerning overlapping themes from their joint findings. The conversations were dynamic interactions in which these emerging adults and their disciplemaker encountered their questions and beliefs in the context of community.

Reflection. After five weeks of this (they were up to 1 Chronicles) and some amazing "light bulb" moments together, Lynn saw that there were some areas that needed more time. She made a list of questions, identified gaps and asked the Lord to lead them in how to proceed.

Intentional strategy 2. Lynn brought her list to the group, and together they decided to go back and clear up a few areas before moving ahead with their study. Kaelee put together an explanation of the major Hebrew festivals, Heather took on the task of making a list of good versus bad kings, and Lynn traced the bloodline of Christ through the characters they had studied. The learning and sharing continued to be dynamic!

Reflection. Kaelee, Heather and Lynn met weekly for four months. At the end of their meetings, each person was able to articulate a greater knowledge of God's movement through history and, more importantly, a better understanding of how to ask and seek out answers from Scripture. Kaelee and Heather shared stories of how what they were learning was impacting their ability to minister to and mentor others, and they expressed deeper trust in God's wisdom as they saw it play out over time. The three of them kept in touch and continued to encourage each other about personal study times. They enjoyed remembering the exciting adventure they shared that brought both insight and relief to an area of felt need.

MORE DISCERNMENT, INTENTIONALITY AND REFLECTION IDEAS

Kaelee and Heather came to the disciplemaking relationship aware of their spiritual need and hungry to learn. Their growth entailed gaining knowledge and skills for additional seeking. The need for spiritual growth, however, can come in many forms. Working with an emerging adult who does not have an idea of how he or she wants to grow underlines the need for the disciplemaker to develop discernment. Here are more ideas for working with the spiritual challenges of emerging adults.

Discernment

- *Discern growth frontiers.* It's essential to ask the obvious: "Where do you sense the Lord wants you to grow right now?" One young woman, Becky, was able to express to me (Jana) that the Lord was challenging her in regard to frustration with her parents for mistakes they made with her as she was growing up. We had previously talked about other struggles she experienced in relating to others. Lack of forgiveness was an obvious theme. I was grateful for her self-awareness in regard to her parents, and as a result of careful listening, we were able to identify the roots of this spiritual roadblock and begin to address it.

- *Discern potential strongholds.* At times, growth obstacles stay in place because of spiritual strongholds. Ed Silvoso defines a stronghold as "a mindset impregnated with hopelessness that causes one to accept as unchangeable something known to be contrary to the will of God."[10] Second Corinthians 10:4 reminds us, "We use God's mighty weapons, not worldly weapons, to knock down the strongholds of human reasoning and to destroy false arguments" (NLT). Strongholds require a different level of spiritual confrontation in the life of the disciple. Prayer disciplines, fasting, Scripture memorization, ministry prayer (others praying over the disciple) and engaging the armor listed in Ephesians 6 can all be helpful practices for breaking strongholds.

- *Ask pacing questions.* For example, How is she responding to God's invitation to walk closely with him? When does he sense God's flow of grace? What things seem to block that flow? Where does she find herself having difficulty (or success) in trusting, submitting or loving like Christ?

- *Explore the young adult's expectations for living the Christlife.* What beliefs do they hold regarding what it means to follow Christ through life? Perhaps they think living the Christlife is about behaving well morally, receiving God's blessings, or the eventual outcome. You might also explore disappointment or disillusionment they may have with God. A look at what drives them—or what demotivates them—in their walk with Christ can provide an opportunity to refocus on a faith that is receptive and responsive.

Intentionality

- *Confront unwillingness in submission to the Father.* My (Jana's) friend's toddler has an interesting strategy whenever he doesn't want to do something she asks him to do. He simply pretends he didn't hear her. He continues to play or run or color even when she makes louder and louder appeals. Adults often do the same thing, whether by being deaf to the call to obedience or by a stubborn unwillingness to follow Jesus. They may be so self-focused in regard to their own needs that they cannot see what others need. Even if they tell you that they value living for Christ in all areas of their life, you might observe fragmentation. When disciplemakers see contradictory behavior they need to be an accurate mirror to help young adults see when they are living inconsistently with their desire to live with trust, submission and love.

- *Be a truth teller so they can connect with God's wisdom.* A young man asked me (Rick) to help him share Christ with his unbelieving fiancée. He was convinced that if I spent time with her, she would become more open to the truth of the gospel. After a period of time, I discerned that he was seeking to manipulate a religious outcome rather than submitting to the heart of God for his life—and for hers as well. Therefore, I agreed to spend time with her on one condition: he had to call off the engagement, explaining to her that he loved her but that his love for Christ was greater. I told him that if he really wanted his fiancée to see the value and worth of Christ, he should demonstrate this to her in his own life before asking me to talk with her. Speaking truth can be hard, but it's essential. (Note, however, that responding to a disciple in such a confrontational manner should not be done casually; being blunt and bold must be coupled with both discernment and compassion.)

- *Connect them to other growing adults.* Help emerging adults gain a vision for connecting with others for interdependent, life-giving spiritual growth. Examine their connection to the "virtual" community of believers and help them see how they might take advantage of on-line connections for encouragement in faith matters. Refocus adults who are overwhelmed by transitional challenges on the availability of the Father's wisdom in prayer and Bible study but also in community. Take time to explore with them how connection to the local body can provide them with support in times of need or confusion through resources or presence.

The women's group Pam belongs to, for example, deeply fulfills the definition of peer discipleship. This steady, consistent, godly group of women meets regularly and are committed to being present in each other's lives in order to support each other and call each other upward in Christ. In each group meeting they seek to identify the issues that lead them away from their loving Creator. Their work is to lovingly yet firmly lead each other back into a place of unhindered connection with him. For each woman, this involves self-awareness, confession, integrity and a willingness to allow others to speak into her life. For the group, it means a willingness to be discerning and intentional about reflecting reality—whether that is helping each other see areas of hidden sin or gain a clearer picture of God's grace. Ultimately, it calls them to a vulnerable place of submission to God's loving leadership in their lives. Their pursuit of the Christlife together is a beautiful picture of courageous and caring interdependence. Of this close-knit circle of believers, Pam says, "God uses this group of women as one way to work out my salvation with fear and trembling, and to continually turn my focus back to him."

- *Empower them with skills that are needed to pursue spiritual growth goals.* Skills needed might be "holy habits" like solitude, deeper Bible study or prayer. Or they may be skills that counter spiritual erosion such as decision making, problem solving, spiritual-warfare strategies or apologetics. As emerging adults reassess purpose and impact, assist them in forming a balanced perspective or in setting new goals. Spiritual growth is holistic. The development of trust, submission and love reaches all aspects of our lives; becoming like Christ involves our whole self. Thus, holy habits also need to be formed in beliefs, attitudes, relationships, approaches to life. We believe Scripture, prayer and worship *are* central to becoming like Christ, but Bible study is not something that should be limited to a fifteen-minutes-a-day quiet time (though this may be helpful too); instead it should inform us and be consulted by us as we go through our day. Indeed, we cannot surrender to the Father's wisdom if we don't know what he has said in his Word. And the act of surrender at any point *is* worship. Therefore, emphasize an integrated, whole-life approach to these disciplines—which is how they ought to be practiced in our lives—in your disciplemaking.

• *Challenge emerging adults to explore and resolve spiritual doubts.* Questioning their faith and trying to understand where Christianity fits within our increasingly diverse culture is a healthy way for emerging adults to pursue their Christian identity. Wise disciplemakers therefore help them unearth and then address spiritual doubt. Someone once said, "By God's grace, truth is revealed, not exhausted, by investigation."[11] In the history of our faith, many great Christians have encountered doubt: John the Baptist, Augustine, Martin Luther, Josh McDowell, Billy Graham. Help young adults find resources and biographies to investigate how others have resolved issues of faith.

Reflection

• *Ask questions that allow you to assess movement.* Jacqui was discouraged about her mentoring times with Alissa when she came to talk with me (Jana). She felt like the time she was spending pacing with Alissa was keeping her from making progress. I let her talk for a while about her frustrations and then I asked her, "As you look back over the last six months with Alissa, where have you seen her change or grow?" She looked at me, cocked her head to the side and thought for a few minutes. Slowly she began to tell me about how they had come to a place of mutual trust in their sharing. Then she listed two or three areas where Alissa had taken positive steps in her walk with Christ. A significant step had been taken in a family relationship as well. I sat back and smiled. Then she smiled. Then we took some time to celebrate the movement of the Lord in Alissa's life. Understanding how the Lord had been working in Alissa's life gave Jacqui insight into how to facilitate further movement in their times together. Realizing that the Lord *was* at work even if she did not always see it also gave Jacqui more peace about the process. Other reflection questions you might ask yourself are

- Where do I see God growing him in regard to the Christlife (trust, submission and love)?

- Where does our relating/studying/praying (etc.) feel dynamic? Where does it feel stagnant?

- What would draw us into a deeper conversation with Christ?

- How do I sense the Spirit nudging her in the area of loving others in her life? How responsive is she to that nudging?[12]

- *Help them reflect on a vision for purposeful living in everyday circumstances.* Though it's worthwhile to set long-term spiritual goals, young adults also need to be challenged to find spiritual purpose and live out their identity in everyday ways. Integrating our "spiritual persona" with our "everyday persona" means living with a spiritual mindset in the nooks and crannies of our day. We never really know all that God is choosing to accomplish in the spiritual realms through our everyday actions.

A story is told of a Mr. Genor in Sydney, Australia, who spent a portion of each day standing at a corner on George Street. His goal was to be a simple witness to ten people every day. After forty years of being faithful to that goal, he had never heard that even one person turned to Christ on his account. Without knowing of Mr. Genor, a pastor from England continually rubbed shoulders with people who talked about the influence one particular man (whose name they didn't even know) had had on them. He decided to track down both the man and his impact. An extensive count determined that at least 146,100 people from all walks of life had been influenced for Jesus by the faithfulness of this little, unknown man.[13]

Especially in the late twenties and early thirties, emerging adults may feel like they're giving up their big plans for small ones. In God's economy, however, small acts of obedience and faithfulness may have far-reaching effects that elude detection! Encourage them with the impact a life of everyday faithfulness can have.

- *Map growth in the Christlife postures.* Create a chart to assess growth areas being pursued. For example, you might map growth in trusting God's wisdom, submitting to the Father's heart and leadership, and loving as God does in the young adult's relationships with others. Is there evidence of progression, a reason to celebrate or a sense that they're stalled? Looking for these kinds of patterns is not meant to overcategorize a complex relational dance or judge a person's maturity. It is merely the beginning point for further exploration. It may reveal areas to bring before the Lord and/or to discuss with the disciple. Mapping must be done with humility, grace and flexibility to provide insight in how to serve the other well.

- *Seek God through fasting.* Fasting can be used to reflect with the Lord or to wait on him for redirection. Don't be afraid to be creative with it. Fast from food (to create space and a physical reminder to listen to God), from noise (constant use of media as background noise may hinder you from hearing the Lord clearly), from social networking or technology, from others' opinions (especially if you rely on others' feedback and need more time to listen for the Lord's insights), or from some other type of time waster or distraction (like video games or recreational shopping). The idea is to create space and energy for reflection.

One example of the fruit that can come from fasting: Claudia felt like she was hitting a wall every time she tried to develop the habit of regular Scripture reading. She and I (Jana) had brainstormed, scheduled and planned different ways to help her succeed. None of them seemed to bear fruit. She was stuck. Together we decided to take some time to fast from noise and reflect with God about this issue. She turned off her radio on her forty-minute drive to a friend's house and I resisted the urge to listen to a Cubs game for the same amount of time. God spoke to her as she drove. Now she listens to Scripture on CD and makes an effort to discuss what she is "reading" with others. God knew how to address her as an extravert and an external processor. Reflection with the Lord broke us out of the box we had this discipline in and restored the flow of grace in her life.

GROWING SPIRITUAL FRUIT

My (Rick) wife, Teresa, loves gardening. I . . . well, I love my wife. So every year I help her with her vegetable, herb and flower gardens. Last year we planted several tomato plants in a small patch of ground near our house. For the most part, these were just healthy, normal tomato-bearing plants by mid-July. One plant, however, channeled its "inner beanstalk" and grew to be eight feet tall (and I'm not exaggerating; I even have pictures to prove it!). I have no idea what happened. (The topsoil was from nearby Oak Ridge, home of the world's largest burial grounds of nuclear waste. To be safe, I kept my dog and all small children from going near the plant just in case it mutated and became carnivorous.)

You would think, being a guy, I would be proud of an eight-foot tomato plant. In reality, I did not like that atomic tomato plant in the least. I had no respect for it at all. Why? Because it was all stalk and no fruit. While all the normal three-foot plants threw tomatoes right and left, the eight-footer hardly produced a tomato all summer. Committed to growing its big stalk, it absorbed all nutrients for the show of its Godzilla-like presence. Frankly, I was glad to see it go by the end of the summer.

Tomato plants should be more committed to bearing fruit than they are to becoming big and impressive. So should churches. So should Christians. That's why the Christlife matters so much to emerging adults. The temptation to create a great impression at the expense of dealing with doubts, disillusionments and disappointments is very real. Being all stalk and no fruit is pretty easy—but it is, on many levels, pointless and fruitless. Restoring life to the spirituality of emerging adults means helping them press into the uncompromising trust, humble submission and relentless love of Christ. Restoring life means helping them continually face the reality of their hypocrisy and the authenticity of his grace, even as we do so in our own lives. Restoring life means helping them learn to embrace the joy of covering themselves with the glorious spiritual fruit of Christ's righteousness, the spiritual hope of glory for the world.

RESTORING LIFE IN THE
EMERGING ADULT'S RELATIONSHIPS

A. J. IS TWENTY-FOUR and is living
with his parents on and off. After college he spent a year and a half
teaching English in a foreign country, and after *that* his parents graciously allowed him to move back home so he could save money and
discern his next steps. He is dating seriously but not sure he's ready
for the responsibilities of marriage. His mom and dad have differing
opinions on what his next step should be, and he is unsure which parent to listen to more closely—or if he should be looking for guidance
from them at all. His girlfriend is pressing him to find a stable job so
he can live on his own as they anticipate potentially getting married.
But is this really the right time to "settle down"? There are some ad-
vantages to having a "home base" from which he can freely follow
God's leadings . . .

Chantal is twenty-one and struggles to find her way in both her career and her relationships. Feeling like she truly belongs anywhere is
complicated. She is ethnically different from her Christian adoptive family and doesn't like to remember her difficult background prior to adoption. Though she hears that she is valued and loved from both her parents and her church, she has difficulty believing it. Her friendships are
great as long as they stay at a certain level. Her work is fulfilling—for
short periods of time. She attends college classes when she feels up to it
but isn't very far in pursuing a degree. She finds herself moving from job
to job and from person to person. She has lived away from home but
returned twice—so far. Relationships—whether work-related, church-

related, friendships or dating—never seem to work out. She is desperate to find inner healing and guidance.

Jin is thirty-four and unattached. His parents moved back to Korea when he was twenty-seven, and though they expressed a wish for him to be married, he had gotten so used to living life on his own terms that he put off moving in that direction. When he was thirty-one, he began to feel bothered by the fact that he didn't have a "significant other," so he signed up for an Internet matching service. None of the email conversations he started with women panned out. Friends told him he was too picky. In reality, he felt that if God wanted him to marry, he would be strongly compelled to pursue one of the women. He enjoyed the email interactions, but he took his continuing passivity as a sign. Sure, sometimes he feels lonely, but he likes his job and has friends at church. The pastor talked him into volunteering in a ministry, and Jin hopes God is using him. Things are fine. At least for now.

A. J., Chantal and Jin are experiencing multiple relational challenges. Their stories highlight the fact that relationships are important to emerging adults and acutely on their radar. Yet young adults all struggle with figuring out how to negotiate their own constellation of relationships.

In the midst of relational challenges, the transitional nature of relationships in young adulthood creates God-ordained encounters that provide the opportunity to mature. In an article regarding the friendships of emerging adults, professors Carolyn Barry and Stephanie Madsen propose that these all-important relationships serve several functions:

1. They support emerging adults' identity development.

2. They elevate mood and promote adjustment during times of transition.

3. They help emerging adults understand how relationships work and develop in them the ability to see from another person's perspective.

4. They offer companionship (with people both near and, through technology, far away).

5. They develop skills of intimacy and interdependence, which are important for future friendships and romantic relationships.[1]

Relationships hold a key place in the emerging adult's experience. Friendship networks are largest during early emerging adulthood and then generally undergo a process of reduction as adults progress in age.[2] Christian Smith points out,

> These years involve complex processes of incorporating new relationships and experiences into ongoing, developing lives, while sustaining and renegotiating old relationships with parents, siblings, friends, former adult mentors, and others.[3]

Indeed, young adulthood poses some unique relational challenges with regard to both family and friends. Navigating the uncertainties of dating and potentially choosing a life companion also add to the complexity of relationships for emerging adults.

NEGOTIATING PARENTAL RELATIONSHIPS

One key relational transition from adolescence to adulthood involves taking over responsibilities that were previously handled by our parents, such as bills, decisions and dealing with the consequences of our actions. For emerging adults this transition may feel abrupt, take longer than expected, introduce greater relational harmony or, conversely, increase conflict. In the early part of the twentieth century, once a young adult left home for college or a career, only 20 percent returned to live with their parents. At the end of the twentieth century, however, nearly 50 percent did so.[4] A return home may occur for a number of reasons (with finances as the foremost issue) and can be rough for both parents and emerging adults. Parents may be resentful of the increased financial burdens the situation creates or that the empty nest is once again inhabited. Emerging adults may have to give up aspects of freedom already enjoyed. A. J., for example, became accustomed to independence but now has to adjust his decisions to acquiesce with parental standards. And every time Chantal returns home, she has to renegotiate her relationship with her parents regarding family expectations, rent and household duties.

A transition back home isn't always bumpy. In fact, sometimes it is welcomed and negotiated in a way that is beneficial for everyone. In A. J.'s case, despite his parents' differing opinions on his future, they were glad to have him home and were careful to give him space to make his own decisions and yet allow him to save for marriage if that was his next step. Emerging adults appreciate it when parents loosen their grip and see them as functioning adults. Parents appreciate that their children are gaining the maturity to recognize the value of how they were raised. It is not uncommon for young adults to become closer to their parents during this stage of life. Indeed, in less individualistic societies and some European countries (where apartments may be scarce and expensive) parents don't expect that their young-adult children will move out to gain independence. For example, in Italy, 94 percent of fifteen- to twenty-four-year-olds live with their parents, and only 8 percent of them perceived this as a problem.[5] So while some societies react to a young adult's move home as a step backward, others embrace it as a part of the young-adult journey.

FRIENDSHIPS

What new opportunities or concerns face emerging adults in their relationship circles? What factors affect the way they develop or maintain everyday relationships? First, it's important to note that friendships are still an influencing factor at this age. Emerging adults report that the behaviors of their friends—whether from school, work, church or their neighborhood—affect life outcomes (including church attendance) both positively and negatively.[6] Unfortunately, Smith reports that emerging adults in their early twenties are more likely to feel a sense of relational belonging among nonreligious groups (like a sports team or a fraternity) than at church, though they are not necessarily uncomfortable at church and may even describe it as a friendly place.[7] We wonder if this implies that the relationships they find inside church walls have remained either too distant or too shallow to create the kind of safety and belonging that generate relational influence.

Overall, making generalizations about how emerging adults "do" friendship is a difficult task. At the very least, we know that cultural backgrounds, gender and technology often affect how relationships are approached. For example, an article exploring friendships in emerging adulthood identifies differing friendship qualities sought out among various American ethnic subgroups:

- Asian Americans tend to seek an amicable exchange of ideas.

- African Americans tend to emphasize acceptance and respect.

- Latino Americans highlight the importance of relational support.

- European Americans focus on meeting the individual needs of each friend.[8]

It's a little bit easier to generalize according to gender. Women's friendships tend to be more focused on companionship, emotional security and affection, and women usually have a greater number of close friends than men. Perhaps the emphasis on deeper friendships explains why women tend to maintain a similar-sized friendship network even when they start a career. In contrast, men's friendships are more likely to provide assistance, alliance and self-validation. Men tend to have fewer close friends but larger friendship networks pre-career. As they move into a career, however, their friendship circles tend to shrink.[9]

Overall, emerging adults are more open to male-female friendships than their parents were—especially in the context of pursuing education. It is somewhat less common for men and women to be friends beyond college years or after one or the other marries.[10]

Young adults are flexible and creative in maintaining friendships using current technology. Many stay friends with former boyfriends or girlfriends online, whether through a social network site or email. Research seems to indicate that cell phones, texting and social networking support existing friendships rather than displace them;[11] technology use is more likely to displace involvement in the larger public world and civic life. Most of us are submerged in technology at some level, but young adults seem to be even more so in their own "fluidly constructed, private networks of technologically managed intimates and associates."[12] Since technology keeps them connected 24-7 through instant messaging, blogs, texts, Facebook, Twitter, cell phones (etc.), they are often initiating or responding on the bus, in the car, at work, in class, during conversations in restaurants and even in church. They appear to have difficulty *not* multitasking—or, to say it another way, they have difficulty patiently *concentrating* on one thing at a time.

One longitudinal study indicates that, partly due to the popularity of laptops and smartphone technology, Americans are now spending more than half their waking day interacting with media.[13] Research hasn't yet determined how this may affect long-term relational satisfaction, but mediated contact has a tendency to produce a sort of "relational skimming" effect, a phenomenon that I (Jana) have observed and discussed with the young adults I interact with. Many of them feel at a loss in knowing how to engage meaningfully with others. Facebook, texting and email have trained them to connect frequently but with fairly shallow sound bytes. They long to know how to deeply understand and be understood. It seems like a forgone conclusion that, unless our mediated contact is supplemented with personal relational skill development, it will hinder the ability to develop the kind of depth and patient endurance important in keeping friendships and marriages viable.

DATING, MARRIAGE AND PARENTHOOD

Marriage and family add even more layers to the complex relational landscape of young adulthood. Barry and Madsen point out,

> Given the many transitions that emerging adults face, it is not surprising that their friendships change as well. Transformations in friendships and friendship networks relate to life stage rather than age. So knowing that a person is 20 versus 26 does not tell us much about their friendships. Instead knowing whether they are romantically involved or have children is much more informative than age alone.[14]

In the area of marriage-related decision making, emerging-adult men and women are more similar than different. Arnett observes:

> Both want to find someone who is similar to themselves in key ways and is easy to live with. Both want to have a period of years in emerging adulthood to learn to stand on their own, to make independent decisions, and to explore the possibilities available to them before committing themselves to marriage. Both get more serious about finding a marriage partner once they reach their late twenties and see the age 30 deadline looming only a few years off.[15]

The arbitrary "age thirty deadline" for marriage is in the minds of many emerging adults. While in his mid-twenties, Scott explained, "I'd like to be focused by 30, be settled down and working in my long-term job or whatever. I'd just like to be focused by that age."[16] Women may feel more pressure because of biological deadlines and are more likely to have an ideal timeline in mind. If they're married by age thirty, for example, they reason that they'll still have time to establish a marriage relationship before pursuing a family—preferably before their mid-thirties. These deadlines may also be reinforced by pressure from parents or other married friends.[17]

Jin hit his "age thirty crisis" when he was thirty-one; that's when he decided that he needed to make an effort to find a spouse. Emerging adults most often date within their friendship network. The diversity found within that network influences the likelihood that they will date someone of a different ethnicity[18] or faith. Since Jin's social circle was shrinking as he immersed himself in a career, he probably experienced a decrease in both time and suitable contexts for finding a life partner. He knew his parents wanted him to marry someone within his ethnic group, but his social circles were mixed, so he thought using an online dating network would be easiest.

Despite pressure to find a spouse, Jin still has choices. He could choose to forgo actively looking for a mate and enjoy the gifts and opportunities that come with being single—including more freedom to focus on how to please the Lord, as Paul encourages (1 Cor 7:32). Or he can confront his pattern of passivity and actively pursue healthy relationships with those of the opposite sex, whether online or in person. Disciplemakers can help emerging adults look at the freedom they have to actively make decisions to pursue relational and life goals instead of feeling trapped as a victim of life's circumstances.

Couples in this age group retain outside friendships at the beginning of romantic involvement but tend to invest in those relationships less as they move toward marriage. The energy of establishing a new marriage may mean that their relational attention will be focused toward their spouse for a time, but young couples benefit from the support of friends, family and especially established couples who are willing to walk alongside them. Relational satisfaction for married couples in their twenties is unrelated to gender, race or education, but faith commitment, interestingly, *does* seem to play a part in increasing satisfaction. Couples who attend religious services weekly or almost every week show a higher level of happiness with their marriage versus those who don't. For example, 73 percent of couples in their twenties who attend church regularly say they are very happy with their marriages; only 58 percent of those who don't attend regularly claim the same thing.[19]

Parenthood causes the most radical reorganization of the emerging adult's friendship networks. New parents have fewer friends, with fathers reporting less satisfying and less supportive friendships than they experienced before.[20] A previous focus on enjoyable activities with friends shifts to caring for children with immediate relationship needs or providing respite from the demands of childcare for a weary spouse. While young adults don't feel that having children is a necessary requirement for becoming an adult, they do report feeling like childbearing ends the gradual pursuit of adulthood they may have been on and instead thrusts them immediately into greater maturity.[21]

Emerging adults' relationships provide a foundation for identity development and support during their many transitions. Relational challenges with parents, the process of reducing their social network and the pursuit of relational intimacy can all be significant relational transitions. Success in negotiating the challenges and learning to give and receive love can set the young adult up for a rich entrance into the life of home, church and community.

THE CHRISTLIFE IN RELATIONSHIPS

Over the years I (Rick) have been fascinated by how people are drawn together. Just this last weekend I watched hundreds of people gather for a community race that raised awareness and money for cancer, three thousand people gather for our weekly Sunday-morning celebration services at my church, and one hundred thousand people gather to watch the University of Tennessee play the University of Mississippi in a South Eastern Conference football game. (Yes, the numbers reflect the reality of my community's passions!)

I have come to conclude that two very important conditions need to be in place in order for people to come together: a worthy *cause* and a relational *community*. The more strongly people sense the presence of these conditions, the more likely they are to gather; we flock to places where we sense that we're simultaneously contributing to the achievement of a worthy goal and building relationships in the context of a larger community. Whether it's a group of people at a race all wearing shirts that say "Can you imagine a walk without a cause?" or a stadium filled with orange-clad, "Rocky Top"– singing Tennessee fans who believe they've urged their team to an important SEC victory, it all boils down to cause and community.

The Christlife fulfills both conditions. It's causal because trust in the Father's wisdom, submission that embraces the Father's heart and love that fulfills the Father's will compel a person toward a kingdom vision. It's also causal because the endgame of this life is meaningful kingdom participation. Ultimately, it's causal because it has a transcendent purpose: the glory of God. The Christlife is communal because trust, submission and love are all inherently relational experiences. It's also communal because walking in the Christlife means we're entering in to the community of the Father, Son and Holy Spirit. Ultimately, it's communal because it's an incarnational expression of Christ in the relational contexts in which we live. The Christlife, properly pursued and expressed, is therefore the ultimate causal and communal experience.

A. J., Chantal and Jin find themselves in different relational situations. A. J. is caught in between the causal and communal. He feels pressured by the potential of a marriage commitment that will require him to say no to freedoms and possibilities (causes) that he still enjoys. Yet the pull toward his girlfriend is a powerful relational (communal) force in his life. Chantal represents the "lostness" emerging adults experience when there is neither a cause nor a community that meaningfully captures their hearts. Like a sailboat with a torn sail and no engine, Chantal is adrift in a sea of experiences that take her everywhere but lead her nowhere. Jin is pretty content for the moment because he has found a cause through ministry at his church. Moreover, there are new relationships that may provide Jin with an initial sense of belonging to a community. Thus, the *potential* exists for both the causal and communal conditions to be fulfilled in Jin's life and to lead him to a fuller maturity in the Christlife. All of this depends, though, on the depth to which he builds relationships and the degree to which he invests himself in his work and his volunteer ministry.

The Christlife calls emerging adults to invest deeply in the causal and communal contexts in which they live. The greatest challenge, of course, is relinquishing ultimate control of the outcomes of these investments. Trust in the Father, submissive humility in response to his heart and love as an expression of the Father lead to increasing freedom in giving ourselves without strings attached. The emerging adults who will have the strongest relationships will be the ones who learn to build the strongest relationships. The emerging adults who will have the deepest impact will be the ones who make the deepest investment.

I often tell emerging adults, "Don't chase the idea of the person you want to marry. Rather, become the person your future spouse would want to marry. You cannot control if you ever find someone to marry, but you *can* choose to become a person who offers love to others." Learning to release control of relational outcomes through trusting the Father gives maturing emerging adults confidence to open their heart and hands to care. Others will be attracted to them because of the difference they make in people's lives. Such people may or may not get married, may have a large or a small circle of friends, but will never be alone.

SHEPHERDING WITH DISCERNMENT, INTENTIONALITY AND REFLECTION

Case study: Roberto (28) and Emilio (37). Roberto was anxious to develop friendships at his new church that were deep enough for him to give and receive the kind of spiritual encouragement he read about in Hebrews 10:24-25. He wanted to take risks and pursue others, but time and again he found that though these relationships started well, they became strained or fizzled out after a few months. Finally, he gave up. *The body of Christ has failed me,* he thought bitterly, and he concluded that initiating relationships any more would be a waste of time. Some time later, Roberto complained about this to Emilio (a small group leader who began reaching out to him). This began a process in which Emilio helped Roberto face both his tendency to be self-focused in his friendship attempts and his pain from the rejection he felt at church, and choose forgiveness instead.

Initial discernment. It was pretty obvious to Emilio why others seemed to shy away from Roberto. He observed that Roberto approached others with such friendliness and force that it was hard to resist his invitations. But after they responded, he seemed impatient if people didn't respond to further invitations to spend time together, and would try to guilt or bribe them into hanging out. What Emilio didn't know was why Roberto was like that. He told Roberto that he'd like to explore his "complaint" with him, so they set up a time to have coffee together. This gave Emilio some time to pray and listen to what God might want to reveal to him before their conversation.

Intentional strategy 1. Emilio decided that spending some time with Roberto to create a foundation in their relationship would enable him to share some of the observations he had made about Roberto's relational skills. He set up a regular coffee appointment with him and also connected with him on email or Facebook at least once in between appointments so that Roberto would *be pursued* instead of being the pursuer. This enabled their friendship to grow.

Reflection/discernment. Emilio prayerfully watched for indications that Roberto was ready to hear about the blind areas that were keeping him from finding and sustaining friendships. He also took time to reflect on his own experience of the relationship, which would enable him to balance some of what he had seen with others with Roberto's relational strengths. Self-reflection caused him to admit that he had some reluctance about "speaking truth in love" because he didn't want to face a potentially negative response. In addition, Roberto had made several comments about how Emilio was the *only person* at the church capable of real friendship. Though he knew this praise wasn't accurate, it still felt good to be highly thought of; fear of losing that esteem added to his reluctance to cause waves. He submitted his reluctance to the Lord and asked to be an accurate relational mirror for Roberto—both in areas to celebrate and in the dysfunctional relational patterns where he needed to grow.

Intentional strategy 2. The next time they met, Emilio shared with Roberto the relational strengths he had seen in him. Then he told a story about a man on a first date who caught his reflection in a window and discovered that he had a big glob of spaghetti sauce in his beard. The reflection was, naturally, both upsetting and beneficial to that man. Emilio then asked Roberto, "If you were that man, would you be glad or upset that you had seen your reflection?" Roberto replied that he would rather know so that he could take care of the flaw that others could plainly see. From there Emilio carefully reflected his observations about how Roberto's approach had hindered his ability to reach out effectively to others. Roberto was a little defensive and embarrassed at first but ended up thanking Emilio for his honesty. They even laughed together as Emilio shared about discovering some of his own relational blind spots. They then turned to Christ together and asked for the Spirit's help in transforming their relational weaknesses into strengths.

Reflection/discernment. It would take too long to describe all the cycles of reflection and intentionality that Emilio went through with Roberto. Suffice it to say that eventually they discovered some of the roots that had led to his destructive pattern of "overpursuing." A deep wound of rejection and abandonment that Roberto still carried from school had clouded his ability to freely give as well as receive.

Emilio's intentional care for Roberto helped give him the courage he needed to recognize, grieve and turn over that wound to allow the Spirit to bring healing. And Emilio knew not to underestimate the power of Scripture and prayer in the healing process. He valued Scripture's ability to expose innermost thoughts and desires (Heb 4:12), revive the soul (Ps 19:7) and instruct in how to bring healing (Jas 5:16). Instead of fearing that he would say the wrong thing as Roberto exposed his wounded heart, Emilio often asked the Holy Spirit to prompt him with both Scripture and words, which created space for God to speak into Roberto's life directly. Eventually, Roberto was able to reenter some of the broken relationships at his church and begin to care for others with a Christ-centered, instead of a Roberto-centered, love.

MORE DISCERNMENT, INTENTIONALITY AND REFLECTION IDEAS

Though Emilio used the intentional strategy of challenging unawareness with Roberto, we've included another example of how to use it here. These ideas are relevant to other topics, but we will include some discernment approaches, intentional strategies and ideas for reflection as they relate specifically to relational issues.

Discernment

- *Wait on God for insight.* Whether you hear from God through a Scripture verse, an impression or insight, a sense of redirection in previous ideas or plans, or peace about the direction you're pursuing, listening to him is key. Elizabeth meets with Chantal (from the beginning of the chapter) every other week. Her time and care are a godsend to Chantal, but their times together are not always easy. Knowing that she has to rely on "God's mighty weapons" (2 Cor 10:4 NLT), not her own, to disciple Chantal, Elizabeth uses the thirty minutes before an appointment with Chantal to listen to the Lord on Chantal's behalf once more before they meet. It's not surprising, then, to hear stories about how God works in their times together.

- *Ask pacing questions.* Where does he feel inadequate in his relationships with others? How well does she do in *receiving* relationally? In *giving to others* with intentionality? Does she tend toward trusting the Father for her relationships or toward trying to control relational outcomes? Is he more focused on investing in others or on being invested in by others?

- *Discern the level of contentment in present life situations.* Young adults may see themselves as victims of either singleness or marriage. Being single in your late twenties or early thirties, however, does not necessarily brand you as unmarriageable for life. Singleness can be viewed as a choice, and proactively embraced. Only the Lord knows whether this stage of life is temporary or permanent for them. Alternately, being married with children need not be viewed as a static stage. As children grow they bring new dynamics and challenges to parenting. Moreover, illness, accidents or even divorce could cause a stable married person to find themselves suddenly without a spouse.

  In 1 Corinthians 7, Paul encourages his readers to be satisfied with the state the Lord presently has for them. His words apply to marital state, social circles, career or location alike. If you discern discontentment, help young adults actively *choose* to embrace their situation— as long as that situation is not counter to godly values or does not involve them running from following his will. Lead them toward actively embracing life in submission to the Father's wisdom rather than allowing themselves to be swept away by life's circumstances (Eph 4:14).

Intentionality

- *Challenge unawareness in the call to love others.* Emilio used this strategy with Roberto, but here's another example of it might look: Disciples who are young believers simply may not know God's call in regard to loving brothers and sisters in the church and others outside the faith. Explore this with them in Scripture. Read 1 John together, study examples of how Jesus loved those around him or look for relational commands in the Gospels. In addition, make sure the disciple finds ways to connect to a small group, service project or outreach opportunity so that they have a context for building loving relationships.

- *Invite young adults to be proactive in connecting and caring for others.* Fulfilling the Father's will by reaching out to love others requires initiative. Passivity, self-focus or fearfulness must be dealt with before we can be self-giving and relate to others with generosity. Help emerging adults evaluate the present state of their relationships: with their parents, with friends, with coworkers, with their spouse, with children. Then help them learn to become purposeful in those relationships by considering opportunities for growth and deciding on specific steps they can take to move in those directions.

- *Confront resistance to the Father's wisdom for healthy relating.* A ministry volunteer in my (Jana's) leadership core was adamantly convinced that she did not have an emotional side. Her father was dying of cancer and she was experiencing some sizable disappointments in her relationships at church, but she was refusing to surrender to the God-ordained place of emotions in our lives as a valuable means of bringing us to the Lord and connecting us with others, and as an indicator of areas in our soul that needs attention. I knew I needed to confront her with the truth, as confrontation is appropriate when a person is resistant to the wisdom or the work of the Lord in their lives. Slowly her initial resistance gave way to an embrace of this God-given gift in her life. Her relationships are richer because of it.

- *Shepherd relationally apprehensive adults into the security of God's embrace.* Christ was able to live courageously in the midst of uncertainty and transition because he understood how deeply his Father welcomed him and trusted the affection of his Father even in the midst of painful circumstances. A young woman who wonders if she will ever find marital love needs to know she is securely wrapped in her Father's embrace in order to wait out the answer with grace. A young man who fears an inability to succeed in his career needs to know he is deeply accepted no matter what his career path looks like. A brand new parent needs to feel the stability of being lovingly parented by *the* Father in order to face the daunting task of bringing children up in this world. Connecting young adults to the fact that they are deeply embraced by God frees them to make commitments and decisions with less fear.

One note of caution about this: pay attention to extreme levels of relational anxiety and be ready to suggest that the emerging adult consider gaining support through counseling. A yellow flag here for the disciplemaker is when you sense that you're in over your head or if the young adult makes no progress even with your attentive and proactive shepherding.

- *Explore relational wounds that hinder fulfillment of the Father's will.* The intentional disciplemaker pays attention to two very practical means God has provided for addressing relational wounds: forgiveness and reconciliation. It is tempting to offer comfort to hurting souls by assuring them their response is justified or their pain is beyond repair. Even for those who have truly been victimized, however, the wounds will not be fully healed until they choose to forgive or potentially work toward reconciliation with others. This warning from Jeremiah 6:14 reminds us not to ignore this reality: "They offer superficial treatments for my people's mortal wound. They give assurances of peace when there is no peace" (NLT). "Superficial treatments" are easier to provide than challenging someone to forgive or reconcile. But in the end it's always worthwhile to help disciples face their wounds in a way that empowers them to walk forward in freedom and humility.

- *Encourage involvement in peer mentoring opportunities.* Verizon Wireless used to run commercials where an ordinary person was made stronger because of his connection to a whole network of people. A guy would be cleaning his bike, get a phone call, look up and notice there were five hundred people standing behind him. In much the same way, emerging adults already have a "disciple network" available for spiritual transformation. The perception that disciplemaking *only* occurs in relationships where an older person is the spiritual mentor is misguided thinking. If you are that "older adult" in a young adult's life, encourage them to be intentional in their friendships so that they can mutually participate in calling *each other* to surrender to God's wisdom, submit to his heart and fulfill his will. A healthy relational posture for all of us to take is one of proactive pursuit in encouraging peers toward growth in Christ and humble receptivity in accepting encouragement and being challenged by our peers.

- *Teach specific skills for healthy relating.* Familiarize yourself with resources that can be used to sharpen relational skills in struggling disciples.[22] Address media-created "relational skimming" gaps with by teaching skills like attentive follow-up, expressing desires versus demanding that needs be met, speaking the truth out of genuine love, appropriate self-disclosure, being responsible *to* but not *for* others, developing and communicating boundaries, creating relational space, and creative relational problem solving.

  Emerging adults may also need help deepening their capacity for relational intimacy. You can guide them to refocus or gradually reduce their social network. Trying to connect with the same number of friends from college days while adding a full-time job and/or young family will leave them without the time or energy for true and enduring relational intimacy. You can also instruct them in specific skills that build relational intimacy. Here are three:

  1. *Pursuing the inner world of another.* Safety and security are built as people feel esteemed or valued by others. A problem occurs, then, when spouses or friends assume familiarity and cease to be curious about each other's worlds. Relationships can stagnate if effort is not expended to know or understand the world of the other. Teach the disciple to ask questions about the activities, thoughts and relationships of others and to become present to other people's worlds (e.g., read what they have written, watch

them exercise their spiritual gift, see them engage in a favorite hobby or meet people who mean a lot to them). Along with this, help young adults avoid extremes in their pursuing by asking others what pace of relationship is comfortable for them.

2. *Communicating care with words and affection.* Guide disciples in building on the security appropriate involvement creates by expressing not just esteem but also warmth and care. Moving beyond *thinking* a person is great to actually *telling* that person deepens the relationship! This may sound obvious, but all too often lack of practice, fear and self-protection will get in emerging adults' way. Emotional generosity seeks to move past fear and self-protection to love like Jesus loved. The NLT version of the Bible translates many of Jesus' interactions with "Dear children," "My dear Martha," "This dear woman," "Dear friends." We *feel* his embrace of others through his words.

Learning to engage with words and affection can be tricky because people have different definitions of what sounds or feels loving. An important skill to teach, then, is "checking things out." When an emerging adult comes to you in confusion because he received an unexpected response to something he said or did, coach him to find out how the other person received his communication. Relational skimming teaches emerging adults to receive and move on quickly rather than pursue understanding. Instead, we should consider that every person we meet is like a foreign country and coach young adults in translating others' language and culture as well as interpreting themselves for others. It's at this level of relational understanding that relational warmth can best be given and received.

3. *Engaging when it's difficult.* Perhaps the most critical skill necessary for longevity in relating well to others is learning how to engage during tense or stressful relational seasons. Andy never learned it. He became overwhelmed when things became difficult in his relationships—whether it was at church, with his wife or with his children. Instead of sticking around and working things through, he ended up leaving his position at the church,

divorcing his wife and living estranged from his kids. He started out as a dynamic Christ-follower with every intention of loving others as Christ did. A combination of unexplored wounds and an inability to engage relationally in difficult seasons sidetracked him so dramatically from living the Christlife that he became lonely, depressed and hopeless.

Openness, creativity and persistence are key elements in engaging through difficulty. Knowing how to use distance appropriately in order to come back and work things through together can mean the difference between a disagreement that escalates to isolation and one that comes to resolution. Finding courage, strength and insight through taking time to meet with Christ can bring hope instead of resignation. Learning to problem-solve and brainstorm to overcome a relational impasse can provide new relational energy for emerging adults. Mentoring them in these skills will greatly deepen their capacity to negotiate a changing relational landscape.

Reflection

- *Talk less and pause more.* Pausing is vital in creating space for God to reveal a new approach when you, as a disciplemaker, are stuck. It's also a lost art in our society. Things go faster and faster, not slower and slower. Life rushes by us so quickly that we can be out of touch with what just occurred, whether positive or subtly damaging. We are conditioned to get results and move on. Sitting silently with God, a trusted friend or the mentee deepens the reflective process, creating a holy pause.

  Holly grew up in a family that loved to debate. Personalities were strong. It was considered a mark of respect to challenge someone else's ideas. This worked well in her family of origin, but it was not working well in relationships with those in the new church she had joined. Holly felt more and more marginalized because of her tendency to debate. Functional in one context, it was disrupting in another. Bianca tried to help Holly see how her communication style was affecting her relationships as they journeyed together. True to her pattern, Holly countered with arguments justifying the communication patterns she grew up with. This severely hindered Bianca's ability to help Holly grow. She decided to stop pushing for growth and instead entered into a time of reflection with the Lord. Bianca was open to whatever emerged from her prayerful time of reflection, but she was surprised when she discerned that she should approach Holly with deeper humility and vulnerability in response to Holly's abrasiveness.

Bianca followed her discernment by communicating to Holly that she felt sadness in their relationship and by inviting Holly into her own heart. She shared about the walls she experienced when she tried to challenge Holly or give her feedback, and about the fact that she was beginning to put up walls now as well. Bianca then asked Holly if they could begin to work together, to open both of their hearts to be better listeners and encouragers of one another through times of reflection *together*. Holly was prepared for a power struggle, but her heart softened when someone modeled for her true humility and vulnerability. Gradually Holly began to perceive Bianca's feedback as a gift, not a threat.

- *Create a diagram of relationships.* A diagram of relationships also proved helpful in Bianca and Holly's relationship. When the Lord revealed to Bianca that she needed to change the *way* she approached Holly, they began reflecting together using a chart that explored three categories of Holly's relationships (family, work and friends) and her communication styles in each. They looked at areas of overlap in the styles she used, which gave them the chance to see what was going on in a way that facilitated discovery. Then they walked the Christlife together as they sought God's wisdom through prayer. Bianca's choice to reflect and then respond with humility made Holly feel safe enough to explore her relational patterns. Holly was now able to recognize her past resistance to receiving challenges and became open to growth. The key was making the journey a shared one.

- *Observe relational patterns.* One of the most powerful contexts for relational rewiring for emerging adults is their relationship *with you* as a disciplemaker. Taking time together to reflect on your relationship provides a safe place to look at relational tendencies. Write a timeline highlighting the highs and lows of your disciplemaking relationship. What patterns emerge? What do you wish would have gone differently? What were the moments that facilitated good relational results? Acknowledge that you are on a journey together toward living in a Christ-centered relationship. Strive for authenticity, transparency and humility in interactions with emerging adults. Occasionally take stock of how each person is experiencing the relationship, especially noting expectations that are or are not being met. Submit areas of disappointment to the Lord and celebrate areas where you both experienced relational richness with the Lord.

Selina checks in with the young woman she is mentoring at least twice a year regarding their relationship. In creating six-month timelines, they have been able to identify both destructive as well as constructive relational patterns. This not only helps them relate well but also opens the door for discussion on similar relational patterns experienced in other relationships.

- *Help emerging adults reflect on the benefits of relational consistency.* The increased mobility of young adults both geographically and socially means that "relational staying power" muscles are weak. They may not have learned how to persevere in relationships when things are difficult. Help them evaluate the strategies they use and adopt mindsets that allow them to fulfill the Father's will by choosing to stay and work through relational sticking points when it would be easier not to.

- *Reflect on how you are modeling relational skills.* The way you relate to emerging adults can empower emotional and relational intimacy. What are they learning from you in regard to speaking the truth to others out of love rather than principle alone, attentive follow-up, listening deeply and responding meaningfully, being responsible to but not for others, communicating boundaries, creating relational space and creative relational problem solving? These skills can serve them in powerful ways for the rest of their lives.

GROWING IN COMMUNITY: INTERTWINED ROOTS

The largest living things on earth are the various species of redwood trees. With branches that reach nearly four hundred feet toward the sun, trunks large enough to build a road through and lifespans that stretch across millennia, these trees are amazing creations of God. You can't help but worship him when you're standing in a circle of redwoods looking up toward barely visible treetops.

Even with the stunning outward majesty of these mystifying towers of nature, one of their most fascinating—and almost incomprehensible—qualities lies beneath the surface. Redwood trees of all varieties do not have deep roots. That deserves repetition. Redwood trees of all varieties do not have deep roots. They have one root that is set deep when they are young. From that point forward they extend their roots outward, two feet wide for every one foot high. And because they grow together as a community of trees, they intertwine their roots below the surface, providing mutual support and stability. In other words, they reach their enormous size only because they are able to rely on one another for the strength required to stand hundreds of feet tall. No redwood can stand alone—so none of them grow alone.

No one who stands alone stands strong, stable or tall in the Christlife. A deep root in Christ is required of all mature adult disciples. Mutual support and stability, with spiritual lives intertwined around one another in community, are also necessary for disciples of Christ to reach their full, magnificent potential. And standing in the midst of such disciples is, without a doubt, reason for worship.

RESTORING LIFE IN THE EMERGING ADULT'S SEXUALITY

JERRY WAS FINALLY IN the position he'd dreamed of for so many years: employed as a full-time youth pastor in a young church, one semester away from completing the seminary degree he'd been working on for four years and engaged to Molly, a college senior whom he loved with deep devotion. Today, though, he feels like he's in a nightmare. Molly is pregnant. Jerry and Molly had often crossed boundaries they'd set for their physical relationship. The guilt Jerry has felt about it as a youth pastor has been almost too much to bear. Still, he's reasoned that they'll be married soon—and they only had intercourse on two occasions. Now Jerry's dream world is being shattered from every angle. How will he explain this to the church? To his professors and mentors at the seminary? To Molly's father, who has so often expressed his respect for Jerry? What should he do now? Molly's ideal entry into her post-graduate future has likewise imploded. She feels guilt, but she also feels anger—toward Jerry as well as the church for the fact that what should be the joyous anticipation of a child may now be looked down upon as a "mistake" and a "result of sin." Furthermore, she fears that the community around her will be more focused on how this affects Jerry than on the impact all of this will be having on her life—and her heart.

Derrick's committed Baptist upbringing and Rosita's devout Catholic heritage make things interesting when it comes to spiritual matters. After a lengthy search, they have finally found a church that both of them can consider a true church home. The large, nondenominational megachurch is just twelve minutes from their new condo. Now, in their interview process to become members, they learn that the church frowns on their choice to live together before marriage. They're not unfamiliar with this kind of moral thinking; they're just shocked that such a progressive, contemporary church would be so "old school" about sex before marriage. Derrick is also concerned with how the church might view his brother Devin and Devin's life partner, James. Derrick and Rosita do not understand how the church, which is supposed to be about the love of Jesus, could assent to such rigid judgments on what is and is not true love.

Nicole had thought that, having been so thoroughly transformed through her conversion to Christ six years ago, she would be forever free of the past that had kept her so bound emotionally and relationally. Being the daughter of a distant mother and an absent father, as well as repeated sexual abuse by a close male relative while Nicole was growing up, had left her soul in many pieces. Steeped in self-loathing and feelings of abandonment, Nicole had fallen farther and farther into a life of sexual promiscuity, shocking even herself at the frequency with which she "hooked up" for relationally meaningless sexual encounters. When Nicole was twenty, Christ rescued her from her despair, giving her a new hope and a fresh vision for her life moving into adulthood. Meeting Carlton her first year in grad school seemed to be the final severing of her ties with the past. They maintained a sexually pure relationship all through their dating and engagement. Now, however, only months into their marriage, Nicole is suffering from feelings of worthlessness, self-condemnation and memory flashbacks. Far from enjoying her sexual relationship with Carlton, she is experiencing him—through no fault of his own—as a "trigger" that takes her back to the past. Ashamed and desperate, Nicole feels the one person she most cherishes in her life, Carlton, is beginning to pull away in hurt and confusion.

Lisa was born to a teenage single mom who, at sixteen, was kicked out of the house by her very religious parents. Lisa's childhood was filled with constant change but empty of the vital resource of extended family support. She remembers her mom having a series of live-in boyfriends who made big promises but eventually broke them all. Desperate on many levels, Lisa's mom finally began to move forward in her life after turning to Christ and to a local church that accepted her as a single mom rather than treating her as "less than." Lisa became a devoted follower of Christ at age fourteen, though she still wrestled with deep feelings of insecurity. When she arrived on campus for her freshman year at a large state university, her insecurities surfaced and she felt more alone and unlovable than ever before. During her first semester, she only developed one meaningful relationship. Jill, a junior, was accepting, nurturing and very committed to listening without judgment to Lisa's doubts and fears. Last week, soon after a small group Bible study ended in Jill's apartment, Lisa and Jill's emotional intimacy led them into physical sexual intimacy. Since that moment, Lisa has been conflicted like never before. She feels such love for Jill, but shame for their sexual encounter. That this happened just after a Bible study further confuses Lisa. She knows that Jill has no trouble reconciling same-sex relationships with her faith in Christ, but this is not what Lisa was taught. Lisa is too scared to continue her relationship with Jill and, at the same time, too scared to end it.

These are the stories of seven emerging adults facing challenges regarding their sexuality. Let's consider another story—the Story of all stories—that begins with a wedding:

> So the LORD God caused a deep sleep to fall upon the man, and while he slept took one of his ribs and closed up its place with flesh. And the rib that the LORD God had taken from the man he made into a woman and brought her to the man. Then the man said,
>
> > "This at last is bone of my bones
> > and flesh of my flesh;
> > she shall be called Woman,
> > because she was taken out of Man."
>
> Therefore a man shall leave his father and his mother and hold fast to his wife, and they shall become one flesh. And the man and his wife were both naked and were not ashamed. (Gen 2:21-25)

The Story of all stories also concludes with a wedding:

> Then I heard what seemed to be the voice of a great multitude, like the roar of many waters and like the sound of mighty peals of thunder, crying out,

> "Hallelujah! For the Lord our God
>   the Almighty reigns.
> Let us rejoice and exult
>   and give him the glory,
> for the marriage of the Lamb has come,
>   and his Bride has made herself ready;
> it was granted her to clothe herself
>   with fine linen, bright and pure"—
>   for the fine linen is the righteous deeds of the saints. (Rev 19:6-8)

Throughout Scripture, the image of marital union is used as a carefully crafted metaphor for how God pursues, loves and relates to his people. The mystery of his love for the church is likened to the sexual union of a husband and wife (Eph 5:31-32), and the nature of his commitment to his people is described as spousal fidelity (as in Isaiah 54:5: "For your Maker is your husband, the LORD of hosts is his name; and the Holy One of Israel is your Redeemer, the God of the whole earth he is called"). Furthermore, spiritual rejection and rebellion by his people is consistently referred to as "adulterous" (Ezek 16:32-33; Jas 4:4-5). The story line of the book of Hosea is astounding in its portrayal of the raw emotion of a God who experiences his people like a husband whose wife repeatedly, blatantly betrays him sexually.

Sexuality, sex and marital sexual union are not, therefore, simply creations of God's handiwork; they are articulate, self-revealing expressions of the very nature of God. Scripture clearly communicates that the God-intended expression of marital sexual union is unique in its capacity to reflect the image of his spiritual nature. However, Scripture also warns that sexual union apart from marital intimacy, where God intends for it to exist, is equally capable of distorting and damaging our bodies and our souls (1 Cor 6:18). We cannot overstate that our sexuality and our spirituality are inseparable, and at the core of who we are as whole persons. Even as we write we are once again reminded—with great sorrow—of the devastating relational, spiritual impact that sexual disobedience has had in the lives of those we love and lead. Thus, living the Christlife in their sexuality, especially in a sexually charged culture like ours, is one of the most critical spiritual challenges emerging adults face.

SPIRITUAL CASUALTIES FROM THE SEXUAL FRONT

As a casual but enthusiastic student of the Civil War, I (Rick) have been particularly fascinated by the infamous moment known as "Pickett's Charge" in the battle of Gettysburg. Pickett's Charge was an ill-fated march by twelve thousand Confederate soldiers "over one thousand yards across open ground" ordered by General Robert E. Lee on July 3, 1863.[1] The assault lasted fifty minutes and resulted in more than ten thousand casualties.[2] After the slaughter of Confederate soldiers was finished, history records that General Pickett returned to Lee's side, only to be ordered by Lee to reassemble his division of men and engage the Union army once again. Pickett responded respectfully but sorrowfully, "General Lee, I have no division now."[3] By the end of Pickett's Charge, many portions of the open field were so strewn with bodies that soldiers could walk a great distance on them without touching the ground.

Whether I'm having a pastoral counseling conversation or listening to the transparent stories of men gathered in spiritual community or watching previews for Hollywood's latest comedic offerings, I often feel like I'm standing in a spiritual battlefield that rivals the aftermath of Pickett's Charge. The wounds in people's lives from impoverished sexual decision making have created a new level of devastation that the church is only now beginning to acknowledge and address. I'm not suggesting that all emerging adults are in sexually dire straits. Recently I've spoken with several college-age men and women who articulate a joyous vision for their sexuality and demonstrate with their actions a faithful obedience to sexual purity. These emerging adults do, however, represent the minority. In a discussion, established-adult men currently mentoring emerging-adult men were asked, "What percentage of the young men you disciple can be described as struggling significantly with sexual purity in thought and action?" One man's response was telling: "I would say eleven out of ten." The point of his humor was not lost on the men in the room—in regard to themselves as well as the emerging-adult men.

My wife, Teresa, is a licensed professional counselor and a certified sex therapist. (I have already warned my children that, since I pastor an evangelical Christian church and Teresa is a Christian sex therapist, no one will ever want to marry into the family!) I asked Teresa to describe her feelings as she repeatedly encounters the wounded on the battlefield. Here's her response:

> I will never forget the words exchanged in a momentary interaction following a talk titled "Sex and Chocolate." The event was planned as a launch for our church's women's ministry year. After I had concluded the frank but compassionate presentation on a biblical vision for whole-person sex and sexuality, a petite gray-haired lady approached me cautiously. I was instantly struck by her piercing blue eyes, made even more like blue crystals by the tears brimming on her lids. With deep sorrow she said, "I wish some one had told me this sixty years ago. It would have changed my life. Please keep teaching this to women. We need to know." I was deeply moved by these words. Somehow that brief encounter was used by God to fuel a passion to communicate and pass along God's truth and design for sex and sexuality. Suddenly I realized that the need was far greater than I had previously imagined. Imagine this with me: if this woman, growing up as a teenager in the 1940s, needed to hear a biblically truthful, compassionate, whole-person vision for sex and sexuality, how much more do twenty-first-century teenagers and young adults long for the hope and healing of God's designs for our hearts and our bodies?
>
> I find I need to do very little convincing either within or outside the Christian community that the current twenty-first-century Western cultural approach to sex and sexuality is leaving men and women less relationally satisfied than ever before. The evidence is irrefutable that each successive generation becomes increasingly disillusioned, profoundly aware that something is askew and missing. When confronted with the growing emptiness around sex and sexual relationships, the broader culture's response is: more variety, more exotic and erotic experiences, more people, more, More, MORE! And, in a very real sense they find themselves finding "more," but it is not the more they had envisioned. With each new partner the sexual participant experiences more emptiness, more longing, more hopelessness regarding the existence of intimate love. Sadly, the impact of these losses results in an increasingly desperate search to fill the need or find a way to numb the need so the pain goes away. The impact is pervasive—and growing:
>
> - 16 percent of adults between 18 and 23 have *not* had intercourse. By age 27, that figure decreases to 8 percent.[4]

- Among young adults ages 18 to 23 who are in any form of romantic relationship, only about 6 percent are *not* having sex of some sort.[5]

- About a quarter of males and 12 percent of females in their late twenties have had 15 or more sexual partners, also representing a much more "diverse" history of sexual experiences (heterosexual and homosexual, oral sex and anal sex, etc.).[6]

- Cohabitation by opposite-sex couples living together rose from 6.7 million in 2009 to 7.5 million in 2010.[7]

- Nearly half of women ages 20 to 24 are infected with HPV (a sexually transmitted virus).[8]

- 87 percent of university students are having virtual sex over webcams, instant messenger or the telephone.[9]

While these stats are astounding, stats are impersonal and therefore easy to set aside as intellectual facts. What is not so easily set aside are the weekly conversations in my office of men and women, young and old, who are trying to pick up the pieces of these realities in their lives, marriages and families. Sex experienced outside the context God intended has left countless men and women deeply wounded not just physically and emotionally but spiritually and relationally as well. If I am truthful, even as a therapist, at times I find it difficult to press into this area partly because it is "sacred ground," partly because it is such a vulnerable subject. This intimate, hallowed ground is not to be dialogued about casually. No one—therapists, pastors, teachers, disciplemakers included—should approach this subject lightly, thereby cheapening sex to the level of a topic like the latest sports scores or stock market trends. Having said this, we must create dialogue and not shy away from this area because it is one of the front-line battles that we are losing for the cause of Christ. Leaving profoundly soul-wounded believers bleeding and crying out on the battlefield fails to fulfill our calling to be "ministers of reconciliation" (2 Cor 5).

Smith, in *Lost in Transition: The Dark Side of Emerging Adulthood*, articulates the extent of the damage that has been done to this generation's capacity to make wise, meaningful connections between sexual experiences and relational health. Smith writes,

We think it is a matter of empirical fact that it is good for sexual intimacy to be protected within proper boundaries. . . . We think it is good for people to protect their physical, mental, and emotional health in intimate relationships. We think the good of sex is ruined by exploitation, coercion, or pure self-gratification. *The majority of American emerging adults [however] seem to have little awareness of those understandings of sex and the good.*[10]

Summarizing the research on sexuality among emerging adults, the author sadly concludes that *"not far beneath the surface of happy, liberated emerging adult sexual adventure and pleasure lies a world of hurt, insecurity, confusion, inequality, shame, and regret."*[11]

Not surprisingly then, the spiritual battlefield is layered with young men and young women who are "soul-wounded" by sexual sin, confusion and addiction. Standing beside this relational massacre and simply lamenting the effects of a fallen world or choosing to self-righteously condemn others like the Pharisees did with the woman caught in adultery (Jn 8) must not be our response to such pain and suffering. Rather we, as disciplemakers, must choose to enter the battlefield, even while the war still rages, and seek to save the wounded, leading them to a glorious, healing vision for living the Christlife in the midst of a sexually explicit and perverse world.

BIBLICAL VISION, GUIDANCE AND SUPPORT

Much of what passes for Christian teaching and leading in the area of sexuality should be called "management" rather than "leadership." Too often the emphases of a Christian message will focus on how to manage our behavior: don't watch pornography, don't go "too far" in dating relationships, learn how to resolve conflicts over sex in marriage, learn how to be a better lover. Of course, there's much value in learning the managerial aspects of dealing with our sexual longings in a biblical manner, but without vision, the motivation for managing sexual energy, whether emotional or mental or physical, typically gives way to urgings that are being powerfully stirred by the images and stories that bombard young adults daily through their experiences in popular culture.

To lead people well in the area of sexuality, then, requires messages and modeling that cast a clear, compelling vision for a person's sexual identity and sexual behavior. Discipline and management motivated by a spiritual vision fuel a heart's desire to love God, creating a relational process. Management disconnected from vision, however, burdens the heart with a duty to "get it right" for God, thus creating a religious process. When it comes to sex and sexuality, only a relational process sustains over the long-term; the needs are simply too great to manage by a religious force of will. (Thus the dismal results from "Just Say No" programs when they're relied on as the *only* means for leading students toward purity.)

Emerging adults need a biblical vision for participating in the Big Story of the God who expresses and reflects his glory in human sexuality and marital sexual union. Lost in a maze of distorted cultural mirrors that reflect untruth, young adults long for practical guidance and relational support in moving toward God's exceptional design for human sexuality. And the context for that vision, guidance and support must be the anticipation of the spiritual union that will be experienced in the wedding feast that awaits us in his presence. The goal of sex, therefore, is not simply physical pleasure or emotional passage; it's also more intimate participation in the design of the Christlife, a life that will ultimately be spiritually culminated and consummated in our eternal life with God. Sex was not designed as an end in itself but rather as a means for experiencing a "spiritual sampler" of the banquet that awaits us in heaven.

Without a well-formed and well-informed Christlife vision for sex and sexuality, emerging adults in the twenty-first century will drift along on the changing tides of the broader culture, tides which are heavily influenced by popular cultural media. And, lacking both a moral compass and a spiritual conscience, cultural media often sends incorrect and conflicting messages about sex, sexual orientation and sexuality. In an essay on sex and emerging adults, Marla Eisenberg argues that the degree of difficulty in sexual identity formation has increased dramatically within the brief lifetime of the current generation of emerging adults. She offers a sobering observation of the challenges that young adults are up against:

> A young man might be deeply attracted to other men but have sex only with women and consider himself straight. A young woman might have had both male and female partners but think of herself as a lesbian because she has only achieved orgasm with female partners, even though

she is really more attracted to men. Young people may have an isolated same-sex experience that has no real impact on their heterosexual identity. Some may strongly identify as gay or lesbian even if they have not had any sexual partners at all. In short, no single component defines one's sexual orientation, and sexual orientation is viewed as more fluid by today's emerging adults than by previous generations. . . .

Whether one is having a lot of sex, just a bit, or none at all, 20-somethings are engaged in a complicated and often confusing developmental task: they must make sense of the divergent messages they receive about sexuality, clarify their own sexual values, and take charge of their sexual health in adulthood. Unfortunately, the gap between the onset of sexual maturity, first sexual experience, and—typically much later— commitment to a single sexual partner is dangerous terrain. And although sex is everywhere, real support for making healthy and sane sexual choices is scarce.[12]

To say that the tides of change regarding sexuality in the broader culture are not headed in the direction of Christ's grace and truth would be a vast understatement. The critical need for "real support" in the lives of emerging adults, therefore, cannot be overstated. Connecting sexuality and sexual behavior to the Creator's vision becomes a sacred, life-altering experience for the emerging adult. While an entire book could be written on this topic, there are three implicit components that comprise the foundations of a vision for sexuality that leads to a deeper experience of the Christlife of trust, submission and love: (1) humanity as a self-portrait of God, (2) human satisfaction as a gift of God's grace, and (3) human sexual intimacy as an expression and experience of God's divine love.

TRUSTING GOD'S SELF-PORTRAIT

In the fall of 2008, a traveling presentation titled "Leonardo da Vinci: Drawings from the Biblioteca Reale in Turin" was on display for six weeks at the Birmingham Museum of Art. While it was there, our daughter, Jessica, invited us (Rick and Teresa) to attend a reception at the museum. During the evening we got to spend about an hour perusing the rare, historically invaluable works by da Vinci. Among the famous pieces on display, including *Codex on the Flight of Birds* and *Madonna of the Rocks,* the one that stopped me in my tracks was da Vinci's self-portrait. I lingered for quite some time, looking at each feature of his artistic representation of himself. The eyes, the posture, the expression all seemed to say something about what he was thinking and feeling as he studied himself and reproduced his own image. I'm quite certain that, in that moment, he could never have conceived of millions of people worldwide traveling to locations like Birmingham to observe his work almost six hundred years after his death!

When God created man and woman, however, he did so with the express purpose of putting them on display—to the whole universe—as a self-portrait. The original language in Genesis 1 and 2 is explicit about the fact that we were created in the "image" of God, in his "likeness." Literally, the Hebrew words used communicate the process of "carving out of" in order to create something "like the original." Newly created humanity, connected to God and to one another prior to sin, is the finite self-portrait of an infinite God. The "one flesh" component of marriage, where "likeness" experiences union with "likeness," further reveals God, a God who exists as three-in-one. Sexuality, as male and female beings, and sexual relationships, as male and female being joined in God's perfectly designed one-flesh physical union, are God-intended ways for him to say to the world, "This is Who I am. I am like this. I possess these qualities and I experience this level of intimacy—infinite, holy, passionate intimacy."

As Teresa explains it,

> Sex was intended to be the natural fulfillment of the oneness that is developed first emotionally, mentally, relationally and spiritually. It is the gift God created to communicate in a physical representation the kind of intimacy and relationship he longs to experience with us.

This, however, is not the understanding of sex and sexuality that most emerging adults seem to have. "When I communicate this to Christian young adults," Teresa notes, "there is almost a physical recoiling regarding putting God and sex in the same arena. Most think of sex as 'naughty' and certainly nothing God would be enthusiastic about."

Young adults need to be led toward this vision of humanity and human relationships as God's self-portrait. In each new generation, the powerful imagery and influence of sex in the broader culture must be confronted with godly reality. The problem is not that our culture makes too big a deal of sexuality. Being created male and female with the potential for whole-person union is actually a much bigger deal than the Romans and the Greeks and Americans in the 1960s and every other sensually hedonistic culture has ever realized. Likewise, sexual union is much greater than the hyperfocus on physical pleasure promoted by Hollywood and hardcore pornography. In reality, the image and likeness of God are meant to be on display in the way humanity experiences and expresses sexuality.

Before we seek to help young adults manage their sexual urges in areas that require mature discernment, such as masturbation or choosing appropriate physical boundaries in dating relationships, or in areas that require less discernment but great amounts of self-control, such as view pornography or have oral sex or sexual intercourse outside of marriage, we need to help these men and women understand the biblical vision for who they were created to be as self-portraits of God. Ultimately, to choose sexual purity in mind and body and soul is to go against the desires of the flesh and the pressures of the world. It requires an ever-deepening trust that surrenders to the Father's wisdom. He created human bodies with their passionate design for intense, intimate sexual pleasure. He knows the why, how and what of his creation.

Trusting his wisdom isn't just about embracing his vision, however; it does also include embracing his prescribed boundaries for sexual purity and sexual self-control. Those who refuse to trust this part of his wisdom do so at their own peril. Indeed, to choose to go outside his design is not simply "immature" or "unwise"; it's a choice to become the god of our desires. In biblical language, it's an act of idolatry. First Thessalonians 4 provides this warning for the person who disregards the will of God for human sexuality:

> For this is the will of God, your sanctification: that you abstain from sexual immorality; that each one of you know how to control his own body in holiness and honor, not in the passion of lust like the Gentiles who do not know God; that no one transgress and wrong his brother in this matter, because the Lord is an avenger in all these things, as we told you beforehand and solemnly warned you. For God has not called us for

impurity, but in holiness. Therefore whoever disregards this, disregards not man but God, who gives his Holy Spirit to you. (1 Thess 4:3-8)

Before going further, one thing should be noted. Everyone has struggled in some form with the confusing passage through young-adult sexuality. *Everyone.* Much grace, mercy and compassion must accompany all teaching on sexuality. This section of 1 Thessalonians, however, makes two things clear. First, disregarding biblical teaching on sexual purity is a direct defiance of the Holy Spirit of God. Second, God's expectation of those walking in the Christlife is that they will learn to manage their sexual behaviors in a manner consistent with his vision for their sexual lives. While there is grace, mercy and compassion available in Christ, it'd be foolish to suggest that we will escape all the consequences that follow a failure to obey his will.

The damage done to the soul and the distortion of one's view of God are among the most devastating results of sexual sin. Having noted this, however, God is a Father who reaches into our souls and minds to rescue, redeem, restore and re-create. For those who, by his grace, embrace his vision for sexuality and yield to his healing of their brokenness, there is enduring hope for sexual purity to be returned to the soul and mind.

HUMBLY SUBMITTING TO THE SATISFACTIONS OF CHRIST

John Piper's prolific teaching and speaking has fueled the spiritual passion of multitudes of young-adult followers of Christ. His compelling vision for young-adult Christians to forsake all idols and worship God alone can be summarized in this statement from his book *Desiring God:* "God is most glorified when we are most satisfied in Him."[13] While Piper's thesis can be applied to innumerable spiritual contexts, nowhere is it more profoundly necessary than in the context of human sexuality.

From Mick Jagger's rock anthem "(I Can't Get No) Satisfaction" of the 1960s to the cable series *Sex and the City* of the early twenty-first century to the insatiable worldwide appetite for pornography, it's clear that an abundance of sexual opportunity and experience does not correlate with characteristics such as integrity, moral strength and satisfaction. In fact, the inverse is true. Pursuing extramarital sexual experiences as a means of satisfaction is like drinking ocean water when you're dying of thirst on a raft adrift at sea; the salt-laced ocean water actually speeds up dehydration, causing death to occur much faster. And yet, it seems counterintuitive to avoid drinking when you're thirsty—just as it seems counterintuitive to resist the urges of sexual desire, especially when surrounded by people who seem to be guzzling ocean water at an incredibly rapid rate with no visible consequences.

Submitting to the Father's heart with humility by accepting his provision for human sexual desire consists of both "indulging" and "denying" as acts of worship. Most young adults are much more familiar with the acts of denial in sexuality: set boundaries on what you see, what you think and where you touch. Certainly these are critical; we can't fully engage the heart of the Father without controlling the sexual activities in our life. For a single person, this means maintaining sexual purity in all relationships. For a married person, it means protecting the sexual purity of the spousal relationship (by abstaining from adultery, from degrading your spouse, from fantasizing about sexual relations with someone other than your spouse, etc.).

On the flip side, telling young adults to "indulge" themselves in order to experience the satisfactions of Christ in relationship with the Father requires a *great deal* of clarification. Indulging in the satisfactions of Christ calls the young adult to join Christ in looking to the Father continually for authentic fulfillment. To review, we described Christ's humble submission to the Father's heart in this way in chapter three:

> Christ humbly and passionately looked to the Father as the source of life in all things and exhibited a heart that was continually surrendered to the Father. That surrender fueled perfect submission to His Father's heart and leadership. He considered the Father's affirmation, affection and glory to be greater than any earthly pleasure, comfort, achievement or possession. He relied fully on the Father's provision and considered anything that minimized the Father as the eternal source to be idolatrous.

A never-depleted spring of water awaits the soul dehydrated by the battle with the emotional longings, mental images and physical urges of sexual desire. To learn to experience the Father's affirmation and affection through Christ, as an individual within community, is to *begin* the journey of leading our sexuality toward Christ rather than just trying to manage sexual desire for Christ. In the end, failing to lead in this way makes us vulnerable to sexual temptation. The desire is too great, the temptations too accessible and the culture too complicit. Denying inappropriate expressions of sexual desire is therefore best empowered by experiencing in Christ the Father's gracious gift of human satisfaction.

INTIMACY AS AN EXPRESSION OF FULFILLING THE FATHER'S WILL

Earlier in the chapter, we named three foundational components for a vision of godly sexuality: humanity as a self-portrait of God, human satisfaction as a gift of God's grace, and human sexual intimacy as an expression and experience of God's divine love. The third component is a much higher calling than just denying sexual desires, remaining a virgin before marriage or not committing adultery. Fulfilling the Father's will in loving others calls a young adult to express his masculinity or her femininity in all relationships as an act of *leading the other person toward a deeper experience of the Father's love.* Marriage adds one more component to this: expressing ourselves sexually with our spouse *in a manner that leads him or her to a deeper experience of the Father's love.*

Note the language in each of those statements: *lead toward the Father's love.* None of us can control how another person pursues or responds to God (though we all try very hard to do so at times). What can be controlled by each of us, however, is whether our words, touch and overall approach to others genuinely have their best interests at heart. And there is *nothing* that is more in the best interest of another person than helping them more deeply engage the heart of the Father's love for them.

For those who marry, the reward for trusting God's design, submitting to God's leading and loving with sexual purity is an indescribable foundation for building marital trust and intimacy. Indeed, when a commitment to Christ triumphs over a commitment to fulfill their desires on their own terms, young married adults can experience a deep, shared reservoir of life in marital sexual union and intimacy. For those who do not marry, that same reservoir of life can be experienced in deep friendships, characterized by integrity and purity, that reflect the heart of a God who offers himself for the benefit of those whom he loves.

What all human beings crave more than anything—including the air they breathe—is to be loved and to love. Scripture teaches, "We love because he first loved us" (1 Jn 4:19). Being loved well by God, then, is what enables us to love well. Ultimately our greatest gift to a person is not our affirmation but God's; not our affection but our loving Father's; not our attention but our compassionate Creator's. Thus, loving well, including sexually, fundamentally means loving in a way that exposes God's heart for the other person.

In chapter two we wrote, "Christ's deep *love* for sinful human beings was like a river of life-giving water that flowed directly from the gracious, pure heart of the Father." With millions of people sexually adrift on the unforgiving seas of popular culture, and with more and more of them guzzling the deadly ocean water of sexual experiences outside of God's design, what a source of life and refreshment the next generation of young adults could be were they to become a riverbed for that flow of life!

THE CHRISTLIFE IN SEXUALITY

The stories that open this chapter each illustrate a different challenge in walking with young adults toward godly sexuality. Jerry, the seminary student and youth pastor, possessed clear convictions for an authentic commitment to sexual purity before marriage, yet he found himself increasingly crossing boundaries with Molly. He either lacked wisdom or humility or courage—or all three—and failed to get the help he needed to fulfill his vision for their relationship. Jerry thus fell into deception, losing sight of God's perfect design and failing to be "strengthened by the grace that is in Christ Jesus" (2 Tim 2:1).

What Jerry needs now is someone who will approach him with a view toward a redemptive, restorative experience with Christ and his local church; he is in desperate need of compassion without compromise, and conviction without condemnation. Grace and truth, mercy and accountability must be mingled so that Jerry will not only find forgiveness for the past but also strength for the future.

Some churches respond harshly to leaders, subtly communicating that a leader who has failed has somehow committed the unforgivable sin. On the other hand, in an attempt to not be "rigid and unforgiving," churches can fail to press into weaknesses and to hold their leaders accountable. Jerry does not need to be abandoned or coddled; he needs to be led in the grace and truth of Christ. If he responds with trust in the Father, humble submission in response to the Father's heart, and love for Molly and all those whose lives his decision has affected, Jerry will experience Christ much more deeply. Moreover, doing so will prepare him to become a much stronger, Christ-dependent leader and husband than he could have been before all of this happened.

Molly likewise needs to experience Christ's truth, grace and love. Large doses of support and challenge, conviction and compassion, will be necessary for her to turn to Christ to heal the hurt in her heart. She needs to be led to face the full reality of the forgiveness of Christ offered to her—and to others—in and through the gospel. Trusting the wisdom of God's commands to release guilt, anger and resentment will spare Molly from developing a sense of bitterness toward the church and even Jerry. Submitting to the heart of a forgiving Father rather than being held captive by emotions and experiences will set her free to be spiritually transformed into a much stronger woman than ever before, one who will relate to others with an open heart that seeks to love them rather than a self-protective, self-absorbed closed heart. And she'll become a more powerfully loving wife and mother, as well as a more life-giving part of the body of Christ in her local church. In this way, the baby born to Molly and Jerry will be not a symbol of sexual failure but rather a reminder of the matchless, glorious, life-giving Creator and Redeemer.

In contrast to Jerry and Molly, Derrick and Rosita lack any substantial vision for godly sexuality. So much of what is taught culturally—even within the church—elevates the experience of human love to a near transcendent level, and the cultural embrace of the constitutional right to "the pursuit of happiness" often trumps the biblical understanding of living in the satisfactions of Christ. Perhaps Derrick and Rosita are just ignorant of biblical teaching but would be open to following Christ's commands if exposed to solid teaching and modeling. On the other hand, they may simply be shopping for a comfortable religious experience, and would therefore be unwilling to surrender to anything or anyone that doesn't fit their own agendas. At the end of the day, the question once again is, Who will be god of my desires?

The motivations of Derrick's and Rosita's heart will only be revealed as someone confronts them, speaking the truth in a loving way. Offered the wisdom of God, will they respond with a desire to know and understand more? Or will they take offense and cry foul with the always popular, "You have no right to judge me!"? Offered the heart of the Father's compassion for them, will they humbly express a desire to be pleasing to their Father and ask for help on their journey? Or will they respond with defiance, suggesting that the church clearly does not understand them and their love for one another? Offered a vision for living life as a loving act of worship, will they begin to seek a deeper understanding of how God has designed them for his purposes? Or will they simply choose to go on creating their own idols by the plans they make for their lives, including seeking a church that will either avoid the issue of premarital cohabitation or support their right to do as they please? Their response cannot be controlled. What can be controlled, however, is the response of the church community—a response that should begin with a compassionate adult disciplemaker and that will instruct them as well as model for them the glorious picture of godly sexuality.

Then there's Nicole, who represents the increasing reality of a culture adrift on the tides of boundary-less and meaningless sex. She may be moving around on the battlefield and even standing upright, but don't be fooled; she is the walking wounded. While she has made much progress, experienced genuine healing, and adopted biblical convictions and commitments, she is so internally shattered that she'll find herself wading through new layers of pain in the aftermath of the abuse she suffered. To communicate to Nicole that she is somehow doomed to a life of sexual dysfunction in her marriage would be inaccurate and cruel. To tell her that she should be completely free of the effects of the past would be equally inaccurate and cruel, as she would then assume she's doing something wrong—and letting down God and her husband in the process—by not "getting over it."

Nicole needs deep communal relationships with God's people—loving sisters and brothers in Christ who will walk her through being renewed by God the Father. In addition, she'll need to continually revisit what it means to trust God's wisdom in the process of redemption and restoration. Ultimately, Nicole and her husband, Carlton, will need to walk the journey toward the intimate, secure experience of God's design for marital sexuality together. Carlton must comprehend and lovingly embrace his role as God's primary agent for Nicole's healing process.

Their sexual relationship must become the *byproduct* of trust and intimacy, not the *basis* for them.

Along the way, Nicole will have to be almost daily reminded of the Father's heart of authentic love for her and unconditional pursuit of her. Without this reinforcement, she may be tempted to live in "reverse pride," unwilling to humble herself due to a sense of shame and self-condemnation. This is a false form of humility, one that refuses Christ's grace-filled embrace.

Finally, Nicole will need support as she learns to love with Christ's love. Rather than running in fear from the struggles in her marriage, she needs to be strengthened to run toward Christ in the struggles and to trust that even those things she fears most will be used by Christ to form her and her husband into his image.

Last we come to Lisa, who finds herself navigating the intimidating terrain of emerging-adult sexuality with severe doubts about her inherited moral compass and with no one to turn to for guidance. She represents the lost, lonely journeys of far too many students who have emerged from within the context of the church. High-school youth group worked great for Lisa—but now what?

Culturally, same-sex orientation and gay and lesbian relationships continue to be hotly contested issues. While full acceptance of homosexuality exists in many countries, particularly in the Western world, in the United States the debate rages. For emerging adults in twenty-first-century America, however, the trend is strongly toward not just tolerance but celebration of the freedom to choose a lifestyle of same-sex orientation. For Lisa, and for many of her peers in similar situations, the conflicts felt in regard to this issue are mentally, emotionally and spiritually overwhelming.

Lisa needs to experience the Christlife in a disciplemaker who loves her in response to being loved by the Father through Christ. She needs to hear grace and experience nurture from a heart that seeks to connect to her heart as well as address the specific issues of her sexuality. And she needs to hear the affirmation that her longing to be loved, her longing for intimate connection and her pursuit of friendship are God-created desires that should not be ignored or suppressed. Her disciplemaker will need to be someone who can join her with humility as one who is also in much need of a Father's guidance and strength.

Lisa is also in desperate need of the wisdom of the Father regarding his creation of and vision for human sexuality. The truth should be spoken in love regarding the elegant, holy design of marital sexual intimacy between a man and a woman, and she needs to be assured that the Father can be trusted with her sexuality because he created it to teach her more about himself. Being loved well and being led to the Father's wisdom will then provide the context for calling Lisa to step away from her relationship with Jill. However, she will need the support of others to fill the emotional and relational void that will be created by Jill's absence; asking her to step away from Jill with no nurturing relationship to step toward will be very difficult. Her longings that are met in Jill are legitimate longings, but she will have to learn how to redirect them toward relationships that reflect the perfect wisdom and love of God, her Father. Ending this relationship must be accompanied by a process of genuine godly repentance, lest Lisa conform on the outside but remain resistant in the heart.

Lisa should also be provided with counseling and support to deal with the guilt and shame of her relationship with Jill and the way this connects to her childhood experiences as well. The journey toward sexual identity and maturity has been complicated by her relationship with Jill—but it has not been damaged beyond repair (though Lisa may feel this way). Healing takes time, but Christ's grace only increases as the need increases in the Father's children

Finally, it's possible that Lisa will not choose to end this relationship with Jill. Her sense of attachment to Jill may be stronger at this point than her sense of conviction regarding the biblical vision for marital sexual purity between husband and wife. In this case, the disciplemaker should always care for Lisa and always be available as a friend. However, the relationship will be forever changed if Lisa rejects the Father's wisdom and pursues her own solutions to her deep needs. A disciplemaker can love but cannot effectively lead someone who specifically is unwilling to submit to the heart of the Father. Accepting this reality and learning how to remain a person who cares but who also does not endorse sin is one of the most difficult journeys that disciplemakers will ever be asked to walk.

SHEPHERDING WITH DISCERNMENT, INTENTIONALITY AND REFLECTION

Case study: Ted (25) and Gary (39). Ted was tired of the cycle of giving in, repenting, making promises and spending more time in the Word only to fall again and again to the lure of pornography. Emotionally exhausted from keeping the struggle to himself and trying to access God's power for self-control on his own, he finally asked Gary if he would meet with him on a regular basis to help him gain ground in becoming obedient to the Lord. A prior friendship with Gary, combined with his desperation for victory in this particular area, accelerated Ted's willingness to admit that sexual addiction was *the* area of obedience where he was having the most trouble.

Initial discernment. Gary didn't need to discern Ted's growth issue, but he did need to discern the direction their times together would take. He felt at a loss, since he had not personally struggled to this depth with pornography. To gain a sense of where to start with Ted, Gary began to read some articles by trusted Christian leaders on the issue and discovered that accountability alone was usually not enough to help a person make a change in this kind of struggle. Several readings mentioned that assisting the person in finding distracting but fulfilling activities was a more successful approach. Gary committed his commute home from work to listening to the Lord for whatever he might want to say to him about how to move forward with Ted.

Intentional strategy 1. First Gary asked Ted to share more about his struggles. He didn't want to assume that Ted's struggles were exactly like the ones he had read about. Then, after Ted shared, they discussed whether finding activities that were interesting and challenging was a good way to start helping Ted shift his behavioral patterns. Gary asked Ted check in with him every other day. Ultimately, though, as Gary listened, he began to see that Ted needed a deeper understanding of and biblical vision for his sexuality.

Reflection. Gary began to pray about how to help Ted see himself as a portrait of God and find satisfaction as a gift of God's grace. They met weekly, and after four months they were purposeful about reviewing Gary's growth. Where was he experiencing progress? What facilitated that progress and what hindered it? Though Ted had taken several steps in the right direction, he seemed to take two steps back for every step forward, and both disciple and disciplemaker admitted their discouragement. The struggle, it seemed, would require more than the attentive care of a disciplemaker.

Intentional strategy 2. Gary acknowledged to Ted that he could not provide all he needed to move beyond his struggle but assured him that he would still walk alongside him in his journey to freedom. He suggested that Ted either find a support group or pursue counseling in order to make it over the hurdle of his addiction. Together they explored possible options. In addition, Gary committed to exploring a biblical paradigm for sex and sexuality with Ted using a Bible study geared toward unearthing the importance of being created in God's image.

Reflection. After another four months, Gary and Ted sat down again to review his progress. Ted had joined a sexual addiction support group sponsored by a nearby church and had been attending regularly. The combination of exploring a biblical paradigm of sexuality and attending a support group was facilitating discernible movement in Ted's heart. They discussed how Gary might continue to be a support to Ted alongside the other help he was getting and agreed that praying together as well as pursuing a deeper understanding of God's vision for his sexuality were paths well worth continuing.

MORE DISCERNMENT, INTENTIONALITY AND REFLECTION IDEAS

Ted came to Gary with a specific sexual struggle. He was ready to work. But sometimes young adults feel confusion or guilt and need to make sense of their urges and feelings on their way to making behavioral changes. Here are more ideas for assisting emerging adults with sexuality issues.

Discernment

- *Identify growth obstacles.* Explore the core relational needs that remain unmet and discuss healthy ways to meet those needs in accordance with God's design for relationships and sexual purity. Sometimes disciples will tell you what they need, but the emphasis with issues of sexuality is often on behavior. Take time to listen and identify underlying unmet relational needs and misperceptions about

God's design for us as sexual beings. Be willing to overcome your own discomfort with issues related to this area so that you can ask frank questions in a spirit of caring humility.

- *Ask sexual identity pacing questions.* Where or how are their deepest needs being met? How do those needs intersect with sexual desires or longings? What areas bring them shame? Where do their assumptions about sexuality come from? What positive or biblical vision do they have for their sexuality?

- *Recognize when it's time to refer.* If issues appear to be chronic or a threat to anyone's well-being, or if they're beyond your scope of understanding or confidence, quickly refer the young adult to someone who has enough experience to deal with the presenting concerns. A well-intended but naively damaging response to critical sexual issues in a person's life is even more dangerous than a nonresponsive approach. While we have a combined half a century in working with young adults on issues of sexuality, there are still many issues that we quickly refer to wiser counsel.

- *Fully assess what you are up against.* Our enemy, the devil, seeks to destroy God's people by wounding us and shattering our hope in Christ's ability to forgive and heal. Sexual immorality in young adults must be one of his most useful (and definitely most-used) weapons of mass destruction. Prayer, wise counsel, fasting, steeping our mind in the Word and having close godly relationships are therefore all prerequisites for stepping onto the frontlines to protect the innocent and rescue the wounded. If you are not committed to self-care, then you should not attempt to help young adults work through their sexual struggles.

Intentionality

- *Encourage trust in the Father's wisdom through God's truth.* Clarisse was a young woman struggling to stay pure before marriage. She was focusing on the "gracious" aspect of God's character, and his continual forgiveness of her for mistakes she had made, to create her "reality"—one which accepted the lie that purity before marriage was not that important. Her experiential truth about God, however, was not the whole truth. There was wisdom available to her that could recenter her and allow her to make a better decision in her relationship with her boyfriend. Exploring the Father's desires for his children along with the relational and spiritual implications of following the wisdom of the world was enough to reorient Clarisse to a truer picture of God. Truth lined her up with reality and brought relief and life back into her relationship with a man she wanted to love well.

- *Encourage submission to the Father's heart regarding masculinity and femininity.* All the men that I (Rick) walk with in disciplemaking relationships face two major spiritual challenges based on lies. First, they have been bombarded by the false images of masculinity prevalent in our popular culture. Second, they live with the universal masculine fear that they are not enough. When you combine these two challenges, the result is often a man who lives passively in his heart, and passivity of the heart is the source of everything from sexual addictions to emotional paralysis. Through God's Word I lead them to Christ's portrayal of masculinity. Through God's Word I teach them how to wrap their fear in faith. Through God's Word and his Spirit, minds are renewed and hearts are restored.

  Females face different—but no less challenging—lies. Cyndi, a wife and mother of three as well as an author and speaker, recently shared with me how the women she teaches and mentors struggle to find a sense of identity outside of their roles. Their femininity is rooted more in what they do as women in other people's lives than in the woman God made them to be in his image. Consequently, women often lack the self-care and self-confidence that would enable them to risk expressing their individual inner beauty in ways that glorify God and significantly influence the world. Cyndi uses Scripture and her own journey as a woman to cast vision and provide guidance toward a Christ-based feminine identity.

- *Discuss sex as a whole-person issue.* No aspect of life is more holistic than sexuality. A godly "one flesh" relationship in marriage, for example, beautifully integrates the whole of mind, heart, body and soul. Painful circumstances also highlight this fact. Consider the difference in impact on a woman between being mugged and being raped.

Being mugged may leave her bruised and fearful and may require counseling to overcome a sense of victimization, but add rape to the scenario and the impact is exponentially more devastating. We should never approach sexual behaviors or concerns as isolated issues of the body or emotions. Sexuality is by definition tied to our very identity as masculine or feminine portraits of God.

Reflection

- *Assess growth by asking specific questions.* Pausing to regularly reflect on areas of growth in the disciple's sexuality, whether it's in perspective, behavior or attitude, can help them see progress or areas that still need attention. Choose questions that will help you celebrate growth, discern redirection, or repair and assess cooperation with the Holy Spirit, such as What is helping the process of transformation to go forward? Is there anything that is hurting progress? What continues to be an area of struggle? What patterns can be discerned in the areas of struggle? Where is growth occurring? What has facilitated that growth? What places still exist where a vision of God's design for sexuality in the Big Story has been forgotten or misunderstood or ignored?

- *Reflect on your willingness to be present.* When trying to come alongside a person struggling with sexual concerns or questions, do not assume you understand until you have listened thoroughly and repeatedly. People often avoid, gloss over or completely ignore details related to sex and sexuality due to embarrassment, questions of appropriateness or fear of rejection. So, while there is no need to probe for details that should be kept private, it is important not to form conclusions too quickly as to "what's going on." More often than not in dealing with sexual issues, the presenting problem and details only represent the tip of the iceberg in terms of what is happening in the heart. Be patient and resist the urge to prescribe too quickly what a person's next step toward healing should be.

- *Be very attentive to your own feelings and thoughts, and lead out of love for the other person, not as an attempt to "heal yourself."* Who does not have regrets, insecurities, repressed memories or concerns about their sexual selves? The temptation when dealing with emotions or experiences of others that are "close to home" in our own lives is to attempt, unconsciously, to make ourselves feel better by helping another person through a similar issue. In doing so, we are relating to the other person for our own benefit rather than theirs. Much prayer and wise counsel from others should be pursued if the issues are stirring emotions and memories in your own life.

TAKING RESPONSIBILITY: CARE FOR THE WOUNDED AND PROTECTION OF THE INNOCENT

It would be imprecise and overstated to say that the church leadership of our (Rick and Jana's) generation is to blame for the spiritual devastation that litters the landscape of contemporary culture. What cannot be overstated, however, is the urgent need for our generation to (1) care for the wounded and protect the innocent and (2) raise up a generation of disciplemakers who are captured wholeheartedly by a vision for human sexuality as a part of the Big Story of God. If we fail to do so, the fallout will be a generation that has emotionally shut down and that is unable to risk trust and experience intimacy. In addition, future generations of Christ's body will walk with painful limps rather than being strengthened to run their race in the power of faith, hope and love. In the words of the author of Hebrews,

> Let us also lay aside every weight, and sin which clings so closely, and let us run with endurance the race that is set before us, looking to Jesus, the founder and perfecter of our faith, who for the joy that was set before him endured the cross, despising the shame, and is seated at the right hand of the throne of God. . . .
>
> Lift your drooping hands and strengthen your weak knees, and make straight paths for your feet, so that what is lame may not be put out of joint but rather be healed. Strive for peace with everyone, and for the holiness without which no one will see the Lord. See to it that no one fails to obtain the grace of God. (Heb 12:1-2, 12-15)

May God grant us favor as we intentionally seek to do our part to "see to it that no one fails to obtain the grace of God."

RESTORING LIFE IN THE
EMERGING ADULT'S DAILY WORLD

KRISTA AND CHUCK, twenty-seven and twenty-six, have been married since they were both in college and have three little ones at home. Krista worked full time after their first little girl was born but decided to stay home with their second and third child. Life feels like sheer survival to them both. Keeping up with finances, preschool schedules, meals, diaper changes, church responsibilities and doctor appointments takes most of their time and energy. When Chuck gets home from work, he jumps in and helps with whichever child is most needy, even though he longs to just sit and tell Krista about his day. Meanwhile, Krista works to make sure meals are healthy and nutritious, both because she wants to and because she feels like it's expected of her as a stay-at-home mom. They volunteer occasionally in the children's ministry (when they actually make it to church) and attend a couple's Bible study as they're able (which isn't often). But the truth is that they both feel exhausted and a bit alienated from each other as well as God. Life is just going too fast. They watch the seemingly carefree lives of their childless friends and wonder if they should have waited longer . . .

Sarita is twenty-nine and finishing a doctoral degree in social policy in Boston. She started college in Arizona when she was almost twenty after a "gap year" working and traveling in South America. Now she is fluent in Spanish and Portuguese and has close friends on two continents, as well as a bachelor's degree in languages and a master's degree in sociology. Though technically she took her time getting to this point, she feels like she's been constantly racing through it all. Working, study-ing, doing internships, writing, attending conferences, presenting pa-pers, and trying to have a social life and maintain some Christian com-munity in the midst of it all has been a challenge. Sometimes she looks at the seemingly simple life of her married friends (who only have to focus on a job and each other) and wonders if her pursuit of higher edu-cation is really worth it. Simply stated, she's burned out.

These scenarios highlight some challenges emerging adults face in their daily life experiences. Even if they're not dealing with significant challenges in regard to their identity, spirituality, relationships or sexu-ality, young adults need assistance in figuring out how to negotiate tran-sitions, set daily living priorities, deal with new time constraints and navigate life in an increasingly diverse culture. These issues arise at home and at work, in their church community, and in actual as well as virtual neighborhoods. Disciplemakers can play a vital role in helping emerging adults navigate—and even thrive—in the often overwhelming details of their daily lives.

CHALLENGES IN THE EMERGING ADULT'S DAILY LIFE

As we (Jana and Rick) have walked alongside emerging adults through-out the years, a few daily realities of adult life consistently come up as points of struggle. Though not an exhaustive list, here are some of the most common challenges.

Negotiating transitions: Is the grass greener? Not surprisingly, a key area in emerging adulthood, according to Christian Smith's book *Souls in Transition*, is *transitions*. He remarks,

> To an extent matched by no other time in the life course, emerging adults enjoy and endure multiple, layered, big, and often unanticipated life tran-sitions. They move out, they move back, they plan to move out again. They go to college, they drop out, they transfer, they take a break for a semester to save money, some graduate, some don't. . . . Their parents separate, make up, get divorced, remarry. They take a job, they quit, they find another, they get promoted, they move. They meet new friends, their old friends change, their friends don't get along, they meet more new people.[1]

Whether they get married or start a family, move to a different country, change faith communities, or make any number of changes in the midst of finding their place in this world, transitions are a way of life for emerging adults. The changes experienced may have a greater or lesser impact, but regardless, they force adults to be flexible and learn how to respond to their shifting lives. Some will get so used to making changes that settling down will feel uncomfortable and they'll wonder what they're missing, like Krista and Chuck. Others will feel exhausted by all the transitions they have had to adjust to, and long for a more settled life, like Sarita. It's likely, though, that Krista and Chuck *feel* anything but settled in their daily life. And Sarita, once settled in to a stable career, location and set of relationships, might have a difficult time adjusting to the *lack* of changes in her life.

Jeffrey Arnett believes that the transitions in this phase—especially job transitions, where young adults may bounce from job to job trying to find their way in the work world—can create a "quarterlife crisis." This is likely more common in the United States than in Europe, he points out, since "there is little assistance in making the school-to-work transition."[2] Nonminority adults from middle and higher socioeconomic strata in affluent countries have the greatest opportunities to explore their career identities through job changing.[3] However, since emerging adults tend to take a meandering route toward a settled career, many of them will work with one eye on new job postings. For Christian emerging adults, this can raise questions about job loyalty, leaving or starting a job well, discerning God's will, and the ever-elusive search for contentment.

Living life transitionally also affects participation at church. For example, there are only half as many emerging adults represented in congregations as in the general adult population.[4] And according to Robert Wuthnow, the percentage of emerging adults in congregations has been declining over the past several decades.[5] Smith speculates about this trend: "Many life transitions and disturbances of diverse sorts—divorce, death of a family member, leaving home, job loss—have been shown by studies to correlate negatively with religious practices."[6] If churches are, in fact, providing guidance and support during major life transitions, emerging adults unfortunately must not be seeking support from the church as frequently as those of previous generations did. This has implications for ministry programming and also highlights the need for adult mentors who can proactively seek to guide young adults in the midst of transitions.

Time constraints and technology: Recreation, time savers and time wasters. When it comes to the challenge of setting priorities, emerging adults need to figure out how to manage their time. At the college where I (Jana) teach, we always warn our busy, stressed students that, contrary to what they think, life doesn't get *less* busy after graduation, though those who have jobs or get married and start a family *during* college probably *are* as busy as a graduated adult. Physically and practically (especially once young adults begin working forty to fifty hours a week), energy and free time lessen the further into adulthood they move. Finding a rhythm of living that allows for rest, work, relationships and play is tricky.

In this age of technology, we are blessed with a plethora of time-saving devices: microwaves help us cook faster; email, texting and social networking help us connect faster; and increasingly quicker Internet connections help us find the information we want faster. Smartphones allow us to learn, connect or be entertained wherever we go. (They don't cook things *yet!*) These can all be good things. In some cases, however, we may need to help young adults challenge the idea that these devices are actually serving them well. Keeping up with texts and voicemail takes a lot of time and energy, and sometimes the sheer amount of information available on the Internet causes our research to take more time, not less. In addition, playing games or checking Facebook on the go on our smartphones, iPads and iPods can distract us from other priorities. Texting instead of calling might save time in the short run but can also cause misunderstandings that take time and energy to resolve.

Just as time-saving technology can also provide time-wasting opportunities, the entertainment emerging adults choose can be more of a distraction than true recreation or rest. Young adults devote less time to watching TV and movies than they did in their younger years but still spend an average of four hours a day watching TV. Approximately 77 percent of them go to the movies and about the same amount watch a DVD at least once a month (making them one of the box office's most frequent consumers). Many, however, prefer to watch web videos online.

They spend less time than their elders with newspapers, books, magazines and radio, but 85 percent of them visit Facebook, Twitter or MySpace daily.[7] Emerging-adult males often form and maintain connections with one another through gaming—much of it online.[8] In all this, emerging adults have trouble figuring out how much time on Facebook or gaming with friends actually enhances relational connection and is life giving versus being draining or relationally distancing.

The term *prosumers* has been created to call attention to the fact that many young adults are not just consumers of entertainment but also producers of content.[9] They film digital spots for YouTube, blog, create iPhone apps and podcasts, and mix music at home on their own computers in order to post playlists on their social network site or webpage. What these tech-savvy prosumers critically need, though, is disciplemakers who will guide and encourage them to pursue their activities with a sense of purpose rather than using them to fulfill a need for a pleasing online persona.

Everyday priorities: Living life meaningfully. How is a young adult to choose where to spend their diminishing time and energy? As they become more aware of their identity and the call of Christ on their life, the importance of having values and priorities match increases. Becoming an adult requires learning things like balancing a budget, setting up a home, paying bills, learning to successfully function in a workplace, developing a manageable social network and making major purchases (like a car).

As we've mentioned, financial independence is a recognized feature of adulthood, so it will be an important aspect of a holistic disciplemaking relationship. In general, young adults are more likely to live below the poverty line. The dramatic increase in the average cost of transportation over the past few decades (especially car-related costs like fuel, insurance and maintenance) has contributed to the strain.[10] In addition, a rising inequality regarding wages has meant lower salaries for adults in their twenties, which means it takes them longer to pay off school loans, car loans and credit card debt.[11] Emerging adults need help understanding how to be good stewards in these greater areas of responsibility.

Regular church attendance is another area that can be a struggle for young adults, as we discussed earlier. If they're not able to see the church's relevance to some of their more pressing issues, like discovering their identity or achieving financial independence, they may view church as an inconvenience in the midst of so many other energy-sapping transitions. As Smith points out,

> We have good reason to believe that the sheer plenitude of life transitions that emerging adults experience themselves has the tendency to lessen the frequency and importance of religious practices and potentially undercut religious beliefs. In the face of these factors, emerging adults staying religiously active . . . requires that the life of faith be made a high priority in life, one that can overcome the countervailing forces.[12]

They need help answering questions like, Why is church important? and How important should it be for me?

As Krista is experiencing, balancing all the aspects of life can be overwhelming. Many young adults try to cope by creating a simplistic priority list: God, Family, Everything Else. The problem then becomes, How should I think about "everything else"? What happens if a demanding career or raising an infant is squeezing out time at church? The emerging adult needs to learn to go before God daily and ask him for wisdom in centering their efforts, allowing them to move into the challenge of "everything else" guided by his peace and wisdom. Then the priorities of each day become less a balancing act and more an act of obedience to the wisdom of the Father.

Living in a diverse world: Neighborhood, work and church. Emerging adults are handling the challenges of negotiating transitions, time and priorities well in the midst of an increasingly diverse environment. About 30 percent of the population in America is made up of minority groups, and an increasing number people identify themselves as "mixed heritage" and "multiracial."[13] Estimates predict that minority groups will make up 50 percent of the United States by 2042, but among young adults it will be as soon as 2027.[14] Professor Gerardo Marti notes,

> Young adults have more frequent and more continuous cross-ethnic interaction in racially diverse settings compared to their parents and grandparents. . . . They are more aware about race and ethnicity in ways that are radically different from their parents, which affects both their social interactions and their own self-identities.[15]

Emerging adults tend to focus more on attitudes, beliefs and lifestyle than on race in forming intimate relationships. One article points to three indicators of this: the existence of churches that draw younger adults where the experience of multiracial relationships is normal (three examples in California alone are Mosaic, Oasis and Evergreen Baptist Church of Los Angeles[16]); college ministries like InterVarsity Christian Fellowship where the goal to increase diversity is being successfully pursued;[17] and an increase in the number of interracial marriages among young, college-educated individuals. Parental pressures and prejudices (especially among Asian and Caucasian parents) might be why there aren't even *more* interracial marriages among this age group.[18] Additional factors, such as the presence of adult children of immigrants who have family members in other countries,[19] the accessibility of international news via the Internet and cable, a higher percentage of adults who obtain a college education, and increasingly diverse urban and suburban areas, may contribute to young adults' tendency to be more accepting of intermarriage and more welcoming of religious[20] and ethnic diversity in their neighborhoods.

These same young adults also tend to think more in terms of the international or global church than their elders.[21] The churches, communities and workplaces of the emerging adult will continue to become more diverse in terms of gender, race, religious affiliation and nationality. Emerging adults will wonder how to relate tolerantly yet hold firm in their beliefs. They may struggle to articulate distinctive aspects of their faith in contrast to other belief systems. They might also wonder if it's acceptable to be inspired by the practices of someone from another religion or culture or if that will compromise their own beliefs, background or heritage. Smith describes this aspect of the emerging adult effectively:

> Religious faith, community involvement, and personal practices are all sorted out one way or another in this larger process of struggling to balance differentiation, consolidation, and integration of relations, identities, goals, and resources. Often an uncomfortable unevenness typifies this period, as emerging adults pursue lives with one foot in what seems like helpless dependence and another in what feels like complete autonomy and total responsibility. Most of them are at pains to keep open as

many options as possible, to honor all forms of social and cultural diversity without judgment or even evaluation, and as quickly as possible to get on the road to autonomous self-sufficiency. Little of that encourages them to put down roots within particular religious communities that engage in committed faith practices.[22]

A disciplemaker will understand this increasingly diverse landscape of the maturing emerging adult.

In light of all this, what might it look like to encourage young adults to pursue the Christlife in the daily details of their lives?

THE CHRISTLIFE IN DAILY LIFE

No one wants to spend their life on something that seems meaningless or unimportant. In truth, though, life is spent one minute at a time; what we do with each minute of our lives ultimately becomes how we spend our life. Christ's vision for "spending" our life is for us to use each moment as an opportunity to deepen the Christlife. No moment captured for Christ, no matter how mundane the task, is wasted in the economy of God's kingdom.

Over the last year I (Rick) have watched Teresa press into a deeper understanding of and commitment to the biblical principle of the sabbath. Some days I wished that she had chosen to explore just about anything other than the sabbath. Nothing convicts me more of my "do first, be later" approach to life than watching her sit with Jesus and listen quietly enough to hear his very heartbeat. Often while I'm busy "doing things for God," she is being captured by his heart for her—which means she's much more effective at discerning which things God is actually asking her to do for him. (I have a lot to learn!)

Krista and Chuck as well as Sarita have fallen into the trap of spending their lives on urgent deadlines. Like a person balancing on a wire, each of them is constantly adjusting, trying to regain some sense of equilibrium, hoping desperately not to slip under the stress of constant movement and instability. Each of them has become, in Eugene Peterson's words, "Sabbath breakers." Rather than living out of the reservoir of the Christlife, they are constantly drained dry because their lives demand more than their shallow inner worlds can provide.

The more hurried, stressed or overwhelmed a person becomes the more vulnerable they are to the seductions of distraction, consumption and possibly even addiction. As one nineteen-year-old remarked, "I don't want to sit still or be quiet—if I do I will have to think about how bad my life is." What a contrast to God's intent. In Ecclesiastes, Solomon observes,

> There is nothing better for a person than that he should eat and drink and find enjoyment in his toil. This also, I saw, is from the hand of God, for apart from him who can eat or who can have enjoyment? For to the one who pleases him God has given wisdom and knowledge and joy, but to the sinner he has given the business of gathering and collecting, only to give to one who pleases God. This also is vanity and a striving after wind. . . .
>
> Behold, what I have seen to be good and fitting is to eat and drink and find enjoyment in all the toil with which one toils under the sun the few days of his life that God has given him, for this is his lot. Everyone also to whom God has given wealth and possessions and power to enjoy them, and to accept his lot and rejoice in his toil—this is the gift of God. For he will not much remember the days of his life because God keeps him occupied with joy in his heart. (Eccles 2:24-26; 5:18-20)

The enjoyment of daily life is a gift from God. Accepting our place in life—whatever that place may be—is the beginning point of cultivating the joy the Father intended. Emerging adults are, by nature, goal-focused: build a career, find a mate, get that advanced degree, start a savings account, buy a condo. However, when these goals become the driving force, hurriedness and busyness soon overcome joy. Many an emerging adult has put off embracing life in order to achieve or consume or accumulate, only to find later that the payoff of a postponed life is often prolonged pain.

On the reverse side, there is an *abuse* of the sabbath principle when an emerging adult confuses the idea of rest and renewal with being constantly preoccupied with leisure activities (video games, movies, "hanging out") or with adopting an unproductive, noncommittal approach to work. Capturing each day for the glory of God cannot be experienced by someone who settles for that kind of lifestyle.

John Ortberg once asked his congregation, "What is the most important moment of your life?" After a pause, Ortberg answered his own question: "Right now. That is the most important moment for all of us."

Ortberg's point was as profound as it was simple. The key to life is connecting our heart and mind and body to Christ. Right now is the only moment in which we have an opportunity to connect to him. The past is gone, and the future has neither arrived nor been guaranteed. Emerging adults need the gift of learning to connect to Christ in each moment and enjoy with him the real life they find themselves in. Simply stated, they (like so many of us, if we're honest) need to learn the art of being present in the present; it is the only moment any of us really have.

SHEPHERDING WITH DISCERNMENT, INTENTIONALITY AND REFLECTION

Case study: Sally (33) and Barb (60). Sally married at the age of twenty-one, worked for six years as a registered nurse and then quit to have children. Her kids are six and four-and-a-half years old. She loves being a mom, but feels badly about her relief over the fact that her eldest is gone for a full day at school and her youngest for part of the day at pre-school. Her husband, Caleb, is an involved and caring dad. Their marriage seems better than ever, especially since they have both learned to ask for what they need from the other. Overall, the thirties are better than Sally imagined they would be, and she hopes they will keep getting better. She's been dreaming of the day when both her kids are in school all day and pondering whether or not to go back to nursing. What would it be like to balance being a mom with succeeding as a professional? She wants her life to be lived meaningfully . . . but she isn't always sure what that looks like in this new phase in her life.

Barb is the leader of the young moms' small group that Sally is part of. She has two children: a daughter, who is living in another state pursuing a career, and a son, who is getting his master's degree at a nearby university. A stay-at-home mom when her kids were little, she returned to work once they were in school all day. Though Sally and Caleb have talked at some length about the possibility of her returning to nursing, she also wanted to ask Barb if she'd be willing to meet so she could get the perspective of a woman who had already gone through the transition from full-time mom to career mom.

Initial discernment. Barb felt honored that Sally wanted to meet with her one-on-one to discuss some life-stage issues. She knew a lot about

Sally already from their small-group interactions, but she needed to understand more specifically what Sally wanted help with. Since they already had an established relationship, she made a personalized mini-questionnaire and sent it to Sally over email. Sally was thrilled to have the opportunity to think and answer the questions on her own time. They set up a meeting for the following week, and Barb committed to praying for ten minutes each day in anticipation of how God might want to use their time together.

Intentional strategy 1. Through the questions she asked, Barb learned that Sally was looking at the possibility of reengaging in a career but that she felt anxious about whether she could continue to be the kind of parent she wanted to be while pursuing nursing. She was aware that it would require greater focus and determination to reach her goals. She was also nervous about how she might deal with time-management challenges that would arise with added responsibilities. When Barb and Sally met, then, the first thing they did was to clarify Sally's career aspirations and parenting goals. Barb shared how frustrating it had been for her at that age to try to *balance* all her life components, and how the Lord had shifted her thinking toward living a life that was *centered and ordered* by her times with him. They began to talk about how to seek the Father's wisdom for aspirations and goals as well as daily life choices. For the next several weeks, they evaluated priorities and sought to surrender each area to God. Then they brainstormed how Sally might handle time challenges with work, marriage and parenting. Specifically, they worked on finding strategies that would enable Sally to look to the Lord for wisdom in those challenges.

Reflection/discernment. After several months of meeting for coffee, Barb tried to imagine the answers Sally would give now to the original questions she had asked her. This was a great exercise to evaluate Sally's growth. And, though Barb was excited to realize that there had indeed been growth, she was also alerted to the fact that an underlying area was still unaddressed.

Intentional strategy 2. The next time they met, Barb asked Sally how she felt about her *present* circumstances. They had spent so much time working through future concerns that they had neglected to address today. Sally admitted that her tendency to dream about the future was partly because she felt unfulfilled as a mom of young children. They began to pray together for a greater experience of the Lord's embrace for her life. Through that, Sally began to change how she approached her everyday life. She felt less of a pull to constantly dream about changing her current situation. And she refocused her perspective on this season of parenting young children, seeing it as a time to experience and explore a different facet of fulfilling the Father's will by loving her small children instead of seeing it as a tedious delay of her previous goals.

Reflection/discernment. Barb and Sally continued to meet and to peel back various layers of Sally's desires. In those precious times together, they shared a journey of seeking the Father's wisdom, learning to live in his embrace and committing themselves to seek the Father's will in how they loved their spouses and children.

MORE DISCERNMENT, INTENTIONALITY AND REFLECTION IDEAS

Sally and Barb started on a journey to help Sally clarify goals and meet upcoming challenges. Through that they began to share a similar journey of pursuing the Christlife. Here are other discernment, intentionality and reflection ideas for helping emerging adults through the challenges of daily life.

Discernment

- *Uncover hidden growth areas.* The press of daily life often conceals our deeper issues. It took a long time for José to see that pride was underneath all of his dissatisfaction at his job. We spent a lot of time working on trust and communication issues before I (Jana) recognized his hidden issue. It was only when transformation *didn't occur* after working on identified areas that he was ready to see and own the part that arrogance played in his discontent in the workplace environment. Search for the issue beneath recognized patterns where the emerging adult has not given the Lord access.

- *Ask pacing questions about their daily life.* Where is he succeeding in living the Christlife? Where is he failing? What would be the hardest thing about _____ for her to face right now? What all is he trying to balance in life? What would it look like for her to allow God to order her life on a daily basis?

- *Take time to discern areas of inconsistency in their daily attempts to live a Christ-centered life.* Examining how well or poorly the young adult actually lives out their commitments may help you identify unrealistic expectations they have or areas that are out of harmony. For example, if a postcollege emerging adult with an overly full schedule is trying to maintain a lifestyle no longer appropriate for her circumstances, telling her to cut back or slow down might be like trying to stop a moving train. Taking time to discern life patterns, however, allows you to thoughtfully reflect to them what you're seeing and provide a mirror that can help them decide what needs adjustment. Are they living a life that is *centered*—centered on responding in obedience to the Father in short-term as well as long-term decisions? A centered approach to living in the midst of our hectic world is more effective than trying to hold all things in balance. Jesus, the disciples, Paul—none of them appear to have lived with a tremendous amount of balance. This struggle is common to all stages of adulthood, so you can be discerning about your own life as well and then intentionally walk *with* young adults in discovering how to live Spirit-filled, centered lives marked by peace instead of haste.

Intentionality

- *Look for truth in God's world to connect to God's wisdom.* Jesus often used aspects of the world around him to help people understand spiritual truths. I (Jana) gardened with one young woman I was mentoring, and as we worked the soil and planted together, we reflected on the importance of making our "spiritual ground" hospitable for growth in our own lives. This gave us a chance to think and talk about where we were open to truth and where we were hardened to it. Using everyday life activities to address everyday life issues is often an effective strategy, and also models purposefulness in the ordinary.

- *Confront unwillingness in pursuing the Father's will in everyday decision making.* The issue may be stubbornness, self-focus or an overly busy life, but regardless, a refusal to look outside themselves or live according to their priorities is a character flaw that needs work. If disciples tell you that they value rest or that they believe that living like Christ means taking time apart with the Father but they fail to live accordingly, you must be willing to speak the truth in love to them. Loving confrontation opens the door to growth in becoming like Christ. As Paul notes in Ephesians, "Speak the truth in love, growing in every way more and more like Christ, who is the head of his body, the church" (4:15 NLT).

- *Refocus adults overwhelmed by transitional challenges on the availability of the Father's wisdom.* Young adulthood is a great time of life to make a renewed commitment to pursuing wisdom from Scripture, listening prayer and the perspective of other adults. Urge the emerging adults you mentor to do so. Strengthening a foundational trust in the Father and renewing the belief that *God is good* and that *God knows the best way for us to live* provide a critical base for the challenges of each new stage of education, career, family and community.

- *Empower them with needed skills for pursuing lifestyle, financial or career goals.* You don't need to be the one to teach these skills, but you should be on the lookout for resources and people to connect the emerging adult to. Each new transition brings with it the opportunity to examine old goals and develop new ones. As emerging adults redefine direction, encourage them to pursue goals that will help them reach their potential. Since becoming like Christ involves our whole self, how we steward our resources, conduct our relationships and order our time matter.

- *Invite young adults to embrace the present through meaningful commitments.* Choosing to serve in multigenerational or multicultural contexts can expand a vision for adulthood as well as provide the context for seeing beyond some of the all-consuming identity questions and decisions encountered in initiating adulthood. Encourage young adults to be willing to make a commitment—at least temporarily—for the good of another person(s). This enhances their ability to experience and embrace the opportunities they have in the present.

Reflection

- *Use a journal to keep track of how God is working.* There is no right or wrong way to journal as a reflective exercise. You can record your thoughts in a journal, on a computer or on a digital recorder. For for-mat, you might journal the answers to a set of reflection questions or write out questions that come to mind about your interactions and encounters with the emerging adult. I (Jana) recorded my prayers in a journal for one woman I was mentoring. The act of slowing down enough to write out your thoughts facilitates reflection, and taking time periodically to look back over what you have written will further maximize your ability to see God at work or discover recurring patterns that need to be addressed. In this case, it was a joy to be able to sit with her later and share this prayer journal with her, looking back on decisions she was facing about further education and relationship possibilities. We were able to review and revisit how God had answered prayers in her daily decisions regarding her future.

- *Help emerging adults recognize stability and new limitations as a gift, not a curse.* Especially as they enter the thirties, emerging adults become aware of their limitations in a new way. Whether the limitation is physical, emotional, relational or circumstantial, take time to discuss the hidden blessing that may be behind it. Search for God's perspective. Paul appears to have lived with a physical limitation that he ultimately learned to accept (see 2 Cor 12). Jesus lived with emotional and physical limitations (after all, he was in his thirties during his major ministry push!); his limitations drew him to regroup in quiet with his Father. We all have limitations in our abilities and gifts put there on purpose by God to draw us to each other (Rom 12; Eph 4) and to himself. Discuss career, evangelistic and relational benefits that can bring new or deeper opportunities. St. Anthony once told someone desiring to follow Christ: "Always have God before your eyes; whatever you do, always do it according to the testimony of the holy Scriptures; *in whatever place you live, do not easily leave it.*"[23] An interesting piece of advice to consider in our mobile society! Help emerging adults reflect on the manifold potential of stability in neighborhoods, jobs or churches instead of seeing themselves as stuck when they reach a more settled phase of adulthood.

- *Reflect with emerging adults on a vision for purposeful living in everyday circumstances.* Being purposeful in the details of our lives, such as how we love a neighbor, serve our spouse or listen to a coworker experiencing turmoil, can be as powerful in building the kingdom of God as leading a spiritual rally for Christ. As young adults approach thirty, youthful dreams may need to be released (either forever or for a time), so understanding the eternal impact *each day* holds is critical. Ask them to reflect on and write out a vision for their everyday life. Or ask them to identify time wasters that keep them from living purposefully. Discuss and lift these up to God together.

WANTED: SPIRITUAL RISK-TAKERS

Wherever Elias was in a room, he had a presence. A twenty-four-year-old student studying for vocational ministry, this young Englishman spoke with sincerity and passion as he unfolded his vision for his life to me (Rick). He lived among the desperately poor of east London, serving as a volunteer pastoral ministry leader in a church committed to imbedding the love of Christ in its impoverished neighborhood. His less-than-five-years-old church had already planted two churches in other parts of east London, and he looked ahead to the day when he would launch another church plant. Newly married, gifted, confident, filled with hope and opportunity, Elias just made me smile.

I remember being at Elias's stage of life. I remember all the hope and opportunity that lay ahead. A quarter of a century later, I'm even more hopeful and excited than I was then. I have a greater sense of both my gifting and why God called that giftedness into being in his kingdom. I experience a deeper sense of confidence as well, though it is much more centered in Christ than myself as compared to twenty-five years ago. The intervening years, however, have been an incredible challenge. Career changes, health issues, multiple graduate degrees, miscarriages, babies born, adoption, failed adoption, moving from the South to Chicago and back to the South, leaving academia for the local church, raising three teenagers who are completely different from each other—none of it has not been easy. Nor will it be for Elias. Nor should it be.

Jesus was straightforward with the disciples: *In this world you will have many troubles,* he told them (see Jn 16:33). Sadly, our prosperous Western culture has too often communicated the view that God's blessing translates into an "easy life." Emerging young adults, in order to mature spiritually, must come to understand that God is not a parent who feels compelled to give us a "soft" life. The apostle Paul said that being a disciplemaker was like being a hard-working farmer, an athlete and a soldier—not exactly professions for the weak! But what a day when the crops come in, when the gold medal is hung around your neck, when captured cities are liberated. The "prize," however, is always won through a long-suffering journey fueled by vision and disciplined commitment.

Ernest Shackleton's leadership of his stranded crew following a failed attempt to cross Antartica in 1914 provides a compelling picture of this. Much of the credit for the survival of all twenty-seven crewmembers can be directly attributed to Shackleton's demeanor and decision making, but without a doubt survival was also possible because of the type of men Shackleton had recruited for the journey. His dubious recruitment simply read,

> Men wanted for hazardous journey. Small wages. Bitter cold. Long months of complete darkness. Constant danger. Safe return doubtful. Honour and recognition in case of success.[24]

Five hundred responded to the invitation. Why? Because we were made for adventure! We, like Elias, were created to risk our hearts on the goodness and greatness of our God. We, like Shackleton's men, have not been guaranteed ease and comfort but rather a chance at being a small part of something much greater than ourselves. Following Jesus is not easy, but there is no greater adventure—and that adventure is lived out in our everyday experiences. Emerging adults who have responded to his simple call to "follow me" have signed up for something risky— even in the midst of the ordinary. The great adventure is also the disciplemaker's journey as they walk alongside emerging adults—often in seemingly ordinary ways. Both the emerging adult and the disciplemaker risk and persevere in large and small ways to follow the One who calls them, as both have attached themselves to a leader who, in the words of C. S. Lewis, is not safe but who is good.

PART THREE

Emerging Adults

and Their Disciplemakers

THE JOURNEY OF
THE ADULT DISCIPLEMAKER

RECENTLY SOMEONE CALLED me (Rick) to ask if I would speak at his church's weeklong retreat. As part of discerning whether or not I should do it, I asked a number of questions. When he told me that I would be speaking eight times in the space of five days, I was pretty sure God was not calling me to this opportunity. Reflection over time has helped me understand my own capacities as well as the kind of speaker and teacher I am. For me, teaching is highly relational and requires a great deal of energy. Teaching eight times would've left me without any energy to connect with people before or after I taught—and for me that's essential. So I declined, freed to accept other opportunities more geared to how God has wired me. A decade ago, I might have made a different choice.

Students at my (Jana's) college regularly approach me for mentoring. I take time to pray and ask the Spirit for wisdom, but I also ask them what they're looking for in a mentor, listening to see if my strengths match up with their needs. And I share with them how I'm best equipped to help others grow. Many times we have together come to the conclusion that another person would serve them more effectively, and I help them find that person. Occasionally God overrides this process—and I cooperate with that too.

Looking back, both of us have gone through several phases as ministers. At first, we thought we were supposed to be Superman or Superwoman by taking every opportunity and doing everything well within each opportunity. In the second phase, we discovered we were *not* superheroes and began to wonder if we brought anything of value to the table. In our current phase, we are more at peace, knowing what gifts we bring to ministry that work really well, but also aware that we lack some gifts and abilities. We have learned to reflect on the challenges of our current phase of life in order to more fully understand what can be brought to the disciplemaking process. Those areas where we're weak are not as much deficits to us any more as they are occasions to invite and empower others to complete what we're lacking. Or they are opportunities for us to lean more deeply into one or more of the postures of the Christlife as we negotiate life-stage challenges.

Adult disciplemakers need time to reflect on the challenges and capacities of their current life stage so they can effectively channel their energy to make a difference for the kingdom. Then, as they learn to cooperate with God and yield to the refining process inherent in disciplemaking, they will be able to move boldly on the journey toward living the Christlife alongside young adults. In this chapter, we hope to help you get a stronger handle on your own journey as a mentor so that you can maximize your ability to shape and *be shaped by* the disciplemaking process.

JOURNEY MARKERS FOR DISCIPLEMAKERS

Each stage of adulthood is different from the next, whether in small or large ways—or at least it *should* be! Adult disciplemakers should not be just like the emerging adults they mentor. If they are, they're likely either not maturing or not paying attention to the changes that come with age. Erik Erikson wrote:

> If we speak of a cycle of life we really mean two cycles in one: the cycle of one generation concluding itself in the next, and the cycle of individual life coming to a conclusion. If the cycle, in many ways, turns back on its own beginnings, so that the very old become again like children, the question is whether the return is to a childlikeness with wisdom—or to a finite childishness. This is not only important within the cycle of individual life, but also within that of generations, for it can only weaken the vital fiber of the younger generation if the evidence of daily living verifies man's prolonged last phase as a sanctioned period of childishness. Any span of the cycle lived without vigorous meaning, at the beginning, in the

middle or at the end, endangers the sense of life and the meaning of death in all whose life stages are intertwined.[1]

How then can adult disciplemakers live with *vigorous meaning* in their current life stage? The first way is by recognizing some markers for their stage of the journey so that potential hindrances can become assets.

Markers of established adulthood. We love this quote in George Eliot's novel *The Mill on the Floss:*

> The middle-aged, who have lived through their strongest emotions, but are yet in the time when memory is still half passionate and not merely contemplative, should surely be a sort of natural priesthood, whom life has disciplined and consecrated to be the refuge and rescue of early stumblers and victims of self-despair. Most of us, at some moment in our young lives, would have welcomed a priest of that natural order.[2]

The adult disciplemaker in what we are choosing to call the "established" years of adulthood (ages thirty-five to sixty) does indeed have the makings of a "natural priesthood." We have been disciplined and consecrated, as Eliot reflects, by God's hand in our life experiences; we see life in broader categories, understand perspectives we only knew as shadows when we were younger and have a better grasp of the finite nature of our time on earth. These can be the most productive years of our lives.

In a book about the passages of adulthood, Gail Sheehy uses descriptive terms for the decades of this "established" stage: "The Flourishing Forties," "The Fearless Fifties" and "The Influential Sixties." She sees forty-five to sixty-five as the "age of mastery."[3] Though we might initially focus on the challenges of growing older, her positive take on the potential of this stage of life should give us pause. God calls us to fearlessly flourish in our abiding and fruit bearing! Some positive journey markers that characterize established adulthood include abandoning our scripts, negotiating time demands, "launching" children, embracing limitations and beginning a legacy.

Abandoning our scripts. My (Rick) initial middle-adult years were the most tumultuous years of my life. During this period, we added two sons to our family, one by adoption and one by surprise following a miscarriage. Our first son, Zach, was chronically ill for the two years that preceded Ben's birth. I left my role as a seminary professor in Chicago, Illinois, to take a church pastoral staff position that had an uncertain future in Knoxville, Tennessee. I severely injured my back, spending months in intense pain while I was still teaching at the seminary in the Chicago area and working in Tennessee on the weekends. I had back surgery at the same time our seventeen-year-old niece who was homeless came to live with us—and then move with us. We left behind our closest friends and both of our chosen professions to go to Knoxville. We struggled with financial challenges as a result of the additional children and the unanticipated move. Once in Knoxville I realized that the position at the church would be more short-term than I had thought, and entered into a period of absolute vocational discouragement. Teresa and I were just coming out of a tough period of being relationally isolated from one another in response to the stresses we were experiencing. Eventually the church entered into a very difficult season, and I emerged on the other end as the interim lead pastor and ultimately the permanent lead pastor, a role I assumed at forty-two years old, with no prior lead-pastoral experience, for a church in deep pain from its transition. That prompted about 30 percent of the people to depart immediately, sending a once thriving large church reeling into a downward spiral of negative momentum. What a welcome to midlife I had!

And yet, what an incredibly gracious gift from God all of this was in my life. It certainly didn't feel that way then, and the "bigger picture" reality I have now doesn't take away the pain of the process. But through all of this—and more, much more—God pried my grip loose from my role as "scriptwriter" (being my own god) and led me to a place of releasing my heart into his hands as my God. I often summarize the experience as God saying to me, "Now that we have seen what you can do with your life, would you like to see what I can do with it?"

Disciplemaking during the established-adult years requires reflecting on our life patterns and recognizing the story that God is writing. Parts of the story will be *through* these patterns and parts will be *in spite of* these patterns. With some of the energy and vitality of young adulthood still present but also a growing self-awareness and life wisdom from experience, established adults are well poised to help young adults anxious in the midst of multiple transitions to comprehend through Scripture, the Spirit, Christ's body in community and their own experiences that he is one who can be trusted with our scripts. Engaging in these established-adult years with an eye toward abandoning our scripts for God's script is a crucial component of spiritual maturity that prevents the disciplemaker from stunting the spiritual fruit that God has intended to grow with increasing abundance as life progresses.

Negotiating the squeeze of time. Amber, forty-four, is a mom—by anyone's definition. Nurturing and providing environments of care are like breathing for her. First and foremost she's a mom to her three children—two high schoolers and a college student. At church, Amber, being a single mom herself, leads a small group of twentysomething single moms who live in a nearby apartment complex. For these less experienced and much more overwhelmed moms, she feels like having a mom they can turn to for support is important. She is also the team mom for at least one sport each season of the year. She has washed more uniforms and served at more team fundraisers than she can remember. When she shows up for school sporting events or concerts or special assemblies, she's still amazed by how many of the students yell, "Hey, Mrs. Z, how you doin'?" Several of them do not even call her Mrs. Z; they just call her "mom."

Amber loves being a mom, but in her heart of hearts she had thought that she would carry a broader title than this by age forty-four. An avid reader and a gifted writer, she had once dreamed of writing novels about the lives of women who faced and overcame great odds through difficult historical periods like the Civil War era and the Great Depression. The lead characters, including their dreams and fears, still occupy a silent part of Amber's mind. When she actually has some peace and quiet—quite rare for this "super-mom"—they come to life, and she longs to give voice to their passionate struggles to keep faith alive in the midst of hopelessness. In the end, however, thinking about writing just makes her sad, because she realizes that choosing to write would mean sacrificing the investment she has chosen to make in her children, her church and her community. Still, in the midst of her daily journal writings, she often wonders whether there could ever be some alternative option and fantasizes about a world in which she cares well for her children, invests in the lives of young adults transitioning to adulthood *and* writes a novel.

She intentionally empowers the dreams of others—but what is she supposed to do with her own dreams?

One developmental theorist characterizes the earlier years of established adulthood as a time in which life's demands cause adults to feel overwhelmed by all that needs to be done: "The time squeeze is not only felt at work but also in relationship with their children with whom they are fast losing influence."[4] Though emerging adults also feel the time crunch, established adults have extra challenges as they navigate the added work responsibilities that come with career advancement or struggle with raising teenagers. Time with teenagers tends to happen on the teen's terms, giving parents the nearly impossible task of being readily available. And even when teens are not present, the time spent worrying about them can be draining.

The time squeeze is not just felt by established adults with children, however. Single adults in this stage of life are often at a point in their careers where much is demanded from them; with more expertise and connections, they're often asked to contribute on more fronts. In addition, church leaders frequently assume that single adults in this stage have more availability than adults with children and therefore press them to contribute to multiple ministry efforts. And for both single and married adults, this is often the time when their parents begin to decline and need extra help from adult children.

David wrote in Psalm 39, "LORD, remind me how brief my time on earth will be. Remind me that my days are numbered—how fleeting my life is" (v. 4 NLT). Amber, like David, is beginning to realize that our time on earth is not unlimited, and is wondering, as established adults commonly do, if she can accomplish all she wants to or feels called to before it's over. What a perfect condition to help us realize that we are *not* like God, whose time is unlimited. In the book of Job, Elihu exclaims, "Look, God is greater than we can understand. His years cannot be counted" (36:26 NLT). Emerging adulthood can be a time of embracing our need for dependence on our Father as we come to terms with the limits of our time on earth. Amber needs the daily wisdom of the Father in order to choose what to attend to or how to reorganize her dreams; he can lead her to what is eternal and lasting as well as help her let go of what is superfluous. As disciplemakers, the challenge of the time squeeze can also prompt us to use our time with young adults wisely, purposefully encouraging them toward the postures of the Christlife.

Launching children and the postlaunching period. For established adults who are parents, these years contain the sometimes harrowing task of preparing children to be independent: teens are differentiating, college-age students may leave for school and young adults may strike out on their own. Established adults are left to figure out the steps to the dance that occurs when a child goes away to college: How much support should they give and how much should they withhold in order for their child to learn functional independence? To the extent that an emerging adult is able to receive a parent's encouragement in developing holistic postures of the Christlife, that parent *is* a disciplemaker in their son's or daughter's life. During these transitional years, the key task for established-adult parents is to learn to relate to their children *as* adults.

The postlaunching period begins when children are successfully launched (though boomerang returns because of the economy may mean a parent has to "relaunch" their child at some point). A "role loss" may occur at this time if an individual's or couple's sense of identity has come primarily from parenting.[5] Parents must learn to refocus energy on their marriage as well as develop good relationships with their adult children's spouses and kids. While it may not be a good idea to "replace" your parenting role with the role of disciplemaking just so that an emerging adult will look to you in a way you wish your children still would, it *is* a good idea to take advantage of the space created by a "role loss" to invest in the next generation.

Embracing limitations. A friend of mine (Jana's) in his early forties loved to make light of the changes he was experiencing in his body. "Look at these amazing nose and ear hairs I'm sprouting," he would say. Or, "How do you like my imitation of a young man with energy?" he'd ask after dropping to the ground, exhausted, after doing some yard work. I appreciated his willingness to acknowledge the decline we all feel in the established-adult years. Daniel Levinson explains that often men do not embrace those changes nearly as graciously.

> In his late thirties and early forties a man falls well below his earlier peak levels of functioning. He cannot run as fast, lift as much, do with as little sleep as before. His vision and hearing are less acute, he remembers less

well and finds it harder to learn masses of specific information. He is more prone to aches and pains and may undergo a serious illness that threatens him with permanent impairment or even death. . . . The decline is normally quite moderate and leaves a man with ample capacities for living in middle age. But it is often experienced as catastrophic.[6]

Women, in turn, may struggle with the media-created expectation that they should always look young and fresh—no matter what their age. In established adulthood, both men and women are coming to terms with physical, relational and practical limitations. Roger Gould identifies the period of forty-three to fifty as "a settling-down stage in which people learn to accept the limitations imposed by time and destiny."[7] Sheehy similarly observes, "The crucial innings of second adulthood are neither played by the same rules nor scored in the same way as a young man's game."[8]

However, both technology and medical advances are allowing men and women to live longer, more active lives; today an adult in their forties is really only halfway through the average life span. And though it's true that established adults experience a tangible decline in capacities and capabilities, typically they only have to make some adjustments (such as the focus or pace of life) to accommodate those changes. The sooner this is realized, the more fruitful and productive the second half of adulthood can be. And this kind of focused productivity can be instructive for emerging adults. With the number of options they're trying to juggle and the difficulty many of them have in acknowledging new limits in their capacities as *they* age, seeing an established adult embrace limits and refocus energy can provide valuable insight they can apply to their own challenges.

Beginning to focus on legacy. Alex, fifty-one, is a builder, in every sense of the word. He owns his own construction company—which he built from the ground up—and has a reputation as a builder whose work is of the highest quality and whose word is of the highest integrity. Alex also works hard at building a financial future for his wife and three children (two of whom haven't gone to college yet), especially given the fickle economic nature of the construction industry.

Beneath all of these layers of "building," Alex is "becoming" as well. Having established the foundations of his adult life relationally, professionally and financially, he is now becoming increasingly aware of who he is and who he is not. And he's confronting the reality that, for all of the building he's done, the real "stuff" of life that God intends for him to enjoy is found in relationships. For all the good that his work brings, it also poses a threat. Not kept in check, his "building" would consume his real life of relationships with his wife, children, church family and friends. He therefore struggles with what it means to be a successful business owner and an effective spouse, father and friend. In his more reflective moments he wonders how he can make loving God and loving others his top priority and still find the emotional energy to deal with the demands of leading his employees. Alex loves being a builder; some days it frightens him how much he loves it.

Established adulthood finds Alex pondering the lasting effect of his life. Levinson notes about this life stage, "The meaning of legacy deepens and the task of building a legacy acquires its greatest developmental significance. . . . This will add both to the personal fulfillment of individual adults and to the quality of life for succeeding generations."[9] It makes sense that God calls adults in this stage to enhance their legacy through disciplemaking relationships! As an established single adult with no children, I (Jana) find great fulfillment in knowing that I am able to leave a rich legacy of faith in the lives of the emerging adults I have been privileged to mentor over the past several decades. They are my hope, my joy, my reward and my crown (1 Thess 2:19)!

Ephesians 2:10 tells us that we are "[God's] workmanship, created in Christ Jesus for good works, which God prepared beforehand, that we should walk in them." The journey will include discovering what in our lives produces the most lasting impact. Rather than an early foreclosure on "this is what I'm good at," we need to be encouraged toward an openhearted willingness to be surprised by who God is calling us to be and how he might be calling us to make a difference in the life of an emerging adult.

In Alex's life, an "open-hearted willingness" eventually led him to create space to invest deeply in a few young men. They're being discipled in the art of spiritually building others up as well as in the trade of building a successful company. Alex's legacy will therefore be much more than a financially successful business, as it now includes several young men who are inheriting the spiritual wealth of his growing vision to make disciples in the midst of his workplace relationships.

Markers of seasoned adulthood. It's being predicted that in 2040 over 20 percent of all the people in the United States will be sixty-five or older.[10] At the same time, social observers note that people are taking much, much longer to grow old in traditional ways—they are working longer as well as staying active and adventurous.[11] Many of them will be single (either never married or widowed[12]) and will be pondering how to spend the twilight years. Seasoned adults often have the unique opportunity to *choose* how they spend their latter years. Investing in the next generation of Christ-followers is one of the most significant choices they can make.

Consider Lloyd Dees. At eighty-eight years young, he visits shut-ins, the grieving and hospital-bound patients and also teaches Sunday school. He has embraced seasoned adulthood as a time of freedom in giving instead of having the right to relax and receive. He says, "Spiritual maturity is giving to others and letting go of your own wants and needs."[13] Like Lloyd, the seasoned adult disciplemaker is venturing into this stage of life deciding how to use new arenas of freedom even as they navigate new limitations. Journey markers for the seasoned adult include the opportunity to reinvent themselves in retirement, a shift from temporal to eternal concerns, and a deepening legacy.

Reinventing ourselves in retirement. Studies show there is great variation as to the degree of satisfaction with retirement.

> Men can experience it as a great reward, withdrawal from workaholic tendencies, or the absence of a fulfilling objective. In contrast, by their retirement age most women have developed a rich network of intimate relationships with family and friends. Thus the retirement years offer the opportunity to enjoy these relationships. . . . Many men, on the other hand, can claim to be intimate only with their wife, meaning they must learn to cultivate relationships beyond the world of work.[14]

Women tend to be less unsettled by retirement since they're used to leading lives characterized by significant change; many move in and out of work and domestic realms in their adult years, and have learned already that even immense changes (like pregnancy and childbirth) can bring good results.[15]

Sheehy notes that with thirty or more years to fill up *after midlife,* there's plenty of time for both men and women to reinvent themselves. What an opportunity to make "the decades after 40 the most exciting and deeply meaningful of all," she adds.[16] The freedoms of retirement provide the possibility of a greater focus on building God's kingdom by helping emerging adults live out the Christlife in their world.

A shift from temporal to eternal. The bad news is that many older Americans are staying tethered to the temporal. An article called "Old Is the New Young" cites studies that reveal that many sixtysomethings are still consuming in similar ways to how they did in their youth (buying motorcycles, rock music and video games, for example), maintaining "adolescent" values of purchasing.[17] By contrast, in this passage from Philippians, Paul shows that he is drawn by the eternal and yet understands the privilege of living a life of trusting God with others.

> As long as I'm alive in this body, there is good work for me to do. If I had to choose right now, I hardly know which I'd choose. Hard choice! The desire to break camp here and be with Christ is powerful. Some days I can think of nothing better. But most days, because of what you are going through, I am sure that it's better for me to stick it out here. So I plan to be around awhile, companion to you as your growth and joy in this life of trusting God continues. You can start looking forward to a great reunion when I come visit you again. We'll be praising Christ, enjoying each other. (Phil 1:22-26 *The Message*)

Like Paul, Davie Hill has perspective on what is important in life. She's been attending the same church for sixty-eight years and says, "My advice to people in this [upcoming] generation is to have a strong relationship with the Lord."[18] At ninety-three years old, Davie has seen so much and knows what counts in the overall scheme of things. The temporal is trumped by the eternal. Cliff Myers knows this as well. As a man who has lived for 102 years on this earth, his priorities have been shaped by what he's experienced: "Your character is your most important attribute. It will follow you for life."[19] He could have added, "and into eternity." Davie and Cliff know what lasts and what doesn't and are the kind of adults the authors of *The Reciprocating Self* call a "spiritually mature individual," someone who is an empowerer of others, seeking to invest him or herself in others rather than needing to be served by others. The mature elderly person is able to combine the strengths of separateness and independence with an interdependence and connectedness within a network of reciprocally caring others.[20]

Spiritually mature seasoned adults dream and reinvent themselves in ways that incorporate their understanding of the importance of the eternal in the temporal. As these adults order their lives to reflect that reality, they can also help emerging adults connect or evaluate their dreams according to the eternal. In a culture that insists that emerging adults consume all the latest technology or experience all that the world can offer before they "settle down," seasoned adults can bring perspective. Furthermore, they can experience the deep intimacy that comes when "individuals empower others in pursuit of their dreams," the authors of *The Reciprocating Self* explain. They add, "This does not mean abandoning one's own dream but having space in the relationship to empower one another's dreams as well as be close enough to dream together."[21] Eighty-eight-year-old Osborne Munroe experiences this as he mentors underprivileged kids. In fact, he still maintains a friendship with a man he mentored as a child who calls him "Dad." He says, "I am proud to be alive and able to help others."[22] The seasoned adult can empower emerging adults to pursue their own dreams and even continue to dream alongside of them.

Deepening the legacy. How do I want to be remembered? What legacy will I leave? Of all the stages of adulthood, seasoned adulthood is when we most focus on these questions. Some of us will look back over our life and feel disappointment in how those questions would be answered. But disappointment can be tempered with hope. It's never too late to leave a legacy by investing in the life of another. No matter what age or circumstance, the seasoned adult has something to offer. Erikson points out, "Wisdom . . . maintains and conveys the integrity of experience, in spite of the decline of bodily and mental functions. It responds to the need of the on-going generation for an integrated heritage."[23] Whether they can articulate it or not, emerging adults long for a heritage that is connected to something larger than themselves. Seasoned adults who are walking alongside young adults can provide that connection to a larger story—of their church, their neighborhood, their family or whatever context connects them—that began way before the young adult was born and will continue longer than they can presently fathom.

CHOOSING AN ETERNAL LEGACY
BY FOLLOWING THE BIBLICAL SCRIPT

I (Rick) turned fifty last year. There are several words and phrases that can describe this age: Half a century old. The "golden" year. Seasoned. AARP. From the perspective of my young congregation, though, the word is *old*. As I look backward and forward on my life, my career, my choices, I have several points that could be classified as "game-changing moments": experiences, conversations and choices that have significantly altered the course of the past fifty years. [24] One is a conversation I had during a class with my doctoral mentor, Dr. Ted Ward. I recently had an opportunity to share this game-changing moment with a group of men, all over forty, who had gathered together to become a community of disciplemakers for the next generation. Here is the story I told them:

"Publish or perish." As a young university professor I understood well that my future vocational success was closely tied to my capacity for publishing articles, chapters and books in my field. This pressure-filled knowledge was daily reinforced as I walked the hallways between my office and the classroom buildings. Along each faculty office corridor I would see on the office doors of my colleagues book covers or reviews proudly displaying their latest publishing accomplishments. One exception, however, was the most effective educator on the campus. Ted Ward, the head of the Ph.D. programs in education and missions, was the least published of all senior ranking professors. In fact, through all of my courses in my master's and doctoral programs in education, I had never read a book he had written. He had taught in over sixty countries, was the first American educator invited into Vietnam after the war and was on the UNICEF Year of the Child board. He was a distinguished professor emeritus of Michigan State University as well as the founder of the Ph.D. program in education for our university. But I had never read a book he had written!

In the midst of a dialogue between students and faculty one day, someone asked, "Dr. Ward, why have you not written more books?" His response shaped me profoundly then and still shapes me today. "Books," he replied firmly, "last for only a little while. Eventually they are sold for a quarter at some used book sale. People, however, are eternal. I chose to invest in the development of people who could develop others rather than in the writing of books that are temporary."

This may seem like a strange story to tell in a book I'm coauthoring! Obviously I see value in writing and reading books. However, since my time with Dr. Ward, I have made disciplemaking—investing in the lives of people—a much higher priority than writing books. My life reflects that value choice.

Dr. Ward taught three leadership principles that have shaped how I view the legacy of my life. First, *how a leader measures success determines how they invest their heart, time, gifts and resources.* In other words, how you keep score determines how you play the game. The investment of our lives in the lives of others—as family members, coworkers, coaches, neighbors, friends, teachers, etc.—for the glory of Christ is an eternal measure (score) of a well-lived life.

Second, Dr. Ward taught me that *when it comes to the effective use of a leader's gifts and resources, the "good" is always in competition with the "best."* So many things scream for our attention and time. Like the carnival "barkers" trying to draw a crowd into their tent, our culture calls to us, "Invest your life here. Get your personal sense of worth and meaning from this experience, this possession, or this accomplishment." Most experiences, possessions and accomplishments are not inherently good or bad, but if investing our lives in the next generation gets crowded out, we have settled for the lesser good. As a leader I use this simple progression to remind myself to invest in people, not stuff or tasks, as my first priority:

THERE ARE:

Hundreds of things that you COULD DO as a leader

Dozens of those hundreds of things that you COULD DO WELL as a leader

Several of those dozens of things that WOULD BE GOOD for you to do as a leader

Only one or two things, however, that you SHOULD BE DOING as a leader

Finally, Dr. Ward's commitment to discipling people taught me that *the biblical strategy for reproducing Christ's heart in the church and expressing Christ's heart in the world through the church is simple: Disciples entrusting their hearts and the gospel of Christ to other disciples who will in turn do the same for others.* The biblical "script" for our lives is not so much about whether we are teachers or surgeons, homemakers or coaches, leaders or managers; these are just roles we fill in the midst of a world where work is an essential component of our dignity as human beings who bear his image. And it's not about whether we are in emerging, established or seasoned adulthood; these are just stages of life we experience, hopefully with growing wisdom and grace, as we journey with Christ. The "script" God has written for each of us is one in which we're increasingly investing our hearts where he invests his heart: in the souls of the people he created for eternity. Of all the things that a person can do with his or her days, whether they be many or few, the one thing that God wills above all is the investment of the life of Christ in the lives of those who will in turn invest their lives in others. It was his plan fifty-one years ago and in all the years that preceded our births and has been his plan since the birth of the church in the first century. It will be his plan fifty-one years from now when we're gone (though Rick's great-grandmothers both lived to be over one hundred, so there may be more time for him than he thinks—or less). The only question that remains, daily, is whether we will choose the best by choosing to participate in the generational chain of eternal life experienced in the disciplemaker's journey.

POSTURES OF AN
EFFECTIVE DISCIPLEMAKER

WE (RICK AND JANA) had the privilege of partnering together for several years in teaching, training and discipling young adults preparing for vocational student ministries. Core to our philosophy of leadership development was this saying: "As you are, so will you lead." The idea, more explicitly, is that disciplemakers most effectively reproduce who they are and who they are becoming. Disciplemaking is intensely relational and intimately personal; it's not like crunching numbers or changing the oil in a car. The heart, the character and the spiritual life of the disciplemaker are the core "relational DNA" from which a disciplemaking relationship is born.

Therefore, while it's important to understand the challenges and opportunities inherent in your particular life stage, that's not the complete picture. Our life stage *and* our character must be submitted to the Master for use or for reshaping. We've been discussing how to encourage emerging adults to participate in the Christlife; we can do no less in our own lives. Disciplemakers must also live in a posture of trust, submission and love. A disciplemaker engaged with Christ in the pursuit of the Christlife is likely to create a relationship with a young-adult disciple that reflects these postures. Conversely, no matter how hard a person tries or how intentional they may be in their discipling, without being engaged with Christ in a relationship whereby these qualities are being formed, they're not likely to be used to foster these postures in the life of the young-adult disciple.

Near the end of his life of disciplemaking the apostle Paul wrote:

Not that I have already obtained this or am already perfect, but I press on to make it my own, because Christ Jesus has made me his own. Brothers, I do not consider that I have made it my own. But one thing I do: forgetting what lies behind and straining forward to what lies ahead, I press on toward the goal for the prize of the upward call of God in Christ Jesus. Let those of us who are mature think this way, and if in anything you think otherwise, God will reveal that also to you. Only let us hold true to what we have attained.

Brothers, join in imitating me, and keep your eyes on those who walk according to the example you have in us. (Phil 3:12-17)

As Paul exemplified, disciplemakers are to live out the postures of the Christlife in all stages and relationships of their life. Indeed, trust, submission and love are integral to our role and journey as disciplemakers.

TRUSTING: COOPERATING WITH GOD ON THE JOURNEY

Saundra was sharp, ministry-minded and proactive in how she walked with others in their transformation. Because she was intelligent and capable, she often looked forward to how things *should be* and moved ahead with purpose. But, though Saundra was good at seeing the goal, she was not as practiced at considering things from God's perspective. It was important for her to take time to examine how well she was cooperating with God on her journey with others. Her frustration in those relationships was lowered when she understood that progress was being made both *through her* and *beyond her: through her* in the cumulative impact that God was having as he used her gifts and efforts, and *beyond her* as she took time to see the work that *God* was doing in people's lives outside of her efforts. As disciplemakers, understanding the shape of our contribution helps us focus our efforts, but understanding the limits of our role from a spiritual standpoint raises our sights beyond ourselves to God. We must measure impact not by experience or worldly standards but as much as possible from a godly perspective—through his eyes and in his economy.

We feel compassion for Peter when we read about his encounter with Jesus in Mark 8. Jesus tells his disciples that he will suffer and be killed at the hands of the religious leaders. Steeped in his own limited perspective, Peter is sure that their mission can be successfully accomplished by a better method than death and suffering. He thinks he's doing the right thing when he reprimands Jesus for being such a downer! But Jesus very sternly says to Peter, "Get away from me, Satan! . . . You are seeing things merely from a human point of view, not from God's" (Mk 8:33 NLT). Cooperation with God in a disciplemaking relationship might include failure, suffering or disappointment—and that might actually be God's chosen way!

Keith Anderson and Randy Reese, in their book on spiritual mentoring, recommend that mentors "become trilingual in their listening skills."[1] By this they mean that disciplemakers should listen to (1) the stories and needs of the disciples, (2) the insight or promptings of the Holy Spirit, *and* (3) their own heart and instincts as mentors. The importance of the spiritual life of the mentor in the disciplemaking process cannot be understated. How can we make sure that our own heart and instincts are a positive factor in the mentoring experience? We must surrender to God by cooperating with his promptings, his design for us and our God-given limitations.

Trusting him first: Creating space for cooperating with God. The Lord's ways are superior to and often different from our ways, which means that the Lord's ways for a person we're mentoring may not mesh with the advice someone we trust has given us or a method we've come to rely on. As one author comments, *"It is easy to shift from faith in God to faith in a method or past experience."*[2] First Chronicles 14 records two encounters between the Israelites and the Philistines. In the first battle, King David followed God's commands precisely and led the Israelites to a great victory. When the Philistines rallied, David once again sought the Lord's will for his leadership. God's unexpected answer comes in verses 14-15: "Do not go straight up, but circle around them and attack them in front of the balsam trees. As soon as you hear the sound of marching in the tops of the balsam trees, move out to battle, because that will mean God has gone out in front of you to strike the Philistines" (NIV 1984).

This image of David is arresting. God told him to circle around the enemy and then sit and listen, when David's natural instinct was surely to head straight into the battle. Of all the ways God could have led, he chose to have David wait on him to show up.

In the new covenant we recognize that we now have God among us and within us. Our Immanuel, Jesus, left us with the presence of the Holy Spirit so that we don't have to wait for God to "show up." However, having God present and actually experiencing his presence are vastly different realities. Creating space to hear him helps us engage in spirit-to-Spirit dialogue and choose to be yielded to the filling presence of his Spirit. Instead of rushing into battle, we, like David, need to learn to slow our spirits and listen for his call.

Being by him requires a sacred conversation of life with God. The time-squeezed lifestyle our culture reinforces leaves little room for waiting under the trees, listening for God to move and learning to trust in his provision. Disciplining ourselves to make space is the art of yielding rather than the science of attaining. As disciplemakers, we must learn to create margins in our lives so that we can submit to being conformed by God. If we are not also striving to be conformed to him, do we really have lives worth emulating? Our own vitality in seeking to live the Christlife is nurtured as we make space to be "grasped" by the loving hands of our Father.

Our twenty-first-century souls have been beaten down by the wear and tear of our "objectifying" culture, so we should not expect creating space for continual renewing of our yieldedness to God to be easy—for us or for emerging adults. However, like water poured on the cracked soil of a farmer's fields, the living water of God's Spirit soon permeates even the driest of souls. As we enter sacred conversation in our dehydrated inner soil, we are passionately drawn to the Source of living water. We develop "irrigated" lifestyles that weather every season, including the longest of droughts.

Spiritual caregiving flows out of wells of deeply lived journeys with God. Those who excel at the external elements of caring for others while neglecting their own spiritual journeys face an impending personal implosion. But those who are themselves on a quest to surrender to the Lord in trust, drinking deeply of his care and learning to value what he loves, can anticipate a life of increasingly intimate relationship with the God they serve. Our own sacred conversation with him is the only means we have for inviting others to join us in dialogue with the God of our spiritual journeys.[3]

Trusting his design: Knowing yourself as a disciplemaker. Learning about yourself can be enjoyable. Look at all the "What color are you?" or "What Jane Austen/*Sesame Street* character/Ninja Turtle (etc.) are you?" tests people take on Facebook, for example! A highlight for many students in our Christian ministries department at Trinity International University is a class where they undergo tests and self-reflection exercises to reveal their personality, ministry passions and spiritual gifts. We don't give these tests because they're fun, though; we give them because they're important preparation for ministry. Knowing how God has wired you and gifted you to serve in the body of Christ allows your energy to be more efficiently focused and uncovers potential weak areas.

Entering into a disciplemaking relationship with the illusion that you can be "all things to all people" is a recipe for frustration and burnout. Taking time to reflect on your own particular ministry "shape" is therefore important. Otherwise disciplemaking can be like reaching into a toolbox blindfolded, grabbing whatever your hand touches and hoping that whether it's a hammer, wrench or screwdriver, it will drive the nail into the wall. Ephesians 4:16 reminds us that *every believer* is equipped in some *particular* way for disciplemaking: *"He makes the whole body fit together perfectly. As each part does its own special work, it helps the other parts grow, so that the whole body is healthy and growing and full of love"* (NLT). The search for godly self-understanding of your "own special work" to help others grow requires a lifestyle of listening to God as he paces with us. Spiritual gifts tests and personality tests may help begin the process,[4] but taking time to reflect on how God best uses us in the lives of others broadens the window through which we can discover our unique contribution to kingdom work. Trusting that design and learning how it applies to our relationships with emerging adults is a part of God's recipe for fruitful disciplemaking. As the authors of *The Reciprocating Self* observe, "To live according to God's design is to glorify God as a distinct human being in communion with God and others in mutually giving and receiving relationships."[5]

We wrote this book together precisely because we have learned to understand our weaknesses and lean into our strengths in facilitating growth in potential disciplemakers. Rick is best at establishing foundations—helping others gain a vision and understand the goal. He loves connecting abstract theological concepts of spiritual formation to life's realities through stories. On the other hand, Jana is best at providing clear categories and helping others understand specific steps for sharpening their God-given abilities. She likes giving examples and real-life illustrations that show people how those steps might look. Because we know ourselves, we understand both what we are most effective at providing and what we need others to supplement for us. In this book, we hope the combination of our strengths minimizes our weaknesses and provides a richer resource for others.

In disciplemaking, when we understand our weaknesses we become comfortable connecting young adults we're mentoring to others who can also help them grow (like Jim did with Lee in the case study for chapter seven). When we lean into our strengths, we can maximize the time we have with others. The net effect is that the whole body is "healthy and growing."

Nate and José were co-disciplemakers in a small group of eighteen- to twenty-two-year-olds. Nate was analytic, introverted, observant and a gifted listener. José was outgoing, energetic, an engaging speaker and good at situations that required an immediate response. They figured out that their ability to journey with their group of guys toward life transformation was enhanced by learning to make space for each other's gifts to be expressed within the leadership of the group.

Trusting beyond God-given limitations: Creating and Setting Healthy Boundaries. Healthy disciplemakers strive to understand where their responsibility stops and others' starts. Consider the example of Sylvie and Raymond. Sylvie experienced a myriad of emotional ups and downs as she mentored some of the young wives in her church. She got angry each time a husband misunderstood one of the wives and was elated when a communication breakthrough in a marriage occurred; she felt strongly tied to the hurts, successes and failures of her mentees.

Raymond often experienced dejection after his once-a-month meeting with the small group of young men he mentored. He believed he had the group focusing on the right things, was fostering an environment where transparency and accountability could take place, and was caring for the guys personally beyond the group. But it seemed like some of them never took steps forward in obedience. He felt a gnawing responsibility for their inaction.

Both Sylvie and Raymond need to develop stronger internal boundaries as spiritual leaders. Though their concern and emotional availability are admirable, understanding that they are not solely responsible for those they mentor is critical. Sylvie needs to recognize the difference between experiencing solidarity with the women she is helping and taking on their emotions. If she simply adopts their problems and successes, she won't be objective enough to speak into their situations. Raymond needs to realize that, although he has an important part to play in providing an environment and the encouragement needed for growth, the men in his group also play an essential role in their own growth process. We are called to create a rich environment for growth to occur, but God and those we mentor are responsible for their progress.

In *Caring Without Wearing*, Carol Travilla lists five unrealistic expectations of a spiritual caregiver:

1. I have the ability to change another person.
2. I have the capacity to help everyone.
3. There should never be any limits to what I can do.
4. I am the only person available to help.
5. I must never make a mistake.[6]

Our responsibility is *to* those we mentor, but not *for* them. Paul understood this, proclaiming in 1 Corinthians 3:6-7 (NLT),

> I planted the seed in your hearts, and Apollos watered it, but it was God who made it grow. It's not important who does the planting, or who does the watering. What's important is that God makes the seed grow.

Personal internal boundaries remind us that God is the primary disciplemaker.

HUMBLY SUBMITTING:
CHOOSING TO BE REFINED BY THE JOURNEY

> The computer makes us fantastically more able to calculate and analyze. It does not help us to meditate. We have instruments to enable us to see everything from the nebulae to the neutron—everything except ourselves.

We have immeasurably extended our gift of sight but not of insight.[7]

Insight is a product of the kind of humility that allows us to connect with reality. Humility is our key to being refined in the midst of disciple-making relationships. The journey we are on is a two-way street. Though God is intent on growing up emerging adults—in part through our efforts—he is also intent on growing us up! We will be refined by the disciplemaking journey as we learn to value it, lean into pain and brokenness, and enter into our relationships authentically.

Humbly valuing our journey. Robert knew how to value the spiritual journey of others; he did not know how to value his own. When I (Rick) first met him, he was on fire for God and intent on making disciples for the kingdom. However, lacking a sufficient experience of God's unconditional love for him, Robert failed to place high value on his own physical, emotional and relational needs. He neglected to develop the habit of self-reflection, so *he did not even see* the burgeoning distance between his zeal for serving and his zeal for God, and became deaf to the Voice calling him, as God's beloved, to the intimacy of sacred, whole-person conversation. Eventually it caught up with him. Empty, tired and spiraling toward personal peril, he spiritually imploded and sought refuge in an adulterous relationship. It broke my heart to hear that he left his wife and children as well as a vibrant ministry to pursue a relationship with a younger woman.

Jeff VanVonderen suggests that the root of such personal devaluing and "dysgrace" can be found in shame. Shame causes men and women to be driven in vain to find "the one button that's going to make God smile."[8] Symptomatic of this shame is a lack of genuine self-care. Sacrificing quality of life for quantity of achievement in an attempt to earn love, shame-based disciplemakers even fool themselves into thinking that ignoring self-care represents a holy sacrifice to God.

The mind, emotions, will and body are integrally connected. In harmony with one another, these distinct yet interrelated components constitute the context within which our souls live with God. To fail to care for any component well while attempting to nurture our spirituality is an exercise in futility. Spiritual service that leaves us no time and energy to be attentive to our own thoughts, feelings, life choices and physical condition puts us in tension with the work of God to conform us to the image of his Son and leads us to root our identity in *what we can do* rather than *who we are* in him.

Valuing our journey prompts us to reflect on our patterns, see where slippage has occurred, and listen for the encouragement and conviction of the Holy Spirit in regard to our own spiritual condition. C. S. Lewis's fictional *Screwtape Letters* consists of letters written by a senior demon (Screwtape) and a junior tempter (Wormwood) who is learning "the trade." In one letter, Screwtape bemoans Wormwood's failure in keeping his charge from Christ: "As a preliminary to detaching himself from the Enemy [God], you wanted to detach him from himself, and had made some progress in doing so. Now, all that is undone."[9] To be detached from our own spiritual journey is indeed the desire of the evil one. Valuing our own journey begins as we resist that "detachment" and look honestly and courageously at ourselves as well as at areas that need to be addressed—whether it means celebrating growth, acknowledging a need for rest or leaning into an area of brokenness.

Humbly Leaning into Pain and Brokenness. I (Jana) was stunned when I heard about Larry. When we volunteered together in ministry in the late 1970s, he was a godly, passionate, caring follower of Christ. He married one of my good friends and went on to become a minister to college students. But on a recent warm summer day, I got an email telling me that Larry had taken his own life. In my spirit I was searching for answers. Why? What brought this dynamic minister to such a drastic end? *Part* of the answer came when I read his daughter's Facebook note reflecting on her dad's suicide:

> My dad walked away from the Lord, he was burned by people in the church and instead of forgiving and remembering there's grace . . . he ran. When his marriage got tuff . . . he ran . . . when we disagreed . . . he ran. My dad ran and ran and ran in the wrong direction till Pride took over his whole mind-set and he couldn't take it anymore.[10]

Larry knew how to run; he did not know how to lean into his pain and brokenness. At its extreme, this kind of avoidance can bring tragic results.

Perhaps some of us resist being refined by the journey because we're afraid of what we'll encounter. Robert, for instance, might have come face to face with the deficit he felt in being able to please God and the emotional distance that was threatening his intimacy with God. Larry might have encountered his growing bitterness toward the church and his feelings of inadequacy as a husband and father. Practicing reflection can be humbling and stir up pain from past or present wounds. It may expose areas where we need healing from the Lord and help from the body of Christ. What we discover might run counter to our conception of what a "good" disciplemaker should be. Shouldn't we have it all together?

I (Rick) initially chose to be a leader partly because the image projected by leaders is a wonderful form of self-protection. I have always wanted to be a mat carrier, not the guy flat on the mat (Mk 2:1-5). Through a series of experiences that were emotionally, physically and spiritually painful, however, I reached the end of myself and recognized that I was hiding my wounded self behind the aura of the ministry I performed. God laid me flat on the mat. I had no choice but to depend on others. I could no longer hide my internal weaknesses. Gradually I began to see the man in the mirror as a broken man lying lame on his mat, and to recognize that I desperately needed God *and* people.

It was only when I reached that place that I was finally ready to begin the deep healing processes the Great Physician had been preparing for me. And only in that place was I prepared to become a true mat carrier for the broken lives around me. I was no longer playing physician; I began living as a fellow paralytic who had found the Healer.

Pain denied or concealed becomes infected. Brokenness not properly set leads to twisted, limp lives. The church is full of silent bearers of pain and brokenness. Weeping alone, believers fight off infections of the soul and bravely attempt to provide spiritual care from wounded relational selves. My own "flat on the mat" experiences reduced me to a daily confrontation of my pain and brokenness. For the first time I experienced what I would call true suffering. I wanted desperately to perform my way out, but I lacked the necessary strength. I had to learn how to lean into my pain and brokenness rather than avoid myself.

Disciplemaking relationships, being by their very nature an authentic spiritual engagement of the human heart, become the means by which

God exposes broken, pain-filled places in the hearts of disciplemakers. A metaphor for this "heart exposure" can be found in my (Rick's) experiences with a twenty-three-year-old partner on a high ropes course. Brad, a young man with no fear of heights whatsoever, had been teamed—unfortunately for him—with me, a person who chooses to conquer but still feels a lifelong anxiety about high places. When we came to the highest and hardest of the elements, we clearly needed a well-choreographed partnership to make it through.

Already balancing precariously on the super-thin cable, Brad asked me if I was ready to join him. My normal response to the anxious feeling I was having would be to pretend and hide; I would adopt an externally calm demeanor to conceal my lack of confidence. Standing on a three-foot-square platform, staring at the thirty-five feet of space below the thin cable directly in front of my feet, I had to make a choice. Would I reveal my weakness? In this instance, I committed to be honest—with Brad and with myself. Looking Brad in the eye, I decided to admit my fear while assuring him I *would* take this step. I asked him to give me a minute while I gathered myself. Brad, my "high ropes disciplemaker," calmly replied, "It's okay. I'll wait. Here, grab my hand to balance your first step."

Reflecting on this experience, I recounted these thoughts in a previous book:

> With that I took my step and together we conquered that particular element. My fear was real. I could not talk myself out of it. Rather I had to face it. Having a partner to listen to, accept and meet me at that place made the first step much easier. It was humbling to tell a twenty-three-year-old that I was scared. I found it even more humbling to have to lean on his sense of confidence to overcome my own deficit. Just as it was humbling for me to go to a therapist to seek counseling for my fears of rejection and worthlessness. Just as it is humbling to reveal to others that I am a naturally fearful, anxious person who wants to hide the real me. Just as it is humbling to write this in a book that will be read by perfect strangers. Being authentic, however, has become my only known path to freedom.[11]

Like so many others who find themselves in leadership positions, I am entirely comfortable as a "mat *carrier*." By contrast, I instinctively resist the need to *be carried* on the mat of my limitations, pain, brokenness and weaknesses. Leaning into my own deep needs for supportive community is, however, an unavoidable prerequisite for creating and sustaining authentic disciplemaking relationships that support the journeys of emerging adults. If my approach to my own pain and fear is persistent avoidance, I'll lack the relational and spiritual integrity required to call others to step into those places in their own lives.

Humbly sharing ourselves: Authenticity. As a young adult, Jackson had a difficult time feeling valued both as an individual and in the body of Christ. Joining Clay's small group and being identified by Clay as a leader was therefore a breath of fresh air. Clay mentored him and groomed him to start his own small group. Within a year and a half, Jackson was leading a group of six guys in a life-giving Bible study and looking for the "next leader" among them as Clay had done with him. His personal walk and his experience in the body of Christ were at an all-time high. That high began to gradually diminish, however, when his mentor, Clay, had an argument with the senior pastor that led to him leaving and, eventually, severing all ties with the church; he became less and less interested in maintaining his relationship with Jackson. To say that Jackson was disappointed is an understatement! He had lost his mentor and a brother in Christ who was instrumental in helping him discover his potential. He also didn't know how to understand the conflict that occurred between Clay and the pastor—a conflict that initially appeared petty to him. Was Clay overreacting? Was the pastor? How could Clay let this disagreement bother him so much that he would leave the church?

Jackson's idealization of Clay contributed to the devastation he felt. We could have chosen worse situations to share—stories of spiritual fathers and mothers who have fallen into moral sin, practiced self-deception or turned away from Christ. Or we might have shared from the other side of the spectrum—mentors who fail in a myriad of minor ways. The point is that *all disciplemakers* are imperfect in following Christ and in relating to those they mentor. We live in an imperfect state between salvation and perfection; original sin has infected everything we do to some extent. We're all in need of grace.

It's therefore crucial for us to help those we're mentoring understand that we are imperfect spiritual caregivers. Our imperfections can be an opportunity and not a curse—an opportunity to point disciples to Christ to find their ultimate worth and satisfaction. Christ is the only perfect model; no man or woman can or should replace Christ as our core reason for continuing the journey of learning to love as God calls us to. Even Paul said, "Follow my example, *as I follow the example of Christ*" (1 Cor 11:1 NIV). Christ is the example we are to follow. Hopefully, though, the example of a fellow brother or sister makes him more concrete for us. We are not to follow our mentors, brothers or sisters, but *Christ in them*. Hebrews says it this way: "Remember your leaders, those who spoke to you the word of God. *Consider the outcome of their way of life, and imitate their faith*" (Heb 13:7). We should help those we mentor evaluate the outcome of our own choices and counsel them to imitate our faith—not our unbelief, not our willfulness or pride, but our *faith,* wherever we've been able to model that well. We can further assist them in seeing us accurately by sharing appropriately about mistakes we have made as well as taking responsibility for our behavior toward them. It's important to acknowledge and apologize when we have acted in an un-Christlike manner toward those we mentor.

Disappointment in a mentor is real, and we may be rightly grieved by a choice they've made. We ought to feel it; we need to mourn it with the Lord. But we also can acknowledge that leaders and disciplemakers are imperfect followers of Christ who continue to need sanctification, challenge and growth. In some ways, isn't that a relief?

LOVE: MOVING BOLDLY ON THE JOURNEY

Someone once said, "Love is a verb." Not just a feeling, love requires us to act on behalf of another. Because of this, disciplemakers cannot be passive caregivers; we must be proactive and courageous in our willingness to exercise reasonable risk for the relationship. We must be bold. As Paul reminds us, "God has not given us a spirit of fear and timidity, but of power, love, and self-discipline" (2 Tim 1:7 NLT). Through his Spirit working in us, we can move forward with boldness in how we hope, care and speak truth in disciplemaking relationships.

Bold hope: With God nothing is impossible. Sometimes we may question the ability of a young adult to move forward in their walk with God when we see them get stuck or spiral back to old patterns. Seeing their very real human limitations, we might want to throw up our hands in exasperation at their lack of effort or progress. But as Jesus reminds us in Luke 18:27, "What is impossible for people is possible with God" (NLT). We need to redirect our attention to the work of the Holy Spirit so that we can turn our attention from their failures to the hope of Christ, who is "making all things new" (Rev 21:5). As citizens in God's kingdom, we have a positive vision for their life in Christ, one in which they're grounded in the truths of Scripture, enhanced by an understanding of how God uniquely created them to function in the body of Christ and sealed by the transforming work of the Holy Spirit. All this is available to every follower of Christ as we allow him to live his life through us.

Twenty-one-year-old Drake was a mess when he participated in our campus ministry. I (Jana) felt like I was constantly trying to get him to understand that his actions had consequences, *real* consequences. He would nod his head like he understood, but it didn't take long to see he hadn't. In all honesty it was a struggle to keep going to the throne to receive God's vision for him so that I could balance our many confrontations with a positive picture of his potential. Today, at the age of twenty-four, Drake is the pastor of a church. A *pastor!* Neither of us saw that coming. God's vision was greater than my own.

No matter what kind of struggle or deficit, perceptive disciplemakers must live into their own need for humble dependence on the Father so that they can gently lead others to a clearer view of self and Creator. A renewed vision of the sacrificial love of God can transform our posture from reactive and self-protective to one that is open and embraces others as we relate to emerging adults. And from that posture we can enter into a bold hope for what God is already choreographing—and what he'll do in the future—for his children. We find great comfort in this verse from Isaiah 60:21: "All your people will be righteous. They will possess their land forever, for I will plant them there with my own hands in order to bring myself glory" (NLT). God will bring his people to righteousness with his *own* hands! Our hope needs to be firmly placed in his abilities, not in our own or in the abilities of the young adults we disciple.

Bold care: Looking out for the interests of others. Loving others with selfless generosity means pursuing others in their desire to effectively live the Christlife. Philippians 2:4 exhorts us, "Let each of you look not only to his own interests, but also to the interests of others." One of the reasons I (Rick) love coaching basketball is that success in the game requires an awareness of, a commitment to and a partnership with your four other teammates on the court; I constantly drum into my players' heads that they have to learn to create success for their teammates. And the key to the offenses that I run is always the leadership of a quick, skilled, *selfless* point guard who will distribute the ball to the other players on the team. The point guard may not shoot very often but ends up being responsible for most of the scoring that takes place. His or her role is twofold: set up the offense and get the ball into the shooters' hands. If the point guard's priority is to "get his points," he arrogantly undermines his teammates' abilities and opportunities to score.

The image I see when I read verse 2:4 from Philippians is therefore that of a point guard. In essence, Paul calls us to "distribute" the Christlife—to use our energy and spiritual gifts to set others up to grow in their spiritual walk with Christ. To act with "bold care" thus requires a vision for others' success, a selfless attitude about our role, and an intentional commitment to "distribute" Christ's grace and truth to others.

I (Rick) remember standing at the end of the pool several years ago as a swim meet my sons were in was finishing up. A man about my age, who went to my church and knew me as his pastor but was largely unknown to me, came up beside me and asked, "How are you doing?" After my short, generic response, Guille pressed further. "No, I meant how are you *really* doing?" Years later, we meet twice a month for lunch. We have challenged and encouraged one another through many tough passages in our roles as husbands, dads and leaders. I cherish our friendship and always smile when I see his name penciled in for a Friday lunch at our favorite barbeque restaurant. Guille is a point guard in my spiritual life. He pursues me, he looks out for me, and he distributes the grace of Christ to my heart so that I can progress in my journey.

In short, being a disciplemaker who expresses bold care means being willing to step out of our comfort zone to enter into another's life. It might seem audacious to tell an emerging adult that you are going to be there for them in a crisis moment. It might feel presumptuous to let them know what you see for their future or to create an opportunity where they can use their gifts and shine . . . but there we must boldly go!

Bold truth: Speaking the truth as an act of nurture. Looking to the interests of the emerging adults we mentor includes speaking truth. *My* interest might be to preserve the congenial and warm atmosphere that exists in the spiritual friendship. But taking an interest in the other may mean muddling through some tense moments for their sake. Done sincerely, this can be a powerful way to model love.

Speaking truth can be challenging to do well, however. Paul's words in Ephesians 4 offer some helpful guidance, giving us a picture of spiritual maturity (increasingly becoming like Christ): "Instead [of being spiritually immature], we will speak the truth in love, growing in every way more and more like Christ, who is the head of his body, the church" (v. 15 NLT). Notice that the means of this maturing process is not just truth; we can get that from reading the Bible. And it's not just love. It's *speaking truth in love:* one person in the body of Christ lovingly communicating truth to another for their benefit and growth.

That's not to say it won't be messy. Speaking the truth even with the best motives is often confrontational. Conflict is not inherently wrong, however. And while it's true that natural selfishness mixed with confrontation and conflict can create an environment where relational wounding can occur, it's still better to speak the truth—risk though it may be—and proceed with care than to avoid bringing things to light.

James 3:13-18 provides insight into how we should approach potentially difficult, tense interactions. First, our boldness should not be fueled by selfishness or ambition. Are we speaking truth because we're hurt or angry and want to get even? Or do we truly have the spiritual growth of the other person in mind? Second, we are to be peace loving (refusing to pick fights), gentle, willing to yield (asking ourselves, *Is there something* I'm *convicted by that I need to own up to or admit?*) and sincere (sharing not just the facts but also our heart). And if the young adult is defensive or reactive, we are not to *react* back but rather proceed with care. Many times we may need to let the emerging adult sit with the truth for a while; it may take minutes, hours, days or longer before they're able to truly receive it. Be patient. Let the Lord work on their heart and in your own.

Bold love, then, is hopeful, practices selfless generosity and celebrates the opportunity to connect with truth—which is exactly what Paul was trying to get across to the Corinthians about their relationships! He says it better than we can:

> Love is patient and kind. Love is not jealous or boastful or proud or rude. It does not demand its own way. It is not irritable, and it keeps no record of being wronged. It does not rejoice about injustice but rejoices whenever the truth wins out. Love never gives up, never loses faith, is always hopeful, and endures through every circumstance. (1 Cor 13:4-7 NLT)

REFLECTIVE DISCIPLEMAKERS: "THE COURAGE TO BE CHRIST'S"

Maturing requires acknowledging and addressing immaturity. Becoming stronger requires moving beyond present weaknesses. Becoming a person of boldness requires facing and moving through our fears. Disciplemaking thus requires putting the heart at great risk—in order to afford the heart an even greater reward in Christ.

As we mentioned, Dr. Martin Luther King Jr., in his own compelling, courageous manner, modeled Paul Tillich's phrase "the courage to be." The Christlife requires courage. It takes courage to trust in and be faithful to Christ's wisdom. It takes courage to remain humbly surrendered to Christ rather than grasping for control. It takes courage to love with the vulnerability required by Christ's love. It takes "the courage to be *Christ's*." Cultivating the courage required by the Christlife is a significant challenge for the disciplemaker and especially for the young-adult disciple facing the challenges of twenty-first-century spirituality.

Without "the courage to be Christ's," the emerging adult will be stuck in immaturity, weakness and fear. Fortunately, that is where the life of the disciplemaker can have its greatest impact. If we as disciplemakers model and share "the courage to be Christ's" through our own challenges with immaturity, weakness and fear, the young adult will become infected with "the courage to be Christ's." Courage, likes its counterpart fear, is extremely contagious.

As a disciplemaker, building that courage begins with the commitment to live a reflective life and apply the same patterns of discernment to our lives as we are teaching young adults to practice. For me

(Rick), the most practical way I do this is to regularly return to this prayer of David's:

> Search me, O God, and know my heart!
>> Try me and know my thoughts!
> And see if there be any grievous way in me,
>> and lead me in the way everlasting!
> (Ps 139:23-24)

Yesterday I discovered some grievous ways in me. I saw fear in my heart. I saw poor spiritual reasoning in my thoughts. So I had to submit to his ways. In humility, I came before God yesterday to receive the grace I needed to be able to stand strong in the midst of my failures. Yesterday I needed to be loved well by him so that I could love others well. What made yesterday such a significant day? What was so unique about it? Nothing really. Because today I will experience these very same things in new ways as I pray this prayer. My spirituality is not a product of my goodness or my grace or my love—it is a product of his. Without reflectively seeking him daily in the postures of trust, submission and love, I am left empty as I approach disciplemaking relationships. Yesterday I needed the Father, Son and Holy Spirit to take me on the journey of discovering my need for Christ. Today I need this same journey—and tomorrow will be no different.

The reflective disciplemaker practices the postures of the Christlife because there is no other way to live in the fullness of his goodness, grace and love. In doing so, the reflective disciplemaker becomes the very picture of courageous spirituality that young adults long to experience. For one hundred generations the pattern has been the same. And for one hundred generations our God has faithfully led his people in the way everlasting, the way of the Christlife. The infection of the next generation with "the courage to be Christ's" begins with our reflection as disciplemakers—with our willingness to join God as he conducts a search and rescue mission inside our hearts and minds. To that end, we conclude this chapter with questions that challenge you to enter in to courageous reflection, remembering, as you do so, that it's only by God's goodness, grace and love that you'll ever be able to cultivate the courage that marks the truly effective disciplemaker.

SELF-REFLECTION QUESTIONS

Invite God to refine you through the disciplemaking process.

- How well am I doing at allowing God to "grasp" and "shape" me? *"Examine yourselves, to see whether you are in the faith. Test yourselves. Or do you not realize this about yourselves, that Jesus Christ is in you?—unless indeed you fail to meet the test!"* (2 Cor 13:5).

- Am I acting in a way that shows I value others' spiritual lives as well as my own? *"Pay careful attention to your own work, for then you will get the satisfaction of a job well done, and you won't need to compare yourself to anyone else. For we are each responsible for our own conduct"* (Gal 6:4-5 NLT).

- Where am I "running" instead of facing pain, hurt or immaturity?

- As I look at how I interact within disciplemaking relationships, where do I think God is calling *me* to grow? *"Be honest in your evaluation of yourselves, measuring yourselves by the faith God has given us"* (Rom 12:3 NLT).

- In my own heart and instincts as a mentor, what is being stirred? What creates consonance and what creates dissonance in me as we move forward?[12]

- What am I learning about how God uniquely uses me in the disciplemaking context? Where do I need to focus more of my efforts? Where do I need others to supplement my weaknesses?

- How do my actions or attitudes contribute to relational frustration or disappointment? Am I thinking about myself (as well as the emerging adult I mentor) from a godly or a worldly perspective? *"From now on we regard no one from a worldly point of view"* (2 Cor 5:16 NIV).

- What do I understand about God's role versus my role in the disciplemaking process? Where have I seen God work through me? beyond me? *"Let us test and examine our ways, and return to the LORD!"* (Lam 3:40).

IGNITING YOUR PASSION FOR REPRODUCING THE JOURNEY

A Conversation with the Authors

BUSINESS PHILOSOPHER JIM ROHN
has said, "Whatever good things we build end up building us."[1] And indeed, when we act on Jesus' exhortation to "make disciples" we find that, in the process, we are "made" as well: built, strengthened, challenged and filled with joy. Writing this book has been a labor of love for us as we have sought to construct a tenable approach to making disciples, one generation to the next. At the same time, this book has been writing us. We have been challenged to be discerning and intentional as we think biblically, critically and compassionately about the emerging generation and their disciplemakers. God continues to deepen and sharpen us even as we revisit what we have already written. We've recorded for you here one particular conversation we had as we reflected together on how what we've been writing about is intersecting with experiences and conversations from our daily lives.

RICK: I have been wondering, Jana, if there is a word or phrase that would sufficiently summarize the unique spiritual challenges of this generation of emerging adults. For me, the phrase that comes to mind is a "lack of rootedness."

JANA: I can see that. Many have roots that can be too easily torn up from the ground. Or, in many cases, there is an absence of spiritual rootedness altogether. For example, just the other day I was in a conversation with a small group of emerging adults. They spoke of the same experience, but in different terms.

RICK: How did they describe the lack of deep roots?

JANA: They talked about a pervasive loss of the sense of "place" in their lives. Nowhere in their lives, including the church, did they have a sense of being in a "place" that kept them rooted.

RICK: That's an interesting way of talking about their lives. I think I've seen that in the emerging adults I spend time with—but I haven't heard that term used.

JANA: It makes sense though, doesn't it? This next generation of disciples travels the world making friends and uses the World Wide Web to cultivate those friendships. They live diffused—cultivating global relational lives alongside their local relational lives. In the midst of all this, they really want the church to provide connection and stability, but are not quite sure what that would look like.

RICK: This conversation reminds me of a conversation I had yesterday with the chair of the elder board of my church. Roger and his wife, Jackie, spent thirty years as missionaries in Bangladesh. Their children were born there and raised there until their late teen years. When they moved permanently to the United States, their children went through training on how to live as the "third culture" people they were. They experienced being part of the Bangladesh culture and part of the American culture, but were not fully rooted in either. Similar to Roger and Jackie's children, the emerging generation has a kind of third-culture experience. Some authors have called them "Mosaics"—that also gives a sense that they really are not of "one place," doesn't it?

JANA: And they have a growing sense of anxiety about that. *Now* is a key time for disciplemakers to fill that vacuum with meaningful, intentional relationships. That would create the stability of their connection to the local church while allowing for and celebrating their diverse, global relational lives.

RICK: There is that word again: *intentional*. It's not going to "just happen" is it?

JANA: No, and as you and I have discussed on many occasions, our generation needs to understand the urgency of the situation. We either move now or miss an important window of opportunity with this generation. For sure, *something* will fill the void. What a tragedy if it's not a movement of the church!

RICK: One of my friends told me a story that relates to the Katrina disaster we started the book with. It made me very sad. Bob, who is a firefighter, told me that while there were wonderful stories of rescue following the hurricane's devastation, there were hundreds of rescue vehicles that sat still and were simply destroyed by the flooding. I asked him how this could have happened. The answer shocked me. According to Bob, hundreds of rescue workers fled the devastation, heading to drier ground rather than fighting to rescue the stranded. Their role was to rescue—instead they chose to evacuate.

JANA: Really? Ouch! We can't do that. We can't evacuate!

RICK: I agree. We have been called to rescue, not run.

JANA: But Rick, so many established and seasoned adults feel untrained and unprepared for the rescue mission. One of the biggest challenges I see is an overall feeling of being out of sync with the cultural realities of the next generation. They feel like the fifty-year-old I was talking to who was trying to make the switch to a smartphone. He kept helplessly repeating, "This new phone is kicking my butt." He felt lost, couldn't find what he wanted, kept choosing the wrong pathway to get the info he needed or just make a call!

Similarly, adults often feel lost trying to understand the tendencies of emerging adults. It's not the path they walked or are familiar with. These adults grow frustrated, asking, "How do I find a way to enter into a relationship with such big cultural and generational differences?" They also grow impatient, wondering, "Why do they take so long to grow up?"

RICK: Honestly, I understand completely. I feel a pull to engage, but I also feel a pull to remain in my comfort zone. After all, it's easier to be a guy who develops theories about emerging adults rather than a guy who develops relationships with them. I can retreat into the safety of teaching about discipling emerging adults rather than engaging in the risky process of building those relationships.

JANA: It is a risk—but taking that risk creates that contagious courage we wrote about earlier. Our risk helps them to risk.

RICK: But because it is a risk . . . it's not easy.

JANA: No, we feel insufficient and we wonder if we have enough time or energy to give. We become aware of the needs of emerging adults, and may be afraid our overextended lives simply cannot accommodate reaching into their lives. We're afraid of burnout. But I don't think we truly understand what they need. They need adults who can be authentic about their weakness and limitations. They need adults who are curious about them and what they are experiencing rather than an expert analyst or a superstar disciplemaker. Furthermore, they don't need adults who overextend themselves, but adults who are mature enough to have boundaries and standards yet relate to them with hope.

RICK: I meet with a group of men who are asking the question, "How do we effectively enter into relationships with young-adult men so that those maturing disciples become mature disciplemakers?" You have to be over forty to be in the group, and you have to be willing to take risks. We are quickly realizing how challenging this is. We have also been forced to admit that we feel threatened by the lack of control we experience as we build relationships with emerging adults. It feels like being on a trapeze without a net—scary!

JANA: You often talk about challenges as a gift, not a threat. Say more about what you mean by that.

RICK: First of all, it is a lot easier to say it to others than to speak it to myself.

JANA: Good point.

RICK: I do, however, genuinely believe that the difficult passages God leads us through, while perceived as threats, can actually become gifts to us. In the places and relationships that spark fear in our hearts—we just want to run, to retreat. We feel out of control, inadequate, vulnerable. We come to the end of our ideas, our strength, our answers. But it is there, at the end of ourselves, we begin to experience the fullness of the

Christlife. In more traditional disciplemaking models, there is a curriculum and a set of established steps to be taken. That model offers some sense of control. The disciplemaker studies and prepares and then transfers what he or she knows to the disciple. In the model presented in this book, we have offered a much different model. In the Christlife model, the disciplemaker presses deeper into trust, submission and love. The transforming grace that follows becomes the context for inviting the emerging-adult disciple to press deeper into the Christlife for himself. Less control, more surrender. Less self-confidence, more faith. Less expertise, more grace and truth.

JANA: The old model seemed like an exchange of commodities. Like, "Here is what I possess; now I am going to give some of it to you." But the Christlife model is more like, "Here is *who* possesses me; now I am going to introduce you to more of who he is becoming to me." It's an exchange of life.

RICK: Yep. The language of Jesus and the language of Paul and Peter always focus on life exchange. Disciplemaking includes the content of Scripture and biblical theology. But it also requires action—obedient response to the truth revealed in Scripture. The context by which the Christlife becomes a shared experience is always the life exchange found in relationships. You can learn the Bible in a class. You can practice application alone. But true disciplemaking always includes relationship.

JANA: What relational challenges do you see in this way of approaching disciplemaking?

RICK: You would ask the practical—thanks! One of the most painful of all challenges is facing disappointment.

JANA: Relational disappointments are common in disciplemaking, aren't they?

RICK: As common as human nature. Inevitably we will find ourselves in a disciplemaking relationship where the other person begins to pull away, creating interpersonal distance. Or the young disciple of Christ makes choices that are entirely contrary to what you know he or she knows to be true. When this happens—it really hurts.

JANA: And we feel inadequate.

RICK: Precisely. After being hurt a couple of times—and it will happen—I am tempted to say, "Well, I am not going to set myself up for that again." No one wants pain, and no one wants to feel inadequate. As a matter of fact, for men, it is our greatest fear. I think that is why there are fewer men in disciplemaking relationships.

JANA: But for men and women both, that's exactly where pursuing the Christlife becomes so important.

RICK: I agree, but tell me more about what you mean.

JANA: We have to love with Christ's love—not our own. That's what the disciple needs—Christ's love. We get hooked into thinking that we have to manufacture something great to give them, when we really just need to be a conduit for Christ. His love is enough to overcome both the pain and sense of inadequacy.

RICK: Yes. That's the whole point, isn't it? We cast a vision, giving them *him* by giving them *us*. That's what he intended, I believe. This is where the reality of Christ's unwavering trust, humble submission and relentless love becomes a necessity in my life and I find only by his gracious presence do I overcome myself and begin to risk true life exchange. I offer *him* because he is all I really have to offer.

JANA: That's important to get—it challenges the idea that you have to be an expert of some kind to do this well.

RICK: Absolutely—we have so overcomplicated and overprofessionalized the relational model Christ demonstrated!

JANA: I hope readers are not disappointed in the lack of formulae offered in this book. We have intentionally chosen to talk about disciplemaking in terms of postures and rhythms rather than steps or activities or programs. Postures and rhythms can't really be put on a checklist. You have to revisit and deepen these your whole life. Each new disciplemaking relationship and each new passage within these relationships will require growth in grace.

RICK: When I think about the discernment-intentionality-reflection rhythms, I am immediately impressed with how truly effective disciplemaking relationships recognize the active presence of the Holy Spirit. But there are challenges disciplemakers will face in experiencing his guidance too.

JANA: Most people get the fact that they are led by the Spirit through reading the Bible or hearing the Word preached. They may even embrace how the Spirit speaks in moments of corporate prayer. However, when it comes to consistently listening for and discerning the influence of the Spirit in the midst of life and relationships, this can be a bit scary. How does the Spirit speak? How do we hear? How do we learn to submit what we hear to the authority of Scripture? When do we risk following what we believe we have heard? What is an acceptable risk? This is only learned through stillness, quiet, prayer and then appropriate risk.

RICK: I remember a Ken Gire illustration in *Windows of the Soul*. He talks about how if we open a window we get the glorious gift of a summer breeze. However, we also get a few flies as well. It's just a risk we take.

JANA: We *will* get "flies" from time to time. We can't go for perfection. We're still in process, with the Lord and as people. So trust, submission and love are essential to learning to listen. We cannot be self-sufficient, arrogant or selfish if we're surrendering to the Spirit's leading. A part of this selfless attitude is a willingness to be wrong.

RICK: With trust, submission and love our commitment to perfection is surrendered to our commitment to grow, by his grace and for his glory.

JANA: Exactly. Growing up and maturing ourselves as well as coming alongside others as they grow up is not an exact science.

RICK: Yes—and as my daughter, Jessica, said, "Growing up is hard." Growing up *is* hard—at every age, including fifty! You know, if I am really honest, Jana, what scares me most about disciplemaking is that very reality: that I have to keep growing up for the relationship to be authentic.

JANA: But by doing so we become the very model of what we are hoping to share. Our journey as a disciple becomes the living picture of what we are teaching through our words. Being a learner with Christ authenticates and validates our role in calling emerging adults to be learners with Christ as well. As we press through our fears, they learn from us how to press through their fears. As we experience trust in the midst of doubt, they learn to experience trust in the midst of doubt. As we fall into the arms of grace, they learn to fall into grace as well.

RICK: Then they become not only maturing disciples but maturing disciplemakers as well. They get that this is about Christ and not about them—and they become potential reproducers in the generation following them.

JANA: That was Christ's vision from the beginning. I sometimes feel like we have "dumbed down" disciplemaking, as if we are simply trying to help everybody have a "good day with Jesus." That's too much like the cruise-ship model. We are on an important mission—and we are preparing one another to take mission-critical roles in God's emerging kingdom.

RICK: I once had a dad thank me for my influence in his son's life. He described how my role had helped his son live more productively. He was thankful that his son had stayed away from the negative things that surrounded him in the culture. I told him how much I appreciated his gratitude—but that I was aiming much higher than seeing his son stay out of trouble. I shared with him my vision that his son would find his place in the kingdom of God and make an eternal difference. It is not enough to "contain" the next generation—they need to be deployed.

JANA: I recently heard a powerful illustration from a former colleague, Dr. Paul Hiebert. Let me read it to you. I don't think I need to explain why I thought it was significant.

> "Nothing grows under a banyan tree." This South Indian proverb speaks of leadership styles. The banyan is a great tree. It spreads its branches, drops air-roots, develops secondary trunks and covers the land. A full grown banyan may cover more than an acre of land. Birds, animals and humans find shelter under its shade. But nothing grows under its dense foliage, and when it dies, the ground beneath lies barren and scorched.
>
> The banana tree is the opposite. Six months after it sprouts, small shoots appear around it. At twelve months a second circle of shoots ap-

pears beside the first ones, now six months old. At eighteen months the main trunk bears bananas which nourish birds, animals and humans, and then it dies. But the first offspring are now full grown, and in six months they too bear fruit and die. The cycles continue unbroken as new sprouts emerge every six months, grow, give birth to more sprouts, bear fruit and die.[3]

RICK: Wow! I need to think about that for a while. It is so much easier to do "banyan tree" disciplemaking than "banana tree" disciplemaking.

■ ■ ■

The banyan versus banana tree illustration paused the conversation. Soon we were each lost in our own thoughts, pondering our spiritual legacies and considering questions like, To what extent are the emerging adults in our lives experiencing the Christlife through us? Where in relationship to us are they encountering authentic expressions of Christ's trust, submission and love in relationship to the Father? How consistently invested are we in the disciplined practices of discernment, intentionality and reflection? If an emerging adult spent a year in relationship with us, what difference would it make in their vision for and understanding of their calling in the kingdom of God?

While we hope each of you will ask these questions as well, we also recognize that the key to realizing a twenty-first-century disciplemaking vision is always, only, found in Christ. The original spiritual tree from which the seeds of disciplemaking come is the person of Jesus Christ. He was and is the ultimate producer of "spiritual fruit." Tax collectors, fishermen, prostitutes, tent makers, racially and socially marginalized Samaritans, and a couple of brothers called "Sons of Thunder" were among the early men and women who became spiritual reproducers of the kingdom of God. What an amazing grove of banana trees that was! Even more amazingly, the one hundredth generation of their spiritual legacy includes a university professor in Chicago named Jana and a lead pastor in Knoxville named Rick. Reproducing the fruit of the Christlife in the next generation has now been entrusted to us—and to you.

We began with an email to Rick from Megan, who was crying out for disciplemaking relationships for her generation, the 101st generation of the church. We conclude now with another email Rick received—this one from a young man he discipled—while we were writing this book. In it, Dan illustrates the generational impact of investing ourselves as a disciplemaker in the life of an emerging adult.

> I had a lot of zeal, a little common sense, and a strong work ethic. You taught me compassion, the importance of listening, the necessity of thinking for myself and the unequivocal need for forgiving and moving on. You always treated me with kindness and respect and that made a life-long impression on me. . . .
>
> Following graduation, I went to seminary and got an MDiv. After that Cindi and I served with a mission agency in Brazil for ten years. For the past five years, I've served as a youth pastor in central Indiana. I can't wait till we get to heaven to introduce you to Chico, Carlos, Wanclay, Israel, Jacob, Adam, Brian, Pam, Brian, David, and the list goes on and on of people who are serving God right now, who know God now, because of you.

"Christ, the hope of glory" dwells within all who are disciples of Christ. For those who choose to risk opening the Christlife to an emerging adult there is an eternal legacy: spiritual grandchildren. For the sake of God's name and the sake of the world, may we be faithful to prepare this 101st generation of the church to take their place as spiritual reproducers in the 102nd generation of the church even as it just begins to dawn on the horizon of human history.

ACKNOWLEDGMENTS

WE WANT TO EXPRESS OUR THANKS TO:

Those who helped shape us in our own early adult years. For Jana: Thanks to Karen Nunn Hubbard and Jon and Francie Byron for their wisdom, care and encouragement. For Rick: Thanks to Craig Williford, Mark Senter, Perry Downs, Linda Cannell and Ted Ward, whose mentoring and modeling shaped my young-adult journey with strong doses of grace and truth.

Family, friends and colleagues. For Rick: Teresa, thank you for your lifelong partnership and support as my wife of twenty-eight years. As with all things that are good and fruitful in my life, you are an inseparable part of my writing in this book. I cannot envision one day—much less my life—without you. Jana, thank you for being a lifelong friend who always takes my ideas at the conceptual stage and not only sharpens the ideas and makes them work, but makes them work so much better than I could have ever imagined. I continue to learn so much from working with you. For Jana: Kath, Kristin, Lisa, Steve, Saundra and Greg—each of you have contributed to this project as you allowed me to bounce my ideas off you, asked me questions, prayed for me and supported me for the duration. Rick, thank you for being my best working partner and a faithful friend as well as a visionary who continues to inspire me.

Our supportive church families. For Rick: Thanks to the elders and staff of Fellowship Church, for all that you have taught me about pursuing the Christlife and engaging the world as a local church. What an amazing, unpredictable, exhilarating adventure the Father has called us to as a leadership community. To Kevin—thank you for teaching me so much about true discipleship and the process of equipping leaders for the next generation of the church. Greg—a specific thank you for teaching me so much about both the communication of the gospel to the next generation and the equipping of that generation to guard what has been entrusted to them by Christ. For Jana: Thanks to Geoff, Cyd and Matt for walking with me during this journey. And to Kristen and Julie for the invaluable, consistent prayer support.

The emerging adults in our lives. For Jana: Thanks to Susanne Osborne, Sarah Beyer, Annie Palubicki and Emily Hennings (the BSGE), and to Jeri, Jessica and all my treasured students over the years from Trinity International University who provided me with a real-life education that impacted my ability to write this book. Special thanks to Laura and Scott for providing space for me to write and adventures to write about. For Rick: Thank you to the emerging adults of Fellowship Church, for your passion for Christ's glory and your submission to the full impact of Christ's grace and truth. Many pages of this book reflect what I have learned by serving alongside you as a partner in the gospel. I am so thankful that you are the emerging leaders of "the church we have not yet imagined." I pray that I will be faithful to serve you as you prepare to lead Christ's body into its authentic twenty-first-century expression. May you trust his wisdom fully, submit to his heart and leadership faithfully, and love with his love wholeheartedly as you engage the world.

Those who helped shape our manuscript. Thank you, Kristin Lindholm Gumminger, for your unofficial editing skills in the early stages. Thank you, Al, and all of the editorial staff of IVP as well the first readers of this manuscript. What a great service you provided to us with your strategic questions, suggestions and refinement of our work. It is such a gift to have people who not only possess editorial expertise but also a passion for the vision for our work.

Though it goes without being said, let us say it: Thank you to our Savior, Jesus Christ, for designing us and redeeming us to be his children and his body. What a privilege to wake up every day with an eternal hope, an eternal purpose and an eternal security, all offered in love by his grace and for his glory. Thank you, Jesus, for allowing us to exchange the deadness of our glory for the eternal life found only in your glory.

NOTES

Introduction: An Emerging Adult's Plea for Disciplemakers

[1]Used courtesy of the writer.

[2]Jeffrey Jensen Arnett, *Emerging Adulthood: The Winding Road from the Late Teens Through the Twenties* (New York: Oxford University Press, 2004), p. 8.

[3]Christian Smith with Kari Christoffersen, Hilary Davidson and Patricia Snell Herzog, *Lost in Transition: The Dark Side of Emerging Adulthood* (New York: Oxford University Press, 2011), p. 15.

[4]Christian Smith with Patricia Snell, *Souls in Transition: The Religious & Spiritual Lives of Emerging Adults* (New York: Oxford University Press, 2009), p. 6.

[5]Robert Wuthnow, *After the Baby Boomers* (Princeton, N.J.: Princeton University Press, 2007), p. 6.

[6]Ibid., pp. 52-53. Regular attendance at religious services for young adults ages twenty-one to forty-five dropped from 31 percent in the 1970s to 25 percent in the years spanning 1998 to 2002. Those who never attend increased from 14 percent to 20 percent.

[7]Cathy Lynn Grossman, "Young Adults Aren't Sticking with Church," August 6, 2007, *USA Today* <www.usatoday.com/news/religion/2007-08-06-church-drop outs_N.htm>.

[8]The Barna Group, "Twentysomethings Struggle to Find Their Place in Christianity," September 24, 2003 <www.barna.org/barna-update/article/5-barna-update /127-twentysomethings-struggle-to-find-their-place-in-christian-churches>.

Chapter 1: The Complex World of Early Adulthood

[1]All the stories in this book are either direct portrayals or quotes of specific persons or they are true stories where names and/or details have been changed in order to preserve anonymity. In some cases we have created composite stories that represent actual people but not the specifics of their individual stories.

[2]Tim Clydesdale, "Who Are Emerging Adults?" *Changing Sea* <http://changing sea.org/papersyn.htm>.

[3]Christian Smith with Patricia Snell, *Souls in Transition: The Religious & Spiritual Lives of Emerging Adults* (New York: Oxford University Press, 2009), p. 6.

[4]Jeffrey Jensen Arnett, *Emerging Adulthood: The Winding Road from the Late Teens Through the Twenties* (New York: Oxford University Press, 2004), p. 15.

[5]Ibid., p. 120. Note that Robert Wuthnow reports a lower estimate but includes twenty-one- to forty-five-year-olds in *After the Baby Boomers* (Princeton, N.J.: Princeton University Press, 2007), p. 37.

[6]Arnett, *Emerging Adulthood*, p. 131.

[7]These various terms have been used by Gail Sheehy, Lauren Docket and Kristin Beck, Daniel Levinson, and Robert Wuthnow.

[8]Gail Sheehy, *New Passages: Mapping Your Life Across Time* (New York: Random House, 1995), p. 13.

[9]Erik Erikson, "Human Strength and the Cycle of the Generations," in *The Erik Erikson Reader*, ed. Robert Coles (New York: W. W. Norton, 2000), p. 210, italics in the original.

[10]Ibid.

[11]Lauren Dockett and Kristin Beck, *Facing 30: Women Talk About Constructing a Real Life and Other Scary Rites of Passage* (Oakland, Calif.: New Harbinger, 1998), p. 27.

[12]Arnett, *Emerging Adulthood*, p. 6.

[13]Peg Tyre, "Bringing Up Adultolescents," *Newsweek*, March 25, 2002.

[14]U.S. Census Bureau, "Families and Living Arrangements" <www.census.gov/population/www/socdemo/hh-fam.html>, table AD-1.

[15]Wuthnow, *After the Baby Boomers*, p. 6.

[16]Arnett, *Emerging Adulthood*, pp. 17-18.

[17]Wuthnow, *After the Baby Boomers*, p. 12.

[18]Christian Smith with Kari Christoffersen, Hilary Davidson and Patricia Snell Herzog, *Lost in Transition: The Dark Side of Emerging Adulthood* (New York: Oxford University Press, 2011), p. 15.

[19]Ibid., p. 3.

[20]Arnett, *Emerging Adulthood*, pp. 49-50. In 1920, 20 percent of young adults moved back in with parents. In 1999, the percent rose to nearly half.

[21]Ibid., p. 146. A typical young adult in the United States holds eight different jobs between the ages of eighteen and thirty.

[22]Wuthnow, *After the Baby Boomers*, pp. 114-16. See his discussion on church shopping (41%) and hopping (81%) among young adults.

[23]Arnett, *Emerging Adulthood*, p. 12.

[24]Ibid., p. 143.

[25]Daniel J. Levinson, *The Seasons of a Woman's Life* (New York: Ballantine, 1997), p. 71.

[26]Erik Erikson, *Identity and the Life Cycle* (New York: W. W. Norton, 1980), p. 34.

[27]Wuthnow, *After the Baby Boomers*, p. 49.

[28]Smith, *Souls in Transition*, p. 35.

[29]"Geographic Center of the Contiguous United States," *Wikipedia,* last modified March 8, 2011 <http://en.wikipedia.org/wiki/Geographic_center_of_the_con tiguous_United_States>, emphasis ours.

[30]Oscar S. Adams, "The Geographic Center of the Lower 48 United States at Leba-non, Kansas: First in a Thematic Extrapolation Series," in *The Center for Land Use Newsletter* (Spring 1999) <www.clui.org/clui_4_1/lotl/lotlsp99/geo.html>.

[31]Smith, *Souls in Transition,* p. 45.

[32]Wuthnow, *After the Baby Boomers,* p. 47.

[33]Ibid., p. 47.

[34]Ibid., pp. 43-44.

[35]Smith, *Souls in Transition,* p. 81.

[36]Wuthnow, *After the Baby Boomers,* p. 49.

[37]Ibid., p. 38.

[38]Ibid., pp. 51-70.

[39]Arnett, *Emerging Adulthood,* p. 172.

[40]Wuthnow, *After the Baby Boomers,* p. 104.

[41]Ibid., p. 105.

[42]Cited in ibid., p. 35.

[43]Arnett, *Emerging Adulthood,* p. 23.

[44]Ibid., p. 120.

[45]Ibid., p. 22.

[46]Levinson, *Seasons of a Woman's Life,* p. 97.

[47]Daniel J. Levinson, *The Seasons of a Man's Life* (New York: Ballantine, 1978), pp. 79-80.

[48]Dr. Alvin Baraff, *Men Talk* (New York: Dutton, 1991), p. 6, italics in the origi-nal.

[49]Dockett and Beck, *Facing 30,* p. 32.

[50]Ibid., p. 2. In the sample of women interviewed by Beck and Dockett, many ex-pected the thirties to be awful. The authors comment, "This notion was con-firmed by our interviews with some beyond-thirty women, who told us they ini-tially suspected that their thirties would suck and then found out that they don't" (also on p. 2).

Chapter 2: Breathing New Life into Disciplemaking

[1]Robert Quinn, *Deep Change* (San Francisco: Jossey-Bass, 1996), p. xii.

[2]Brett McCracken, "The Perils of 'Wannabe Cool' Christianity," *Wall Street Jour-nal,* Opinion, August 13, 2010.

[3]My foundational understanding of the term "missional church" was formed by Alan Hirsch's seminal work, *The Forgotten Ways: Reactivating the Missional Church* (Grand Rapids: Brazos, 2006).

[4]A. W. Tozer, *The Pursuit of God* (Wheaton, Ill.: Tyndale House, 1982), p. 17.

[5]Mike Osegueda, "Fresno Collectors Uncover Rare 1869 Baseball Card," *Fresno (CA) Bee,* December 31, 2008.

[6]The Association of Religious Data Archives, County Membership Report for Knox County, Tennessee <www.thearda.com/mapsReports/reports/counties/47093 _compare.asp>.

[7]EFCA Church Planting Bootcamp, presented by Bruce Redmond, October 2010.

[8]Sarah Kliff, "The Abortion Evangelist," *Newsweek*, August 24, 2009, pp. 45-46, emphasis ours.

[9]Cited in "More Disciples, Fewer Leaders Please," blog entry by Bill Kinnon, December 8, 2010 <www.kinnon.tv/2010/12/more-disciples-fewer-leaders-please .html>.

Chapter 3: Rhythms for Living the Christlife

[1]David Kinnaman and Gabe Lyons, *unChristian: What a New Generation Really Thinks About Christianity . . . and Why It Matters* (Grand Rapids: Baker, 2007), p. 223.

[2]Brett McCracken, "The Perils of 'Wannabe Cool' Christianity," *Wall Street Journal*, Opinion August 13, 2010.

[3]Kinnaman and Lyons, *unChristian*, p. 225.

Chapter 4: Life-Restoring Rhythm 1: Discernment

[1]Jan Johnson, *Invitation to the Jesus Life: Experiments in Christlikenes* (Colorado Springs: NavPress, 2008), p. 51. Johnson writes, "Listening can be an important way for us to 'die to our own desires' and 'live' to the desires of another" (ibid.).

[2]Richard R. Dunn, *Shaping the Spiritual Life of Students* (Downers Grove, Ill.: InterVarsity Press, 2001), pp. 15-16.

[3]See ibid., pp. 18-19.

[4]Keith R. Anderson and Randy D. Reese, *Spiritual Mentoring: A Guide for Seeking and Giving Direction* (Downers Grove, Ill.: InterVarsity Press, 1999), p. 92.

[5]The Johari Window is further explained in Julie Gorman, *Community That Is Christian*, 2nd ed. (Grand Rapids: Baker, 2002), p. 136.

[6]An example of the Johari Window can be found in Clair Raines and Lara Ewing, *The Art of Connection: How to Overcome Differences, Build Rapport and Communicate Effectively with Anyone* (New York: AMACOM, 2006), p. 112.

[7]Dietrich Bonhoeffer, *Life Together* (New York: Harper & Row, 1954), p. 98.

Chapter 5: Life-Restoring Rhythm 2: Intentionality

[1]Richard R. Dunn, *Shaping the Spiritual Life of Students* (Downers Grove, Ill.: InterVarsity Press, 2001), p. 20.

[2]Annie Dillard, *The Writing Life* (New York: HarperPerennial, 1990), p. 32.

[3]Dunn, *Shaping the Spiritual Life*, p. 57.

[4]An example of this is found in the blue-eyed versus brown-eyed exercises conducted by Jane Elliott, a third-grade teacher in the late 1960s. These experiments explored the effect of expectations on children in educational settings. In one classroom, blue-eyed children were told they were inferior to brown-eyed chil-

dren. In another classroom, Elliott switched the exercise so that the brown-eyed children were told they were inferior. Again and again, the children who were subject to Elliott's lowered expectations *underachieved* (see "A Class Divided," *FRONTLINE,* directed by William Peters, aired March 26, 1985 <www.pbs.org/ wgbh/pages/frontline/shows/divided/>). More recent versions of this exercise have focused on adults. For example, in a group of forty teachers, police, school administrators and social workers in Kansas City, "The blue-eyed participants were subjected to pseudo-scientific explanations of their inferiority, and underwent culturally biased IQ tests and blatant discrimination. It didn't take long for these grown professionals to become despondent and distracted, stumbling over the simplest commands" (video description of *Essential Blue Eyed,* 1996 <www .janeelliott.com/Merchant2/merchant.mvc?Screen=CTGY&Store_Code=J&Category_ Code=VV>).
[5]Mark Buchanan, *Your God Is Too Safe* (Sisters, Ore.: Multnomah, 2001), p. 114.

Chapter 6: Life-Restoring Rhythm 3: Reflection
[1]Keith R. Anderson and Randy D. Reese, *Spiritual Mentoring: A Guide for Seeking and Giving Direction* (Downers Grove, Ill.: InterVarsity Press, 1999), p. 52.
[2]Thomas Mertion, *Spiritual Direction and Meditation* (Collegeville, Minn.: Liturgical Press, 1960), p. 17.
[3]Julie Gorman, *Community That Is Christian,* 2nd ed. (Grand Rapids: Baker, 2002), p. 96.
[4]A version of the examen can be found in Adele Ahlberg Calhoun, *Spiritual Disciplines Handbook: Practices That Transform Us* (Downers Grove, Ill.: InterVarsity Press, 2005), pp. 52-55.

Chapter 7: Restoring Life in the Emerging Adult's Sense of Identity and Purpose
[1]Jeffrey Jensen Arnett, *Emerging Adulthood: The Winding Road from the Late Teens Through the Twenties* (New York: Oxford University Press, 2004), pp. 11, 165.
[2]Cited in Robin Marantz Henig, "What Is It About 20-Somethings? Why Are So Many People in Their 20s Taking So Long to Grow Up?" *New York Times,* August 18, 2010 <www.nytimes.com/2010/08/22/magazine/22Adulthood-t.html ?_r=1&pagewanted=print>.
[3]Annette Mahoney, "Marriage and Family, Faith, and Spirituality Among Emerging Adults," *Changing Sea* <www.changingsea.net/essays/Mahoney.pdf>, p. 4.
[4]Arnett, *Emerging Adulthood,* p. 163.
[5]Christian Smith with Patricia Snell, *Souls in Transition: The Religious & Spiritual Lives of Emerging Adults* (New York: Oxford University Press, 2009), pp. 268, 297. The data gathered was specific to eighteen- to twenty-three-year-olds.
[6]Arnett, *Emerging Adulthood,* p. 146.
[7]Ibid., p. 163.
[8]Cited in Henig, "What Is It About 20-Somethings?"

[9]Ken Sande, *The Peacemaker: A Biblical Guide to Resolving Personal Conflict* (Grand Rapids: Baker, 2004), p. 16.

[10]Ibid.

[11]Resources such as Bruce Bugbee's *What You Do Best in the Body of Christ: Discover Your Spiritual Gifts, Personal Style and God-Given Passion* (Grand Rapids: Zondervan, 2005) or the "On-Line Spiritual Gifts Test with Automatic Analysis" found at <www.kodachrome.org/spiritgift/> may be useful in the process of helping emerging adults identify their spiritual gifts.

[12]Lauren Dockett and Kristin Beck, *Facing 30: Women Talk About Constructing a Real Life and Other Scary Rites of Passage* (Oakland, Calif.: New Harbinger, 1998), p. 129.

[13]Alan Deutschman, *Walk the Walk: The #1 Rule for Real Leaders* (New York: Penguin, 2009), p. 2.

[14]Ibid.

[15]Ibid.

[16]Ibid.

[17]Paul Tillich, *The Courage to Be* (New Haven, Conn.: Yale University Press, 1952).

Chapter 8: Restoring Life in the Emerging Adult's Spirituality

[1]Penny Edgell, "Faith and Spirituality Among Emerging Adults," *Changing Sea* <www.changingsea.net/essays/Edgell1.pdf>, p. 3.

[2]Interview with Dr. Greg Carlson, professor of Christian ministries, Trinity International University, October 23, 2009.

[3]Tim Clydesdale, *The First Year Out: Understanding American Teens After High School* (Chicago: University of Chicago Press, 2007), p. 4.

[4]Edgell, "Faith and Spirituality," p. 4. The information is based on the author's own research as documented in her book *Religion and Family in a Changing Society: The Transformation of Linked Institutions* (Princeton, N.J.: Princeton University Press, 2005).

[5]Edgell, "Faith and Spirituality," p. 7.

[6]Christian Smith with Patricia Snell, *Souls in Transition: The Religious & Spiritual Lives of Emerging Adults* (New York: Oxford University Press, 2009), pp. 166-68.

[7]Ibid., p. 264.

[8]Robert Wuthnow, *After the Baby Boomers* (Princeton, N.J.: Princeton University Press, 2007), p. 119.

[9]Smith, *Souls in Transition,* p. 196.

[10]Ed Silvoso, *That None Should Perish* (Ventura, Calif.: Regal, 1994), p. 155.

[11]Rebecca Baer Porteous, cited in *Finding God at Harvard: Spiritual Journeys of Thinking Christians,* ed. Kelly Monroe Kullberg (Downers Grove, Ill.: InterVarsity Press, 2007), p. 31.

[12]Jan Johnson, *Invitation to the Jesus Life: Experiments in Christlikeness* (Colorado Springs: NavPress, 2008), p. 205.

[13]"The Astounding Power of Simple Witnessing: The White-Haired Man on George Street, Sydney" <http://net-burst.net/help/evangelism.htm>.

Chapter 9: Restoring Life in the Emerging Adult's Relationships

[1]Carolyn McNamara Barry and Stephanie D. Madsen, "Friends and Friendships in Emerging Adulthood," *Changing Sea* <http://www.changingsea.net/essays/Barry.pdf>, pp. 6-7.

[2]Ibid., p. 4.

[3]Christian Smith with Patricia Snell, *Souls in Transition: The Religious & Spiritual Lives of Emerging Adults* (New York: Oxford University Press, 2009), p. 280.

[4]Jeffrey Jensen Arnett, *Emerging Adulthood: The Winding Road from the Late Teens Through the Twenties* (New York: Oxford University Press, 2004), pp. 51-52.

[5]Ibid., p. 53.

[6]Barry and Madsen, "Friends and Friendships," p. 7.

[7]Smith, *Souls in Transition*, p. 152.

[8]Barry and Madsen, "Friends and Friendships," p. 3.

[9]Ibid., pp. 4-5.

[10]Ibid., p. 2.

[11]Ibid., p. 9.

[12]Smith, *Souls in Transition*, p. 74.

[13]Market Research World, "Ipsos OTX MediaCT Releases Latest Results from Its Longitudinal Media eXperience Study" <www.marketresearchworld.net/index.php?option=com_content&task=view&id=3450&Itemid=77>, New York, September 28, 2010.

[14]Barry and Madsen, "Friends and Friendships," p. 3.

[15]Arnett, *Emerging Adulthood*, pp. 104-5.

[16]Ibid., p. 102.

[17]Ibid., pp. 103-4.

[18]Barry and Madsen, "Friends and Friendships," p. 6.

[19]Robert Wuthnow, *After the Baby Boomers* (Princeton, N.J.: Princeton University Press, 2007), p. 142.

[20]Barry and Madsen, "Friends and Friendships," p. 5.

[21]Arnett, *Emerging Adulthood*, pp. 215-16.

[22]See, for example, Lynne Baab's book *Friending: Real Relationships in a Virtual World* (Downers Grove, Ill.: InterVarsity Press, 2011).

Chapter 10: Restoring Life in the Emerging Adult's Sexuality

[1]"Battle of Gettysburg, Day 3: July 13, 1863—Pickett's Charge" <www.militaryhistoryonline.com/gettysburg/getty32.aspx>.

[2]"Fun Trivia: G: Gettysburg" <www.funtrivia.com/en/subtopics/Picketts-Charge-151931.html>.

[3]"Battle of Gettysburg, Day 3."

[4]Mark D. Regnerus, "Sexual Behavior in Young Adulthood," *Changing Sea* <www
.changingsea.net/essays/Regnerus.pdf>, p. 4.

[5]Ibid., p. 1.

[6]Marla, E. Eisenberg with Christiana von Hippel, "Sex in Emerging Adulthood: A
Decade in the Sexual Gap," *Changing Sea* <www.changingsea.net/essays/Eisen
berg.pdf>, p. 10.

[7]Sharon Jayson, "Cohabitation Numbers Jump 13%," *USA Today* online, January
27, 2011.

[8]Eisenberg, "Sex in Emerging Adulthood," p. 6.

[9]John P. Splinter, "Biblical Sexuality, Part I; Pornography: A Cancer Killing Our
Nation," January 5, 2010 <www.purehope.net/stlouisArticlesDetail.asp?id=187>,
accessed December 16, 2010.

[10]Christian Smith with Kari Christoffersen, Hilary Davidson and Pat Snell Herzog,
Lost in Transition: The Dark Side of Emerging Adulthood (New York: Oxford University Press, 2011), p. 10, italic added.

[11]Ibid., p. 193, italic added.

[12]Eisenberg, "Sex in Emerging Adulthood," pp. 8, 10.

[13]John Piper, *Desiring God: Meditations of a Christian Hedonist* (Sisters, Ore.: Multnomah, 2003), p. 50.

Chapter 11: Restoring Life in the Emerging Adult's Daily World

[1]Christian Smith with Patricia Snell, *Souls in Transition: The Religious & Spiritual
Lives of Emerging Adults* (New York: Oxford University Press, 2009), p. 34.

[2]Jeffrey Jensen Arnett, *Emerging Adulthood: The Winding Road from the Late
Teens Through the Twenties* (New York: Oxford University Press, 2004), p. 151.

[3]Ibid., p. 22.

[4]Conrad Hackett, "Emerging Adult Participation in Congregations," *Changing Sea*
<www.changingsea.net/essays/Hackett.pdf>, pp. 1-2.

[5]Robert Wuthnow, *After the Baby Boomers* (Princeton, N.J.: Princeton University
Press, 2007), p. 53.

[6]Smith, *Souls in Transition*, p. 75.

[7]Jill Dierberg and Lynn Schofield Clark, "Media in the Lives of Young Adults: Implications for Religious Organizations," *Changing Sea* <www.changingsea.net/
essays/Dierberg.pdf>, p. 1.

[8]Ibid., p. 4.

[9]Ibid., p. 5.

[10]Wuthnow, *After the Baby Boomers*, p. 35.

[11]Ibid., pp. 33-35.

[12]Smith, *Souls in Transition*, p. 76.

[13]Gerardo Marti, "Racial and Ethnic Dynamics Among Contemporary Young
Adults," *Changing Sea* <www.changingsea.net/essays/Marti.pdf>, p. 2.

[14]Ibid., p. 3.

[15]Ibid., p. 2.

[16]Visit Mosaic at <mosaic.org>, Oasis Church at <oasisla.org>, and Evergreen Baptist Church of Los Angeles at <ebcla.org>.

[17]Marti, "Racial and Ethnic Dynamics," p. 9.

[18]Arnett, *Emerging Adulthood*, p. 82.

[19]Wuthnow, *After the Baby Boomers*, p. 186.

[20]Ibid., p. 155.

[21]Ibid., p. 186.

[22]Smith, *Souls in Transition*, p. 280.

[23]Cited in Henri Nouwen, *The Way of the Heart* (1981; reprint, New York: Ballantine, 2003), pp. 22-23, emphasis ours.

[24]Margot Morrell and Stephanie Capparell, *Shackleton's Way: Leadership Lessons from the Great Antarctic Explorer* (New York: Penguin, 2002), p. 55.

Chapter 12: The Journey of the Adult Disciplemaker

[1]Erik Erikson, "Human Strength and the Cycle of the Generations," in *The Erik Erikson Reader,* ed. Robert Coles (New York: W. W. Norton, 2000), p. 205.

[2]George Eliot, *The Mill on the Floss* (1860; reprint, London: Collins Press, n.d.), p. 488.

[3]Gail Sheehy, *Understanding Men's Passages* (New York: Ballantine, 1999), p. 12.

[4]Jack O. Balswick, Pamela Ebstyne King and Kevin S. Reimer, *The Reciprocating Self: Human Development in Theological Perspective* (Downers Grove, Ill.: InterVarsity Press, 2005), p. 201.

[5]Ibid., pp. 211-14.

[6]Daniel Levinson, *The Seasons of a Man's Life* (New York: Random House, 1978), p. 213.

[7]Cited in Balswick, King and Reimer, *Reciprocating Self*, p. 201.

[8]Sheehy, *Understanding Men's Passages*, p. 11.

[9]Levinson, *Seasons of a Man's Life,* p. 221.

[10]Balswick, King and Reimer, *Reciprocating Self,* p. 223.

[11]Sheehy, *Understanding Men's Passages*, p. 10.

[12]For example, in 2009, 45 percent of all women over sixty-five years of age were either single or widowed ("A Profile of Older Americans: 2010," Administration of Aging: U.S. Department of Health and Human Services <www.aoa.gov/AoARoot/Aging_Statistics/Profile/2010/docs/2010profile.pdf>).

[13]Rita Blockman and Kimberly Morin, *Listen to the Wisest of All* (Champaign, Ill.: Elder Press, 2007), p. 71.

[14]Balswick, King and Reimer, *Reciprocating Self*, p. 226.

[15]Sheehy, *Understanding Men's Passages*, p. 21.

[16]Ibid., p. 22.

[17]William Higham, "Old Is the New Young: Flip-Flop Generations," *Adweek,* March 17, 2010 <www.adweek.com/aw/content_display/community/columns/other-columns/e3iff897d5a72be7303b555ee8d58f467fc?pn=2>, p. 2.

[18]Blockman and Morin, *Listen to the Wisest*, p. 65.

[19]Ibid., p. 59.

[20]Balswick, King and Reimer, *Reciprocating Self,* p. 227.

[21]Ibid., pp. 198-99.

[22]Blockman and Morin, *Listen to the Wisest,* p. 41.

[23]Erickson, "Human Strength," p. 206.

[24]The language of "game-changing moments" was adopted from the 2010 NINES Conference, an online leadership conference sponsored by Leadership Network.

Chapter 13: Postures of an Effective Disciplemaker

[1]Keith R. Anderson and Randy D. Reese, *Spiritual Mentoring: A Guide for Seeking and Giving Direction* (Downers Grove, Ill.: InterVarsity Press, 1999), pp. 96-97.

[2]Peter Lord, *Hearing God* (Grand Rapids: Baker, 1988), p. 58, italics in the original.

[3]For a similar discussion, see Richard R. Dunn, *Shaping the Spiritual Life of Students* (Downers Grove, Ill.: InterVarsity Press, 2001), pp. 231-33.

[4]Helpful resources include Bruce Bugbee's *What You Do Best in the Body of Christ: Discover Your Spiritual Gifts, Personal Style and God-Given Passion* (Grand Rapids: Zondervan, 2005) or a website like "On-Line Spiritual Gifts Test with Automatic Analysis" found at <www.kodachrome.org/spiritgift/>.

[5]Jack O. Balswick, Pamela Ebstyne King and Kevin S. Reimer, *The Reciprocating Self: Human Development in Theological Perspective* (Downers Grove, Ill.: InterVarsity Press, 2005), p. 31.

[6]Carol Travilla, *Caring Without Wearing* (Colorado Springs: NavPress, 1990), pp. 50-51.

[7]John V. Taylor, *The Go-Between God* (New York: Oxford University Press, 1979), quoted in Lord, *Hearing God,* p. 26.

[8]Jeff VanVonderen, *Tired of Trying to Measure Up* (Minneapolis: Bethany House, 1989), p. 13.

[9]C. S. Lewis, *The Screwtape Letters* (New York: HarperCollins, 2001), p. 65.

[10]Used by permission.

[11]Dunn, *Shaping the Spiritual Life,* pp. 236-37.

[12]This question was adapted from Anderson and Reese, *Spiritual Mentoring,* p. 97.

Chapter 14: Igniting Your Passion for Reproducing the Journey

[1]Quotes by Jim Rohn, America's Foremost Business Philosopher, reprinted with permission from Jim Rohn International ©2011 <www.jimrohn.com/index.php?main_page=page&id=550#GOALS>.

[2]T. S. Eliot, "The Dry Salvages," in *Four Quartets* (New York: Houghton Mifflin Harcourt, 1968), p. 47.

[3]Paul Hiebert, "Banyan Trees and Banana Trees," *Christian Leader* 53, no. 3 (1990): 24.